In Action with the Japanese Navy

In Action with the Japanese Navy

Two Personal Accounts of the War at Sea
During the Russo-Japanese War, 1904
ILLUSTRATED

Before Port Arthur in a Destroyer
Hesibo Tikowara

With Togo
H. C. Seppings Wright

LEONAUR

In Action with the Japanese Navy
Two Personal Accounts of the War at Sea During the Russo-Japanese War, 1904
ILLUSTRATED
Before Port Arthur in a Destroyer
by Hesibo Tikowara
With Togo
by H. C. Seppings Wright

FIRST EDITION

First published under the titles
Before Port Arthur in a Destroyer
and
With Togo

Leonaur is an imprint of Oakpast Ltd

ISBN: 978-1-78282-594-4 (hardcover)
ISBN: 978-1-78282-595-1 (softcover)

http://www.leonaur.com

Publisher's Notes

The views expressed in this book are not necessarily
those of the publisher.

Contents

Before Port Arthur in a Destroyer

PORT ARTHUR, LOOKING TOWARDS GOLDEN HILL

Contents

Before Port Arthur in a Destroyer

Yokosuka, January 26th, 1904.

In the dockyard, on board the *Akasuki.*

At last I have got a moment's breathing space. These last fifteen days have been days of trial for all of us, officers and men—constantly on the move day and night, sometimes with the squadron, at other times with the Destroyer Flotilla in terrible weather and fiendish cold!

And always, always the same monotony. I cannot understand why they have chosen this dogs' weather for our manoeuvres, for the only result is to sicken us of it all and to damage the *matériel.* If only we were sure that war would be declared! In that case everything would wear a different aspect. But now it has been talked about for so long that finally one disbelieves it.

Certainly at sea we shall give the Russians a good account of ourselves, for although they are good fighters they possess little practical experience, and their ships, with a few exceptions, are not worth much. An officer of our general staff was in Port Arthur a short time ago as a spy—we have been practising espionage for some time now—and is sure that the Russians do not believe in the proximity of war.

They do not manoeuvre, they do not carry out any gunnery exercises, and in a corner of the arsenal there are goodness knows how many torpedoes, quite neglected. For months they have not been inspected by either officers or engineers. What a state they must be in covered with rust! When they want to use them the machinery will probably refuse to work—which is a pity, especially as they are of the latest mark!

I must say I should like to know whether we are manoeuvring for its own sake, or whether the *Mikado* has anything serious in view.

Although he is an advocate of peace, the only remedy he will have will be to make war. Ever since our alliance with England, and the continued advance of the Russians in Manchuria, it has been apparent that the inevitable hour of "the first cannon shot" is drawing near.

It is evident that the English want us to pull the chestnuts out of the fire for them, and we can see that clearly. But let them beware how they play with us, for it may well happen that their turn will come when we have finished with the Russians. But . . . I must keep my mouth shut. The commander is having us called up, probably to repeat his eternal lecture to us. "Naval officers must never mix themselves up in politics."

Perhaps he is right, and it would be better to spend our time drilling our men, and instilling obedience into them, so that the vessels confided to our care may always be in the highest state of efficiency.

Now that the leak which my destroyer had sprung has been stopped, and all the defects have been made good I want to examine the bottom plating and propellers carefully, as I think I heard rather a disquieting noise the last night of our reconnaissance off the Elliott Islands.

February 1st.

When I laid down my pen a few days ago, I little thought that my modest prophecies would come to pass so soon. What a conference that was!

The commander of the Destroyer Flotilla could hardly speak for emotion, and only managed to utter one single word: "Mobilisation! "He could not keep still; kept jumping from one place to another, twisting his legs, and laughing, without coming to the point. More explanations were unnecessary; we knew all.

The moment had arrived, the moment for the whole squadron to mobilise with all despatch, and sail for Sasebo on receipt of orders. As far as one can judge, active hostilities may commence at any time, at last we are going to fight.

What a calamity if we should not arrive in time!

There is a busy day before us tomorrow. We have to clean and wax the deck, so that the ammunition cases will slide easily along it. The boilers are nearly ready, and practically all we have to do is to fill them. The crew cannot be improved upon, for they were already good when I joined, and this "peaceful" winter campaign will have improved them.

We have all learned something, and nothing can surprise us. I am quite certain of that.

February 2nd.

I have just come from a farewell *"fête."* It was pretty, but I do not care about these foreign customs which we have learned from the Germans. My uncle Kato, who now commands the *Iwate*, has often talked to me about these *fêtes*, to which he used to go when he was naval *attaché* in the suite of Prince Kaio in Germany.

On every possible occasion, and there is no lack of these, there are great banquets, a lot of chatter, and protestations of affection. I do not like the Germans; as far as foreigners are concerned, my preference is for the English. At least they are a practical race. This afternoon the contagion spread to me, and to all appearances I took an active part in the general merriment. . . . But I must not fill this diary with nonsense about myself, for in a short time I hope to be able to describe something more interesting. The war is a fact, and our flotilla, according to the commander, will be the first to approach Port Arthur:

The place is very well known to us. During the past winter we have been there at least twenty times, and, as far as I am concerned, every creek and every point are as well-known and familiar as though they belonged to Japan. Perhaps in a short time they will do so.

February 4th.

It would be hard to recognise the city and harbour of Sasebo. It is full of troops, and the harbour is too small for the large number of ships destined for their transport. Every day ships go out with soldiers for Fusan and Masampo. But I hear that the greater number are to disembark in the centre of the Corean coast, to avoid having to move over those terrible roads. The point chosen is Chemulpo. The whole squadron will be under the orders of Admiral Togo, a fact in which we ought all to rejoice, since he took part in the war of '94 and is a very able man. Notwithstanding, I am very glad to have command of a destroyer, and to be at a certain distance from him. He is an unpleasant neighbour for his inferiors. The cruisers will be commanded by either Admiral Uriu or Admiral Kamimura; it is not yet known how the squadron will be organised and disposed.

February 5th.

We are on the eve of a struggle. The government has broken off diplomatic relations with Russia, and has charged us with the defence and safeguarding of our rights, which means, briefly, that we are to assume the offensive as soon as we can.

Very early on Sunday we shall set sail with the whole squadron.

ADMIRAL KAMIMURA

Our destination is unknown, but it is probable that it will be Port Arthur or its neighbourhood. Presumably we may meet with the Russian fleet, and show them that their fate will be similar to that of the Chinese.

It is impossible to describe the animation of this city. No one would recognise the former Sasebo. But this will not last long, and soon the old calm and tranquillity will return.

Today we returned our old torpedoes to the arsenal and drew new ones in lieu, for the old ones have become so worn by constant running, that on the last occasion they failed us several times.

Only fancy a "miss-fire" when the real business is on, and there is a Russian for a target! I think if anything of that sort happened to me I should go off my head. This afternoon we shall have the new steel "cigars," and tomorrow morning we shall sail to join the squadron.

Now I shall have instruction every day, to show the crew for the hundredth time what must be done in every conceivable contingency. And surely on service many things will happen in very different ways from manoeuvres! But why worry before the time?

February 6th.

The whole squadron sailed today from Sasebo. Whither is not known, as the only orders we have received are to follow the flagship. To judge by the direction, we are going to Port Arthur or its immediate neighbourhood—a wearisome voyage. The squadron goes at its usual pace, and we have to follow it slowly. The weather is cold, the sea rough, and the engineer unites with me in complaining about the slow speed. "It would have been better," he says, "to have sailed later and to have gone after them faster." And he is right. But I cannot do anything. I have promised him that when I am an admiral I will meet his wishes in this respect, and have advised him to keep a supply of picked coal in readiness, so that in the event of a night attack we shall not show any flame from the funnel.

The torpedo petty officer spends the whole day with his crew round the torpedo-tubes, adjusting the torpedoes, greasing them, and cleaning them as though he hoped by these means to make them infallible.

On the high seas, and with the prospect of something important happening one of these nights, one feels very different from usual—I should not like any one of my companions to surpass me in anything.

Every Russian *hors de combat* is for me a cause of rejoicing, for I

ADMIRAL TOGO

really loathe that country, which is the only obstacle in the way of the aggrandisement of Japan. Why not confide to my diary my desire for glory and that no one shall surpass me? I simply cannot say what I would not do to prevent such a thing! That which Europeans call "fear of death" is not known here, but I know something about it from having read of it in their books, and my Uncle Kato has told me about it. It seems to me to be simply folly, caused by their stupid religion. Fortunately, our politicians have not introduced it among us, and their half imbecile missionaries will not succeed in making lunatics of us.

I cannot make my lieutenant leave the deck. Now he runs like a squirrel from one side to the other, and now he remains motionless scanning the horizon with his glass. It would be better if he saved his eyes for the night—there will be more need of them then.

They are beginning their preparations on board the battleships, which is very sensible. The admiral thinks, and quite rightly too, that it is best to do things calmly so as to forget nothing.

On board my destroyer there is nothing to do, except to prepare and charge the torpedoes, and also to place the ammunition for the guns in convenient places.

February 9th: at night.

At last I have time to describe what happened. And to tell the truth I have got a great deal to relate—much more than could have been prophesied three days ago.

I must see if I am capable of relating the facts in their proper order, and as clearly as possible, although I am dying of fatigue. Yesterday morning the squadron reached the neighbourhood of Wei-hai-Wei and anchored there. The Destroyer Flotilla received orders to go as near the flagship as possible before anchoring. The order was carried out without much difficulty in spite of the roughness of the sea, and no sooner finished than signals reached us for officers commanding divisions and the commanders of destroyers to go aboard the flagship. A curious trembling shook the whole of my body. Was it, then, settled that we, with the weapon of which we were so proud, were going to open the ball? I cannot help thinking that those stupid Russians were very far from suspecting that matters would come to a head so soon, without any declaration of war coming first—a rather ridiculous and inexplicable European custom which is completely ignored by us.

The commander of our division signalled to us that it was not necessary to change our uniform, as the admiral wished to see us as we were, and as soon as possible.

No one needed the order to be repeated, and a few minutes later, provided with our notebooks, we were seated with our commander in his boat.

When we got on board the *Asahi*, the flagship, we were met by many officers, who congratulated us on being the first to meet the foe.

We went on to the admiral's cabin. There was old Togo with his European face, though he is not to blame for that, and round him were his chief-of-staff, several flag-lieutenants, and the captain of the *Asahi*.

He was holding before him a general map of the Yellow Sea, and another special one of Port Arthur. We sat down round the big table, and an officer of the staff gave us each a map of the roadstead and harbour of Port Arthur, on which was clearly marked the exact position occupied by each of the ships which composed the Russian squadron. The officers of the Second Flotilla received a map of the bay of Talienwan and Dalny.

Then the admiral, in his brief, concise way, addressed us more or less as follows:

> Gentlemen, this very night, after twelve o'clock, the Russian squadron in Port Arthur and Dalny is to be attacked, and I leave it to the commanders of divisions to choose the right moment, after they have decided on the exact point of attack. Probably all the ships, and certainly all the battleships, will be in the roadstead of Port Arthur; but since some may be at Dalny, the Second Flotilla will make a thorough reconnaissance there.

Even now I cannot help laughing when I think of the long faces which the destroyer commanders of the Second Division pulled. It is so nice to find oneself envied by others! For those poor devils realised clearly that the choicest morsels would be in Port Arthur. The admiral went on to say:

> In the plan of the roadstead of Port Arthur which you have in front of you, you can see exactly the places in which the enemy's ships are anchored. We have obtained these data from the accurate information of an officer of the general staff who was some time in Port Arthur, in disguise, and made a plan of the different berths in the roadstead. According to his information it is more than probable that you will take the enemy completely off their guard, for it appears that they do not expect the

outbreak of hostilities for several days yet. However, it is hardly necessary to warn you emphatically not to trust too much to the probability of this, as for some time past the Russians have been having sham fights and practising the attack of destroyers against battleships. From this it can be deduced that, as an opening of hostilities, they expect an attack by our Torpedo Flotilla, arid it is not at all unlikely that they have got a patrol service outside the roadstead.

Although I leave the details of the attack to the intelligence and experience of the two commanders of divisions, I want, notwithstanding, to bring the following point to their notice: let the object of attack for each one of you be the big units, that is, the big battleships. If by chance you meet with small cruisers, try to avoid them as much as possible, only attacking them in the event of finding yourselves picked up by their searchlights and seriously threatened.

I need hardly remind you that the first condition required to get within effective range of the enemy, is the absolute invisibility of your own boats.

You must have your lights extinguished, and those which it is absolutely necessary to keep lighted must be properly screened. I must ask you, besides, to remind your engineers always to keep their fires well banked, and as the moment for attack approaches, to look carefully to the steam pressure. If for a moment, however brief, sparks come up the funnel, your own boat is discovered, and the result of the whole attack is jeopardised. The speed of a destroyer should only reach its maximum at the moment of attack or when discovered by cruisers or battleships; and let me especially remind you that the attack must be delivered with the greatest energy possible, because, gentlemen, we are at war, and only he who acts fearlessly can hope for success. Your duty, gentlemen, is very simple, and I only make one request, a request which on several previous occasions when I have been in command, has produced excellent results in cases much more complicated than this—Show yourselves worthy of the confidence which I place in you, and for which I am responsible to His Majesty the *Mikado*.

With these words the admiral rose, and all of us with him, he added:

I hope that we shall all meet again when your mission has been accomplished; but if any one of you has to die, his is the greater glory, that of having sacrificed his life for the greatness of Japan, and history will place him for ever among its heroes.

Then we gave an enthusiastic cheer for the *Mikado*, and—most unusual occurrence—the venerable Togo made a sign to his head steward, and a few moments later offered us each a glass of champagne—a European drink! The admiral drank to our safety and to the happy issue of our enterprise; and we also drank to our own safety!

He then shook hands with us all and dismissed us.

On reaching the Flotilla we went to the cabin of our divisional commander, where he explained his plan to us briefly. At sunset we were to weigh and proceed in a body until we got very near the outer roadstead, separating then on the order of the commander. He allotted to each one of us a part of the roadstead, so that the attack would take place on all the Russian ships at the same time. It was not known for certain if the Russians had got out their torpedo-nets, so it was decided to fit our torpedoes with the new cutters which are necessary for penetrating them. This was a great pity. For, as I pointed out to the division commander, I felt no confidence that these arrangements would work; and moreover, with them on, our torpedoes had always run badly.

He agreed with me, but observed rightly that if the nets were out the only hope of success lay in using the net-cutters, and to counteract their bad effect on the torpedoes, we must get as near as possible to the ships before attacking. He concluded with the following words:

Do not forget that from the moment the signal to separate is given, each one of you works independently. For this reason, I am neither able nor do I wish to give you any detailed orders; no one can tell how you will find yourselves when the moment arrives. But above all things, be vigilant.

I do not consider it necessary to remind you that no boat, even if damaged, must fall into the hands of the enemy, and in addition to this your one care must be to arrange matters so as to discharge your torpedoes with effect; everything else is of secondary importance. If a destroyer has discharged the torpedoes in her tubes, and is not *hors de combat*, she should get out of sight and range at full speed, so as to load again with spare torpedoes. It is not impossible, usually, to deliver a second at-

RUSSIAN BATTLESHIP *PERESVIET*

tack. The most important thing, on every possible occasion, is to keep one's head.

And this last point, above all, must be impressed on the petty officers stationed at the torpedo-tubes. No shot must miss, for this would be quite unpardonable, in view of the fact that the enemy's ships are anchored. The commander has only to look to the handling of his boat. The lieutenant must see that the tubes are properly trained. Everything must be ready before the enemy discovers us with his searchlights and opens fire.

Moreover, I must ask you, after giving your final instructions to your crews, to let them rest as much as possible. Your personnel is composed of picked men, and everyone knows what he has to do, and how to do it. If the commander is laid low, the lieutenant must take command, then the bo'sun, and lastly a petty officer. As regards any of the enemy's torpedo-boats which it is impossible to avoid, open fire on them at once, and without wasting time; and I ask you not to forget that a hostile vessel, if crippled, can be easily boarded.

If this occasion should arise, do not continue the firing for a long time, for, as you all know, and therefore will probably laugh at me for repeating it, you may damage each other—a most important consideration on these occasions.

These words referred to me, because a few weeks before, in a torpedo-boat attack, I had done a great deal of damage to the bows of another destroyer.

And so he went on for a long time, for the poor man never knows when to stop when he is fairly off, and consequently we had to swallow once more (without any omissions) the instructions on the manner in which the commander of a destroyer should behave in a fight and in attack, all of which we had heard, read, and had impressed upon us hundreds of times.

And I thought, and so did nearly all the others, that to listen to these interminable discourses with patience was much more difficult and wearisome than opening the belly of a big Russian battleship with a torpedo.

At last he finished, and, following a high example, he also offered us each a glass of champagne and dismissed us. He added that in two hours' time we must weigh, and hoped that everyone would join with him in seeing that all was in order for the fight.

When I got on board my *Akasuki* the crew were all on deck, anxious to hear the news. All my comrades were burning with anxiety to show for once, at any rate, of what they were capable. What great satisfaction a man experiences, what security and confidence he feels, when he knows that he can rely on everybody, from the highest to the lowest, and that the same ardour inspires petty officers, seamen, and stokers!

I explained the plan which we had to carry out that night, and I was deeply touched by the shouts and applause with which—contrary to discipline—my words were received.

"We will talk about it afterwards," I told them. "Now we must get our boat ready for the fray."

Not a word more was necessary. In the twinkling of an eye everyone was at his post. Together with the torpedo men I inspected the torpedoes, and had them charged with compressed air to the regulation pressure. We tried the net-cutters to see that they were correct and put them on the torpedoes, and lastly arrived the great moment, so often longed for—that of removing the safety-pin from the pistol.

Certainly none of us forgot that, although in the war of 1894 with China, two commanders, in the excitement of the moment, fired their torpedoes without removing the safety-pins, naturally obtaining thereby admirable results! Ever since, quite rightly, this has been unceasingly dinned into our ears. Attention is called to the mistakes made by others, so that thus we may take care to avoid them. As far as I was concerned, my engineer, an intelligent man who only required a glance from me to understand my wishes, had already made all preparations; everything was spotlessly clean, and lumps of picked coal were stacked on the stokehold plates. Thus, on receipt of the signal, he could get the best speed out of his engines.

In the event of the engine-room telegraph breaking down or not acting, I arranged that my orders should be received in the engine-room by whistle, direct from the lieutenant, bo'sun, or one of the petty officers with whom I could communicate from the bridge.

Afterwards we went round to examine the watertight compartments. In each of them we found the following: tow, levers, shores, plugs, wedges, and pieces of fearnought to block up any possible leak, so that in the event of the next compartment being flooded, the bulkheads could be quickly shored up, and thus the pressure of water could not burst them open. This is what is prescribed in the event of water coming in, but, as will be seen later, at times it is not easy to do. A thing which is very easy by daytime, and all plain sailings is not necessarily so at night when one is getting floods of water from below. The boatswain had tried closing all the doors the day before, and managed easily, making everything work to perfection.

My arrangements, then, being complete, I ordered dinner to be got ready for my men, and warned the cook to let the rations be plentiful. They say in Europe:

With a full stomach, one works badly, but one fights all the better for it!

On these occasions I shall always remember the celebrated remark of the admiral in the war with China, who, when it was announced that the hostile fleet was approaching, merely exclaimed, "Pipe all hands to dinner!"

The divisional commander gave a supper-party, inviting me together with the other commanders, and during supper showed himself to be as sentimental as a German. . . .

He is not married, and under those circumstances it is all the same whether one lives a couple of years more or less, and in any case there can be no better fate than to die fighting against an enemy whom every Japanese ought to, and does hate.

Anyhow we felt strangely sentimental when we separated to go to our boats. We looked at each other, thinking, "Shall we ever meet again?" But this emotion lasted but a moment. As soon as I stepped on board my boat, where steam was up and the circulators throbbing, I felt as though I had mounted some mettlesome steed, who, impatient for the fray, was champing his bit, and the satisfied expressions of all my crew showed that they had complete confidence in me.

At last the whistle sounded, the divisional commander's signal for us to start, and we all got under way together, at half speed following our chief's destroyer, the course being north-east. The darkness soon swallowed us up completely, and the cold was intense.

The distance to Port Arthur, as far as I remember, was thirty or forty miles, and it would therefore be more than an hour and a half before we could meet the enemy.

I again inspected my boat, and fell my crew in to explain to them the situation in which we should probably find ourselves, pointing out that, above all, the most absolute silence must reign, and orders must be given in a low voice transmitted from one to the other. We had practised this so many times that we could be sure of the result. All information as regards damage or losses was to be given me as they occurred, since under no circumstances could I leave the bridge. Arms were served out, revolvers loaded, and again I had the satisfaction of seeing warlike ardour and the most perfect confidence depicted on every face.

I had under my orders a very different lot from those stupid Russians, who obey and execute their duty like automatons, whilst our men know that they are fighting for the greatness and prosperity of Japan.

I ordered everyone to his post and myself went on the bridge. All the lights were screened, and not a gleam penetrated to the outer darkness. Within reach I had a dark lantern covered over with a flag.

We were already about five miles from the outer roadstead, and it was necessary to be very alert and prepared for every eventuality. The signal from our chief, two whistles, "Separate," reached our ears. The boats inclined to right and left and I pursued my way behind the Divisional Commander, who went on much in the original direction.

Now that the thick smoke of the boat which had preceded me was not blowing into my face and removing all possibility of seeing anything, I was able to make out that we were very near Port Arthur. The lighthouse situated between the outer and inner roadsteads was throwing out its brilliant beams; the town also was completely lit up; and the objects which could be seen nearer to us were evidently the squadron, although even with my glasses I could not make certain of it.

Those poor devils, then, had no presentiment, and apparently were wrapped in peaceful slumber, after having said their stupid evening prayers, and asked their God to protect them during their sleep. "Ah," I thought to myself, "tonight your safety depends on what we do!"

The commander's boat suddenly went astern. I naturally did the same, and several low whistles called me up alongside him.

I ran alongside, and my chief then told me that he had been able to make out by the map, that the *Pallada* and *Czarevitch* were the easiest for us to attack.

He proposed that he should attack the *Czarevitch*, while I was first to discharge a torpedo at the *Pallada*, and afterwards attack one of the ships anchored further in.

Moreover, as it was possible, according to the position of the ships in the roadstead, that the *Pallada* was on the watch, I was to make the red and white signal which was used by ships wanting to come into Port Arthur.

The Pallada

My heart thumped hard against my ribs. In a few moments the golden dream of all those years of torpedo work was to be realised!

Innumerable thoughts crossed my mind with extraordinary rapidity, without my being able at the moment to say what they were. I ran up and down from the deck to the bridge, and from the bridge to the deck, and finally called my men together to explain the situation to them, and where I intended to deliver the attack.

The *Pallada* could already be distinguished by her great number of lights. We must have been a few thousand metres away, possibly a little more.

"What current is there?" I asked the pilot.

He looked at his watch and told me that an hour ago the tide had begun to flow, for which reason the *Pallada* must be lying with her bows seawards, which, to tell the truth, was not very favourable for us, for on board the big ships the look-out is always more vigilant forward than aft. But what was to be done? To attack the stern, I should first have to go right into the roadstead, and then very probably I could not attack.

I advanced slowly, as close as I could, and verified the fact that the *Pallada* was peacefully at anchor. In a few moments all the final preparations were made, and I gave orders for the starboard side to be ready to open fire.

We were about two or three hundred metres from our objective, which remained absolutely quiet. At the last I was guilty of an act of insubordination, into which I was led by the pilot.

With a gesture of disapprobation, he remarked that he did not think it advisable to make the red and white signal; for in the event of the enemy taking notice of it and wanting us to continue the exchange of signals, we could not do so. The man was quite right; and another point could be added to this, namely, that possibly another of our destroyers might have the same idea and make the same signal.

And so it turned out; someone made it, probably my chief on board the *Kasumio*.

Through the speaking-tube I shouted to the engineer to go "full speed ahead." The pace of my boat began to quicken little by little, whilst I remained with my glasses fixed on the enemy, whose outlines could now be perfectly distinguished. The night was dark and the enemy's ship well lighted up: a night expressly designed for an attack.

Instinctively I looked at the funnel: the engineer was behaving well; not the slightest spark was escaping. I made the usual signal to

The Kasumio

the engine-room and put the helm a little to starboard, so as to get closer for my shots, since it was natural that in their excitement the men would not shoot as well as usual, and it would be impossible to overestimate the gravity of a wasted shot.

The lieutenant came running along the bridge to tell me that everything was ready.

The great moment had arrived! The engines, funnel, bridge, and conning-tower were quivering, and the whole boat was trembling, owing to the speed. The spray was splashing my face. How strange that one can remember such trifles! I was now near enough to be able to distinguish the outlines of the bridge of the *Pallada*, and I thought I saw a great deal of movement going on on the lower decks, although all the crew ought to have been in their hammocks long ago.

I sent down another warning to say that soon, very soon, our ship would be in the line of fire. The reminder was unnecessary, for the men were already alive to the fact, and the torpedo-man had his hand on the lever, ready to discharge the torpedo. When the bridge of the *Pallada* was approximately forty-five degrees before the beam, we suddenly noticed a great commotion. We had been discovered. Cries of fear, words of command, and signals were heard in all directions.

I had no time to lose, and again ordered the engineer to go on as fast as possible.

At two hundred metres' range, according to my calculations, the first torpedo was fired. As far as I could calculate from my post, it ought to have struck abaft the bridge of the *Pallada*. Scarcely had the "yellow cigar" left its tube, making a great dive into the water, then the Russians began to shoot and work their searchlights.

If it is true that up till then they had been off their guard and not on the lookout, it is impossible to grudge them praise for the great rapidity with which they ran to their guns, clearing them away in less time than it takes to tell, and making their searchlights play all round.

Up till then I had kept perfectly calm, but I had the greatest wish to realise my plan of attacking the *Czarevitch*, and I did not want to be put out of action before doing so. With this object in view, I gave orders to alter course just as the petty officer was discharging his torpedo from the after tube; and naturally the shot was wasted.

When we changed our course again, we were able to satisfy ourselves that the first torpedo had got home; a violent commotion in the water was perceptible long before the noise of the explosion reached us. The men who were on deck, and whose curiosity would have made them die a hundred times before going below, told me afterwards that they saw an enormous column of water rise to a great height, immediately abaft the bridge of the *Pallada*. If that is true, and probably it is, a torpedo must have visited the stokers in their quarters. Anyhow it is beyond doubt that the worthy *Pallada* must have had sufficient to keep her on the sick list for some time, and that is enough for me.

Her restless searchlights were hunting for me from one side to the other. There was a moment when the ball of fire nearly lit up our stern, and in the fear of being discovered, I seized the wheel and altered my course, cunningly allowing the beam of light to look for us in our original position. After a minute they told me that two fresh torpedoes were ready, so we moved in the direction of Port Arthur, where we could see indistinctly a ship of great size, which according to the plan should be the *Czarevitch*. At the same moment I saw a flash on board; a second afterwards her guns went off, and the discharges from at least ten ships rang out. Then we heard an explosion; searchlights were turned on; everywhere we could hear orders being given, while my boat dashed on at full speed.

Forward! That was my one thought. Forward, come what may!

Suddenly, not far from the *Czarevitch*, which, like the *Pallada*, had her bows turned towards me, at about 800 metres distance from us, I saw one of our destroyers appear. If I was not mistaken it should be the *Shinonome*, which was running at full speed towards the *Czarevitch* to attack her. My first act was to run to the engine-room telegraph, for, had we gone on at the same speed, not only would the *Shinonome* have been hindered in her attack, but we should have run the risk of collision.

As neither the *Czarevitch* nor the other ships had discovered me, coming as I did from ahead, while they with their searchlights and guns were watching and firing away on each side, I reduced my speed till I was nearly stationary, watching and hoping that the *Shinonome* would accomplish her task. When, according to my calculations, she had got roughly within range, and was preparing for attack, the searchlights of the *Czarevitch* caught her, and such a heavy fire from guns of all calibres broke out, that I thought the unfortunate vessel's last hour had come. Notwithstanding, she discharged her two torpedoes.

A moment afterwards I heard the noise of a shell bursting, saw a brilliant light on her deck, and saw her disappear gradually into the darkness.

I kept hoping always to hear the explosion of the torpedoes, yet

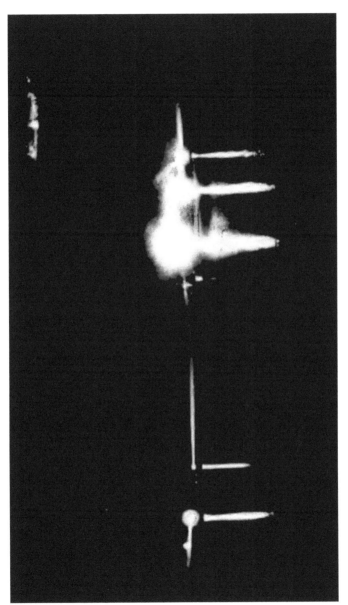

SEARCHLIGHTS IN PORT ARTHUR

strange to say they could not be heard, in spite of the fact that they must have hit the ship.

In the meantime, with indescribable audacity, and without having been discovered by any of the ships with their vigilant searchlights, there was I, silent and watchful; the pilot, seizing me by the arm, called my attention to the starboard side of the *Czarevitch*, which had her torpedo-nets out, and in these the torpedoes from the *Shinonome* were hung up.

This explained everything. I could see perfectly any number of bubbles rising from the water alongside the net, which held the torpedoes firmly suspended by their heads, and the booms which held them standing out horizontally from the ship. As I have already remarked, the antiquated net-cutters with which the torpedoes were provided were no use whatever.

Suddenly we saw another destroyer appear from the same place, evidently detached from our flotilla at the same time as the *Shinonome*. She came on at a rate of twelve or fourteen knots, sure sign that she had been damaged by the enemy.

The commander was a brave man, and intended to attack. But he ought not to have done it in the same place, for the crew of the *Czarevitch*, who were on the lookout on the starboard side, enveloped his destroyer with their searchlights, and before she got within a range of 400 metres, the first shells struck her. "The moment has come," I said to myself. I gave orders for "full speed ahead," and for the torpedo-tubes to be ready, put the helm to starboard, and attacked the *Czarevitch* on the other side. I took a last glance at my colleague, and what I saw was terrible.

He was without torpedoes, for there was a third one imprisoned in the net, and the heroic little vessel was on the point of foundering. Her stem was submerged, and every moment she was sinking more and more. I could see on one side of the bridge the mouth of the funnel, from which a mass of white steam was escaping, showing that one of the boilers had burst, and the conning-tower was almost demolished. She was about to perish, and one could do nothing to help. I had the presence of mind to remove the net-cutters from my torpedoes, as the *Czarevitch* had only her beam defence in position and had her bows as well as her stern unprotected. I hesitated for a moment as to which end was the best to attack, and decided on the stern. This was best, as there was a greater probability of not being seen. It would be impossible now to put down truthfully all the thoughts that flashed through my mind at that moment. It is scarcely possible to reflect at times like these. So many and so strange are the thoughts which cross one's mind, that the nerves and will are paralysed and work unconsciously.

Anyhow I must not fail! I went on at full speed with the helm to starboard, and ran on obliquely till I was under the stern of the *Czarevitch*. I emptied my two tubes, but could not make out which of the torpedoes hit the mark.

At the exact moment when the torpedo-man was preparing to press the levers, the crew of the *Czarevitch* discovered us with their searchlights. There were cries of fear, hasty words of command, and two seconds afterwards the firing began. The first shots came very near my boat. Some fell over, others short, some to the right and some to the left; all screamed and whistled in the air and then plunged into the water. My torpedo had accomplished its mission; a violent commotion in the sea, a loud explosion and high column of water, convinced me that the attack had been successful.

Immediately afterwards I thought that the last moment of my life had come. The hail of projectiles on my boat never stopped for an instant. The deck was riddled. They were probably aiming at the bridge, and consequently at me and my pilot; but they missed their aim. Evidently the Russians are so stupid that they do not understand the theory of raising and lowering their sights.

In spite of being struck by my torpedoes, they nearly destroyed us completely, for a 15-cm. shell hit the bows on a level with the waterline, and afterwards went out near the rudder without exploding. In itself the damage was not of great importance, but in consequence of the great speed of the boat, the water came pouring into the fore compartment and filled it completely. Fortunately, we were able to confine it to one compartment, but anyhow the bows were submerged.

The predicament of the boat became worse every moment. A 15-cm. shell entered the conning-tower, destroying one of the walls and bursting on contact with the other. It brought down the mast, killing a petty officer and two men, and exploded a box of ammunition. The torpedo-tube itself sustained no damage, but the mounting had been torn up, and so the whole apparatus became unserviceable.

The funnel was full of holes, partly made by gun shots and partly by the explosion of a shell which fell short and burst in the water. The shell must have been highly explosive, for the boat was full of innumerable pieces of it, the largest of which pierced and riddled the funnel.

RUSSIAN ADMIRAL OSKAR VIKTOROVICH STARK

Some 4.7-cm. shells would have put an end to my poor engines if they had not entered the coal-bunkers, where they exploded without doing much damage.

I dashed away from the *Czarevitch* at full speed. The bows of my boat continued settling down more and more, and owing to the great speed at which we were travelling the water swept over the deck, making the bows sink yet more. The after bulkhead of the fore compartment was on the point of yielding, and I saw that in another moment it would do so. Moreover, for the same reason, the boat was not under control, and therefore it was necessary to get her into a horizontal position at all costs.

The pumps on board were ready for use, so I had them started, filling the after compartment with water. By this means the whole boat sank a little lower in the water, but at any rate she was horizontal, and in a position which made her capable of being controlled; and the screw now remained completely under water.

While I was running away from the *Czarevitch* the uproar in the roadstead continued, and the light from the searchlights enabled me to distinguish several of our boats here and there.

To judge by the manner in which the Russians managed these appliances, it was fairly obvious that they had not had much practice. They worked them so badly that they illuminated each other instead of our vessels.

Nevertheless, the crew of the *Czarevitch* continued to strike me with their searchlights, but not with their projectiles, which showed that their gunners were in want of practice in night firing. I am of opinion that the Russians are not easily excited. They open fire when and where they are ordered, and to the best of their power and ability. What is more, they do not know what fear is.

Yet the fact remains that although I did not manoeuvre my boat particularly well, I managed to escape. Beyond doubt I owe it to not being afraid, and also to my pilot.

My unfortunate head was bursting from that fiendish noise, and as I listened to the whistling of the terrible shells which set the air quivering, one idea only took possession of me: "Faster! faster!"

As soon as I was out of range of the *Czarevitch*, I glanced at the compass and gave orders to the pilot to go out of the roadstead into the open sea. He did not need the order to be repeated. As I bent forward I noticed that blood was coming out of my back, so I called for my lieutenant, but the unfortunate man was stretched out below with a broken leg; and the pilot, who was safe and sound, came to relieve me for a moment.

I had the wound bandaged as well as was possible by the sick-berth steward, after making him wash it thoroughly, as some rags from my coat had got into it. Doubtless I had been struck by a fragment of shell.

I sat down on the bridge and looked round me. Outside the roadstead, though I was not the least expecting it, and a long way off, I saw the signal "Recall" made by the commander of the flotilla. I was unable to answer with my electric apparatus, which, together with the mast, had been destroyed, so I ordered a rocket to be fired, and went in the direction of the signal. There were already two destroyers in the flotilla, but the *Shirakuma*, which had sunk under my eyes near the *Czarevitch*, was missing.

Soon the rest of the flotilla rejoined, but very slowly, owing to the fact that two or three of our boats were not in a condition to make more than six or eight knots. We set out for the Elliott Islands, where we had to remain till the following day.

We went along very close together, relating our adventures to each other. I think I had been the most fortunate, as nearly all the others had planted their torpedoes in the nets, and none of the cutters had worked. Only the *Yadsuma*, like myself, had noticed the nets, and, in order to attack the *Retvisan*, had taken her by the bows, which were unprotected. Our chief had discharged all his torpedoes, and as he came out of the roadstead, made sure that he saw the Pallada going at full speed towards the inner harbour.

I did not think I had absolutely destroyed her, but this news was a great disappointment to me. The *Czarevitch* and *Retvisan* had not been torpedoed in vital parts, but I was sure of having destroyed one screw and the rudder of the "*Czar's* son," which are difficult repairs to effect; and if the *Retvisan* had a good hole in her bows, the affairs would not prove altogether a joke for the Russians. Our commander says, and he is right:

> Besides paralysing their movements the docks in Port Arthur are not large enough to repair battleships.

The surprise had evidently been complete, and this was clearly shown by the fact that they did not pursue us. If only one cruiser had managed to chase us, she could easily have overtaken our flotilla, composed as it was of cripples, hardly able to manoeuvre, and she would have made a good business of it, either blowing us into the air, or sinking us into the depths of the sea.

During our slow progress towards the Elliott Islands a telegram was received from the rest of the squadron, asking for news. The commander of the division replied, giving an account of our attack, which had taken place at the hour fixed upon, as the result of which three big Russian ships had been damaged by torpedoes, one of our boats sunk, and the others damaged more or less, though all were under control. We had to lament the death of the commander of a destroyer and some of the others wounded.

It was Admiral Togo in person who was asking, and he ordered us to join the flagship.

The weather had become so beautiful and the sea so calm that we could carry out the orders received without the slightest danger or trouble. The commander of the division ordered us to prepare to transfer the wounded to the sick bay of the flagship.

Unfortunately, we only had one surgeon for the whole flotilla, and he had his hands full with the wounded on board our commander's boat.

As soon as we got near the *Asahi*, we were received by the whole crew with "*Banzais!*" I must, however, confess that I felt too tired and worn out to appreciate this sentiment of joy and triumph.

Admiral Togo, with his staff, visited each of the destroyers, and expressed his admiration to all, especially the wounded; nor did he stint his remarks of appreciation to us officers. In particular, he spent a long time with me, owing to the fact that I was the only one present at the end of the *Shirakuma*. I told him that if the net-cutters had worked, there was no doubt that the three Russian ships would have been sunk, as I had seen four torpedoes hung up in the net of one single ship, the *Czarevitch*. The admiral showed a lively interest, but this remark did not please him much; and in point of fact it is not a very agreeable thing to hear, since the chance of attacking the stern or bows seldom occurs.

In order to rest the personnel, and also because the weather was unsettled and it was dangerous with our boats to remain in the open sea, the admiral gave orders for us to go, towed by two cruisers, to one of the islands situated north of the Miastao Straits, so that we could all rest together. No sooner said than done. The cruisers were ready, and a few minutes later we were gliding smoothly over the calm sea, without using our engines.

On the following day we overhauled our boats, and convinced

ourselves that it was absolutely necessary to take them all to Sasebo for repairs.

Not one was undamaged—in the bows, in the stern, on deck and everywhere were injuries of greater or less importance. Two destroyers had their emergency-rudders broken. On board mine, probably from the excessive pressure of steam, a boiler was leaking to such an extent that a lot of tubes would have to be replaced. Even the personnel was in need of repairs!

In a word, for the present we were *hors de combat*. Fortunately for me my wound was simply a scratch, which did not prevent my doing duty; so I told the commander of the flotilla that I had no wish to go to Sasebo.

He answered that he could not give me leave, for the other commanders would all want the same privilege, and naturally all could not remain behind. I had to resign myself and make up my mind to return as soon as I could leave my boat at Sasebo. Nevertheless, I kept my mouth shut, while I thought of the best way of carrying out my project. When, on the following day, the chief-of-staff arrived in the cruiser *Kasagi* to visit the boats and bring orders from the admiral, taking advantage of my long-standing friendship with him, I went on board and implored him not to leave me in inactivity in Sasebo, and at least to post me in the meanwhile to the squadron.

He answered that I must take my boat at once to Sasebo, and afterwards get my wound thoroughly healed.

Sasebo, February 12th.

There were many more repairs to be done on my boat than I thought: even the ammunition, especially that stowed in the bows, was unserviceable, owing to the wet, and they had to change it.

Moreover, after the attack, in the roadstead of Port Arthur, I must have run into something under water, for both my screws were bent, and the rudder damaged. We found this out on reaching the dockyard, and told the commander. The boat was at once docked, and then another injury of great importance could be seen in the after end of the keel. I cannot explain when or how it happened. Evidently the pilot, while I was half stunned on the bridge, touched the bottom in going out of the roadstead. One of the advantages of war! If the same thing had happened to me some months ago I should have shuddered for the consequences, and now the damage is repaired and no one says anything.

In spite of the fact that they work hard and well in the dockyard, and it is impossible to complain, it will be many days before we can put to sea. There is much to be done. In addition to the repairs to the hull we have got to change the boiler-tubes, and lastly test the new torpedoes which have been supplied.

I have heard this very day that they are going to give us net-cutters of a new type.

How much better to leave such useless things alone! At the best they never work. And moreover it is almost impossible that the Russians will let themselves be surprised again at anchor in Port Arthur; and if under way they will not be using their nets, so that in that case also the cutters will be useless.

Sasebo, February 13th.

The *Fuji* has just arrived. She has been taking part in the bombardment of Port Arthur. The officers say that the Russians, and especially the coast batteries, shoot very well. Cautious as ever, Togo kept at a distance of 6,000 or 7,000 metres. The forts of Port Arthur are so high that they are very dangerous to our ships. What can the best battleship do when shells are falling on her deck? The *Fuji* has been struck in the stern by what appears to be a 30-cm. shell. It has not touched one single important spot, but has made a large hole, destroyed two cabins, dismounted a couple of guns, wounded an officer, and killed two men.

Sasebo, February 14th.

My application was successful. Yesterday evening the commander of the flotilla sent for me to tell me that the chief of the staff, through the commander of the *Fuji*, had asked him if he could spare me while my boat was undergoing repairs, which would not be completed for some time, and since he had no objection, I was going to relieve an officer of the Fuji. When my destroyer was ready, my lieutenant would perform my duties till I could take command.

Naturally I am delighted. The *Fuji* will be able to sail in a couple of days, and so perhaps I shall take part in a bombardment.

The attack on the Russian ships at Chemulpo must have been worth seeing. How I should have enjoyed being there!

What a pity that they were given time enough to sink the *Variag*, a fast cruiser which would have been so useful to us! And it was a case of not being able to save her. She must have sunk quickly in view of the fact that the crew could not be saved.

Why allow officers and some hundreds of fighting men to escape, only to return and take up arms again against us?

Sasebo, February 18th.

Nothing has happened yet on board my battleship. The *Fuji* will not be ready as soon as I thought; and on the other hand the work on the destroyers goes on at high pressure, so that we shall soon be able to go out. It appears we are destined for a special mission.

On the 16th the new armoured cruisers, the *Nisshin* and the *Kasuga*, arrived safe and sound. They are now going to Yokohama to take on board ammunition and victuals, and to complete the crews. They seem to be excellent ships, and a proof of it is their having arrived from Genoa in good condition and without developing any defects after such a long journey. On this occasion the English have behaved like good fellows, for the personnel which has brought them out is composed almost entirely of Englishmen, a fact which I never realised until now.

Sasebo, February 20th.

Tomorrow or next day we are going to play a good practical joke on the Russians. We have painted four ships black, and with these we intend to obstruct the passage from the outer roadstead to the interior of the harbour—more or less like what the Americans did at Santiago. We hope very much that the result will be better. The entrance is very narrow, and if we succeed in closing it, the luckless Russians will not escape us and will be caught in a trap. The commander of our division, who has not yet received definite orders himself, said today that the ships must go to the positions indicated under their own steam.

There will be only an officer, an engineer, and eight or nine seamen on board. The transports are loaded with stones and cement so that they will sink quickly, and below will be placed dynamite cartridges which will be ignited by electricity

It all sounds nice and easy, but first we must get the ships into the entrance, and this is rather more difficult than it sounds. The officers of the *Fuji* say that the *Retvisan* is outside in the roadstead, almost touching the coast. She really is a floating battery, and her line of fire is in the very direction in which we have to go with the transports; moreover, her searchlights are always working and lighting up her immediate vicinity. If only I could get within torpedo range of that monster, with what pleasure would I plant a beautiful "yellow cigar" in her belly!

We shall see! Perhaps we shall be successful in the enterprise. Much more difficult tasks have been attended with success; everything depends on the spirit with which one undertakes them. Our men are excellent; the seamen and stokers of the steamers are all volunteers picked from hundreds who have come forward. This is an example which the Russians could not show; I do not think that those obtuse creatures have got any idea of patriotism.

Sasebo, February 21st.

Within a quarter of an hour we shall start with the transports. The *Sadzanami*, not being ready, remains behind. Her commander is swearing and protesting, but without avail.

Elliott Islands, February 26th.

At last I have got a moment's leisure. What a pity it is our splendid attempt to bottle them up came to grief! And if one thinks over things in cold blood, it would really have been a miracle had it succeeded. When during the night of the 23rd of February we arrived with our transports near the promontory of Liautishan, we met the Second Destroyer Flotilla, which had already been under fire. We were twelve destroyers in all so that, with the five big transports, we made up a regular squadron. "If the Russians allow us to approach," said my lieutenant, "it must be because they are blind."

I thought the same, and came to the conclusion that this venture was impracticable and absurd. I should like to know whose idea it was. Obviously, it would be a capital thing to be able to obstruct the passage for the Russians, but how can this be accomplished, when they are on the look-out, have a great battleship in the entrance itself, cruisers which patrol the harbour, coast batteries which are continually working their searchlights, and the whole lot banging away with heavy guns? Knowing all this, I do not know what we could hope for. The commander of the flotilla is right when he says:

> Admiral Togo has no appetite for a fight with the coast batteries; he wants, at all costs, to avoid weakening his squadron. But something must be done, even if for no other reason than to telegraph to Japan, and his chief of the staff has to think out the most extraordinary schemes.

The operations worked out as follows: From Liautishan we got under way slowly, following the coast-line, which in those parts is very high. We proceeded towards the roadstead, keeping all round the transports. Naturally we had all our lights extinguished, and took every sort of precaution.

The leading ship was commanded by a captain, the others by lieutenants. Each of them had received a sketch of the entrance, with the exact positions where they had to sink their ships marked on them. They had to sink them side by side, for which reason it was necessary, if a good result was to be hoped for, to take them to the spot indicated with mathematical precision; and then came the most difficult part of the performance—to sink them there.

In the roadstead there was already a strong current, which, as was natural, got considerably stronger in the narrow channel which led into the harbour. It would have been a sight worthy of being celebrated in verse to have manoeuvred with accuracy under such circumstances! I cannot help thinking the manoeuvre is impossible; yet, notwithstanding, I hear that Togo wants to go on repeating it until he succeeds. Naturally I felt discontented on the night of the 24th.

At three o'clock in the morning we found ourselves, as far as I could calculate, four miles from the channel. There were few preparations wanting. The huge coast searchlights, both on the right and the left, kept constantly illuminating different parts of the roadstead, searching everywhere. Among them we could make out two situated lower down; they could only be those of the *Retvisan*. By a faulty movement of one of the coast reflectors we saw two large ships which were in the roadstead lit up, one after the other—evidently the two cruisers which were watching the harbour.

A quarter of an hour afterwards the leading ship found herself suddenly lit up by a searchlight, and at the same time we heard a loud report. The *Retivsan* had kept watch perfectly, for she fired off all her guns at us. From the coast as well, two heavy and two small guns fired on us. The leading vessel was soon badly damaged, and began to sink, but her captain ran her aground on the sand to starboard. I was approaching slowly with my usual temerity, to save the crew, for I supposed that attention would be concentrated on the others, now that the first ship had been damaged and put *hors de combat*.

At all events, the commander had a boat in tow, into which part of the crew climbed, and the remainder, in bathing rig, were in the water, hanging on to rope-ends attached to the ship. The enemy had not discovered me, thanks probably to the sunken ship which was hiding me; and as a matter of fact they neither fired a single shot at me nor caught me with their searchlights once. Meanwhile the disaster was growing worse. The four other ships, thinking that the position to port was the most dangerous, manoeuvred with the intention of going to starboard; but I do not think they knew what they were doing, for, even if they had not been under a heavy fire, they could not have reached the channel in this manner.

It is impossible to entrust lieutenants with operations of such importance. Even admitting that they are very capable and have the best intentions in the world, they lack the requisite experience.

The second steamer, which had come on, was struck by a projectile from the coast battery on the left shore, owing to the fact that she had left her stern exposed when altering course. In addition to this, her engines could not have worked well, for she could not continue her course, and remained on the sand very near the first one.

We tried to approach to save the crew—but it was impossible, as the coast batteries kept up an incessant fire, and on the other side we were threatened by the danger of three Russian cruisers which were coming right on to us. I think that one of them was the *Novik*. She was curiously shaped, like a big destroyer, and I recognised her funnels. We dashed away as fast as possible; but one of our boats was struck, and, I think, sunk. She must have been one of the Second Division, for ours was complete

It is a wonderful thing, and seems incredible, that one should be indifferent and stoical in the face of such occurrences. When, on February 8th, I saw the *Shirakuma* sink in the same spot, I felt a depressing sensation, for I realised that a similar fate might overtake me. As soon as the first impression has passed away, an indifference remains, and though one may be absolutely certain that one is going to perish alone or with one's ship a few moments later, or be slain by a shell, one Remains as calm as possible.

In the faces of my men I read that they thought and felt thus, and that they had become as hardened as myself. The Russian cruisers showed little skill, for they ought to have made a clean sweep of us; when manoeuvring inside the roadstead they were afraid to come too near the shore, which they approached with the utmost caution.

We had separated, or rather, I should say, each one was working on his own account, and I was trying to reach the roadstead again in order to discharge a torpedo at the *Retvisan* and see if I could save the crews of the steamers.

I should have liked to attack one of the cruisers, but it was impossible, as they were very alert and made most excellent use of their searchlights; besides, it was beginning to get light, and it was necessary for us to retire.

SUNKEN TRANSPORTS IN HARBOUR ENTRANCE, WRECKED WARSHIPS IN FOREGROUND.

Some miles from the roadstead we found the whole squadron, and received orders to make straight for the Elliott Islands to coal from the ships which were there. When we arrived I had the disagreeable surprise of seeing that my boat was badly damaged in the bows, and that it was necessary to take her at once to the dockyard. I very much doubt her being able to reach Sasebo without aid. The last repairs were done too hurriedly, and without care. The two fore compartments are very weak, and I shall not be able to go fast for fear of increasing the damage.

The *Shinonome* has just arrived with some of those who were wrecked on the steamers; the poor wretches have endured terrible hardships. They have been exposed night and day, in an open boat, to hunger, cold, and exhaustion.

The venture could not have turned out worse. All the steamers, except two which remained on the beach, were sunk, and the crews were only saved with great difficulty.

Nevertheless, it is strange that the fugitive boat was not discovered. She came along hugging the coast all the time, and the Russians thought that they had all perished with their ships.

Our commander emphatically asserts that we are going to repeat the performance and that the admiral is going to persist in it. I do not think that it will meet with success.

I have had to report the damage on board my boat, which made me feel very sad. It is not very pleasant remaining inactive, now that there is so much to do. But on the other hand, there is no point in sailing with a damaged boat, with the probability of sinking or being sunk before getting within torpedo range.

Tomorrow a destroyer goes to the squadron to take a detailed account of the operations of the night of the 24th to the admiral. At the same time, she will carry news of the damage to my boat. I have written to the chief of the staff to ask him to allow me to embark in the *Fuji*, whose repairs must now be finished.

Sasebo, March 2nd.

At midday today I arrived with my crippled vessel, towed by a collier. The voyage was not very agreeable; the roughness of the sea and the frequent parting of the tow-rope did not allow us to rest for a moment, at a time when we most needed it.

All my crew are in the worst possible temper, in view of the days of inactivity which await us; but there is no other remedy than to put up with it, for there is no spare boat here, and we shall have to wait till the *Akasuki* is ready. My thoughts coincide with theirs.

Nor was it very pleasant for me when all the people collected at Sasebo asked me in which fight my destroyer had sustained her injuries, whether I had made a successful attack, and questions of that sort, and I had to answer that I have not taken part in any real battle, and that I have not been struck by a projectile, but that my boat cannot move. I know that it is not my fault, but that does not prevent its being a nuisance. It was a good opportunity to curse the workmen in the dockyard, and cast their bad repairs in their teeth.

To resume: we are all in the worst tempers possible, and for the present cannot see the slightest glimmer of light ahead. Only to think that the others will be making a glorious and decisive attack, and that I am condemned to contemplate my *Akasuki*, which has become a positive encumbrance! It is enough to drive one crazy! I feel like turning into a Christian from sheer rage!

What is the good of getting angry? I had better go to sleep.

Sasebo, March 6th.

There has been another fight. There seem to have been losses; but nothing is known here, and the whole truth is never told. It is a pity; but when all is said and done, we, both men and ships, are here for the same reason, namely, that our superiors may make whatever use of us seems best to them.

Not only on account of my exhortations, but because all the destroyers want a lot doing to them, the dockyard hands work night and day to put my *Akasuki* in order. The repairs will last for a short campaign—at least, so I hope; if afterwards they break down, we will do them again.

I think that in a few days we shall put to sea.

Sasebo, March 13th.

Since yesterday evening I have been here again undergoing repairs. And now it will be rather a bigger business, but this time my boat has done good work. Only one thing saddens me and spoils my pleasure—the fact that I have lost two of my men, one of them my best petty officer. I also have been wounded; a fragment of shell grazed my left fore-arm, tearing out a piece of flesh. Fortunately, neither the bone nor the arteries have been touched; but I have lost a lot of blood, and am compelled to carry my arm in a sling. But this will not stop me being the first to resume duty on board the *Akasuki*.

The operations were a success, and although the result is not of great importance, yet I can say that I have had the good luck to get nearer the enemy than most naval officers of the present day. My men and I are continually discussing it: one relates how he wounded a Russian in the head, another how he threw one of the enemy into the sea, or God knows where—perhaps into the heaven which those lucky mortals seem always to have at their disposal. One of the stokers used a steel hammer from the engine-room as a weapon of offence.

But I must tell the story of these operations in due order and clearly; they are so interesting and, as far as I am concerned, unforgettable.

Admiral Togo, at midday on the 9th of March, informed the squadron and the destroyers of his intention to bombard Port Arthur as usual with indirect fire at ten o'clock in the morning.

The First and Second Divisions of destroyers had to place submarine mines in the roadstead and its immediate neighbourhood, on the night of the 9th. Each of us from midday onwards had six mines on board, and I must confess that we did not feel much enthusiasm for our task.

Mine-laying is not a pleasant duty, and it is very dangerous to handle these contrivances. Our ships were not arranged for the reception of such guests and the men had no practice in handling them, so that the same fate which overtook the Russians with their *Yenisei* might happen to any one of us. (On February 11th, 1904, the Russian mining transport *Yenisei* collided with a mine which exploded under her bows, causing the vessel to sink with a loss of ninety-six of her crew).

I must add that we had to lay the mines in the dark, and if one is not very alert one runs the risk of coming into contact with one of them, without the consolation of going to the heaven of the Russians.

About midnight, accompanied by the squadron, we reached a point about five miles from the promontory of Liautishan, where some of the boats went off towards the promontory, while we continued towards the roadstead to place submarine mines across the mouth of the channel, if we could. Circumstances could not have been more favourable: the night was dark, and the sea very calm.

We had hopes of meeting one of the enemy's big ships and being able to attack her; but the roadstead was completely deserted, and not even a tiny patrol-boat could be seen. Our division sailed in a body, and, very wisely, the commander did not hug the coast as we had always done previously, but made straight for the mouth of the channel from the open sea. Everything seemed to presage a good result; the

RUSSIAN ADMIRALS AT PORT ARTHUR

only thing which worried us was that we could not see lights of any kind either in the town or in the harbour, and the intense darkness prevented us from distinguishing the outlines of the coast.

We had to judge by our watches and the current—(the tide had begun to flow)—and make our calculations. Our chief, concluding that we had now reached the pre-arranged spot, gave the signal to separate; his destroyer stayed in the centre, I turned to port, and the *Usugumo* to starboard.

We began the operation of laying mines successfully, and I had scarcely placed one when suddenly the Russian searchlights from both shores flared out, and a second afterwards the coast batteries opened a heavy fire on us. As the distance was very great the fire was not accurate, anyhow at first; some shells fell short, others over: meanwhile I went on quietly placing the mines. I was consumed by impatience at the slowness of the operation, but my men did all in their power, and more than this it was not possible to ask of them.

It was not very amusing lying there almost motionless, with the prospect of a shell dashing us into a thousand pieces; besides which, with our want of practice, it was probable that our work would turn out a very "amateurish" affair. I should certainly not like to assure Admiral Togo on my word of honour that I had placed the mines at the correct depth, and that the anchors had taken hold. It is more probable that one or two of them, as often happens, are floating at liberty over the waves, and have become as dangerous customers for us as for the Russians. At last we finished our difficult task, and about five o'clock in the morning, when day was breaking, we started out of the roadstead.

By a miracle my boat had suffered no damage, but my two companions had not been so fortunate.

On board the *Shinonome* the bridge was a heap of ruins, the funnels were perforated, and the deck in the worst possible condition.

The *Usugumo* could hardly steer at all, and I concluded that her steering gear had broken down and that she had to manage with the reserve rudder, as afterwards proved to be the case. For this reason, the unfortunate boat went wobbling along from side to side. Luckily all our engines were in good condition, and we slid out to sea like eels.

We were occupied for a long time with our mines, and meanwhile saw the flashes and heard the roar of the guns in the direction of Li-autishan.

By the rapidity of the fire, evidently from small guns, it was obvious that the First Division of our destroyers had come into action. With whom? we asked ourselves. Not with the coast defence vessels, for these would have discovered us first; and moreover, as it was impossible that ships of this kind had gone far from the roadstead, the only possibility that remained was that they were Russian destroyers which had gone out into the open sea to look for our squadron and attack it. Our commander ordered us to turn our bows in the direction of the firing; for besides the wish to take part in the action, we wanted above all to help our companions.

Suddenly, although we could not quite see them, we could hear the firing of guns from the coast batteries, and could see the searchlights flashing.

Our squadron, with the idea of provoking a "sortie" on the part of the Russians, had begun a bombardment of the city and harbour. Shortly afterwards the firing stopped, and my crew and I had already lost all hope of an encounter with the enemy when, by the light of day, which was beginning to break, we saw two Russian vessels which were making for the mouth of the roadstead at full speed. We hastened in that direction to cut them off. I ordered all my guns to be loaded, ammunition got on deck, and everything to be prepared for action, when the two Russian ships separated, one of them having evidently sustained serious injuries.

The *Usugumo* and the *Shinonome* dashed at one, and I at the other.

When she saw that her slow speed precluded all chance of escape—for, in spite of her repeated and, I must confess, skilful alterations of helm, I continued to obstruct her passage—she decided to make a fight of it.

She turned on me suddenly with the evident intention of ramming me, in which she would probably have succeeded if my engines had not worked very well.

I gave the signal for "full speed ahead" and turned the boat slightly to starboard, making her describe a circle and placing myself between the boat and Port Arthur. Then I ordered all my guns to open fire; the enemy had commenced firing a little before.

I had given my gunners the order to aim particularly at the 7.5-cm. gun. After putting it out of action I turned my attention to the others, and lastly to the bridge.

We were a hundred metres apart, going along on parallel courses and firing away without a pause.

Apparently the Russians had suffered great losses, for the 7'5-cm.

Sunken Russian vessel at Port Arthur

gun was being fought by an officer, and the working of the others had been entrusted to stokers, judging by their grimy faces. In spite of this they fired rapidly and accurately, and it really was a miracle that the engines and boilers of my boat came out of it undamaged, these delicate parts not being protected sufficiently to withstand anything but 4.7-cm. shells.

The petty officer who was on the port side was struck by one of these, which, after destroying the railings, burst in the coal bunker; a fragment of shell which hit him on the head subsequently killed him.

I could not stand my somewhat passive duty, so I ran to the 7.5-cm. gun and began to work it; but not for long, for we soon dismounted theirs, and the enemy had now nothing left but guns of small calibre—4.7-cms. I believe.

It is difficult to get a proper idea of that fight, and when I think of it it seems to me like a dream, or rather like a nightmare the impression of which remains with one for a long time, even after waking up.

The indescribable noise, the incessant roar of our guns so close to our ears, the bursting of the enemy's projectiles on contact with the water or with our boat, and above all the exhaustion, physical and mental, produced by that din and by the rapidity with which the guns were loaded and fired—all these are things to which we paid not the slightest attention during the excitement.

We were sweating all over in spite of the intense cold, and it was lucky that we were so near the enemy, for otherwise—I ought not to say this, although it is true—my gunners would never have hit their target.

I will not say that my crew would have behaved like the Chinese in the war of '94, who, instead of resting their guns against their shoulders, rested them against their stomachs, shut their eyes, and fired; certainly it did not get to this pitch, but they did not aim with precision, and I seem to have seen a man cursing a 4.7-cm. gun, as though it were to blame for not having hit the mark. A shell from the enemy dismounted one of the 4.7-cm. guns in the after part of the boat, blowing up a case of ammunition and putting all the people who were manning it *hors de combat*.

I had succeeded with my 7.5-cm. gun in planting two shells one after the other, not far from the water-line, into the engine-room. I saw a great column of thick steam escaping and some men trying to get away. These we were killing and wounding with deadly aim. It was indeed a sight which is seldom seen at sea, and from which one derives peculiar gratification—fighting against men full of vitality instead of inert steel.

At that moment an idea seized me. I left the gun in charge of a petty officer and manoeuvred the boat so as to get her as near as possible to the enemy, who was, as a matter of fact, so crippled that she could not escape: steam was coming out everywhere, fire was only being maintained by a single 4.7-cm. gun, and the torpedo-tubes had been destroyed, without our getting the hoped-for result of an explosion; charges of gun-cotton also were burning with a brilliant flame without doing any harm. When I was about fifty metres away I gave the order "Prepare to board!" or rather tried to give it, for it was impossible to make myself heard; but my men have got so accustomed to these manoeuvres that hardly had they heard the whistle than they were ready for anything that might turn up. I whistled as though I had half a dozen pairs of lungs, drew my cutlass, and waved my arm in the direction of the Russian boat, pointing from bow to stern, so as to show that I wanted everyone to be ready, as we should soon be able to board. Loud shouts of delight came from my crew when my order was understood, and they all seized hold of hook-ropes, waving their cutlasses and brandishing their loaded revolvers.

I warned the men in the engine-room to be ready to come up, except a few who were wanted below. Almost immediately afterwards a deathlike and oppressive silence succeeded the previous great uproar; on board the Russian boat not a single shot was being fired, and not a living soul could be seen on the deck. Naturally we also had ceased firing.

It is not likely to happen again that a destroyer commander will be able to approach a hostile vessel in this fashion, and I can never forget my sensations as we climbed up and set foot on her deck.

Climbing up is hardly the word, for my men went bounding along like wild beasts, with myself at their head.

There was nothing to stop us. On the deck lay stretched thirty or forty dead or seriously wounded, many of them horribly mutilated; and lying about the place were arms, feet, a head, a heap of entrails. . . . . . . But nothing could upset us, and my crew turned the corpses over and over to convince themselves that death was real and not feigned. I could not believe that everyone had perished, for that boat must have had at least forty-five men on board, and on deck there were only about thirty; two wounded men fell into the water, but were rescued and made prisoners. In the fo'c'sle there was nobody. One of

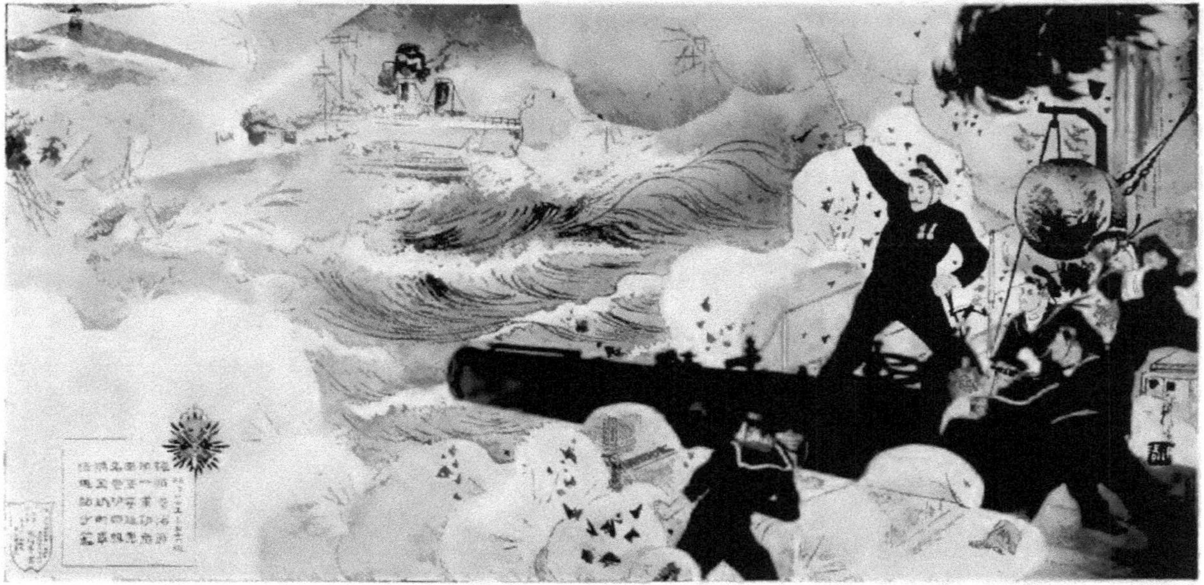

I DREW MY CUTLASS

my seamen came running up in a great state of excitement and told me that the stern hatchway was closed, and that doubtless the rest of the crew would be found down below. Meanwhile the boat began to sink slowly, and if it had not been secured to mine it would have foundered quickly.

I hoped by explaining this to compel the commander to surrender or else to make him prisoner by main force, and for this reason we went down the after hatchway into the cabin, cutlass and revolver in hand. Hardly had we started when two revolver bullets grazed my head and buried themselves in the bulkhead. Without seeing anything I instinctively aimed low, fired a shot and leaped back, colliding with my men, who were following very close behind.

Suddenly the door of the cabin opened from inside, without our being able to see in. The senior petty officer dashed in blindly like a wild beast, and a second afterwards fell with his head blown off. Our situation, to tell the truth, was not a pleasant one, for on such a narrow ladder it was impossible to show a larger front than one man, and those in the cabin could put an end to us one by one.

We contented ourselves with discharging our revolvers, and my pilot went on deck, where he proceeded to remove the hatch of the cabin, which made it quite easy to open fire on those down below.

The Russians would in the end have had to come out so as not to be shot in the back, but their fire ceased owing to lack of ammunition, and we were able to approach them. I took with me the stoker with the steel hammer, whom I mentioned before. No sooner had I reached the bottom of the ladder than someone with a drawn cutlass sprang at me. I was able to ward off the blow, and in my turn attacked him and felled him to the ground. I then saw that he was the commander. We killed half a dozen of the others, and the last two, slightly wounded, surrendered. When we had finished this important task—in the end one becomes so bloodthirsty that one feels a cruel disappointment at not meeting with more resistance when only dead men or prisoners are left—we saw that we had only arrived in the nick of time, for those gallant fellows had been preparing to blow up their boat.

On the floor were dynamite cartridges and other explosives besides the heads of two torpedoes, which altogether would have been enough to make dust of us. Whilst I was quietly looking through the commander's cupboard and desk to see if I could come across any secret documents, instructions, or money, my engineer from on deck began to sing out that the boat was about to sink, and that we ought at all costs to take refuge on the *Akasuki*. I quickly seized what I could and dashed up. I was not a little horrified when I saw my boat on the point of capsizing, having been dragged over by the Russian destroyer. In less time than it takes to tell we leaped on board, and with two smart strokes of our axes severed the hawsers securing the two craft. The *Akasuki* righted herself, and the Russian boat went rapidly to the bottom. When the upper works were hidden, and nothing more could be seen of the unfortunate boat, the whole crew burst into joyful shouts, and I myself joined in the chorus with my whole heart.

My subordinate's idea of taking the flags as soon as we had boarded the Russian boat, gave me immense pleasure. It was a thing I had forgotten to do, and he now presented them to us as actual trophies of our victory while the crew, and I also, were celebrating our success.

Now, as I read over this description of the fight, it seems to have taken an endless time, yet I do not think in reality it lasted more than a quarter of an hour.

One thing is certain, that no one took the trouble to look at his watch at the time; but when I think over the various incidents—first, the fight with the guns till we boarded, then from the actual boarding till the fight in the cabin, then from this point to the sinking, all this cannot have lasted more than a quarter of an hour, and perhaps less.

No sooner had the enemy's destroyer sunk and I returned to my bridge, than I saw our cruisers about 600 metres away, and behind them all the rest of the squadron. So absorbed had we been in our encounter that we had paid no attention to the events of no small importance to ourselves which were happening around us, and up till then we had not noticed that our cruisers were bombarding Port Arthur.

I heard afterwards that what happened was as follows. When Admiral Makharoff was able to see, at dawn of day, that his destroyers were in grave danger, he hoisted his admiral's flag on board the *Novik*, and put to sea at full speed to save his boats, firing on us and driving us back. And he could have fired with impunity at my boat, for both my crew and myself were much too busy to notice anything.

But the Russians reckoned without Admiral Togo, who was waiting with all the squadron not far from the roadstead. The latter, as soon as he saw the *Novik* come out, sent half a dozen cruisers to protect our retreat. When I had discovered this, the *Novik* had retired. I tried in vain to find the other two destroyers which had been accompanying me, and learned afterwards that they had had a fight with the *Reshitelny* without being able to prevent her getting into the harbour.

Naturally I cannot judge of what I did not see, but it seems to me that even if the *Reshitelny* had her boilers and engines in perfect condition, she ought not to have escaped. There were two boats, and double the number of guns, against a single vessel.

One of the two cruisers, I cannot remember which, signalled to me to report my losses and damage. I answered briefly, "Two men dead, six wounded, and my boat still under control."

To tell the truth, I could not make certain of this last fact, but anyhow it was accurate enough, for the boilers, engines, and rudder were intact; but on the other hand, the rest of the boat presented a deplorable aspect. The mast was blown to splinters, and it is strange that an object which presents so small a mark should always come to grief by night as well as by day.

Other projectiles had brought down the bridge and damaged the after torpedo-tube; fragments of shell had penetrated the deck and conning-tower, but this damage was of small importance.

The Russians must have worked their 7.5-cm. gun very badly, before we dismounted it, for only one of their shells had pierced our bows, a few feet above the water-line. I noticed that coal formed excellent protection, for all the small-calibre shells which exploded in the coal-bunkers were, with one exception, perfectly innocuous.

The same result would not have occurred with shells of larger calibre. I had the luck to put the 7.5-cm. gun speedily out of action, thanks to the fact that I concentrated the whole of the fire from my boat upon it, but even so it was a marvel that I got out of it so well. There is no doubt that I owe to luck more than to merit the fact that I was bombarded and fought on an unarmoured vessel and lost only four men altogether. But as luck in the long run only goes to people endowed with good judgment, I believe that my success is owing entirely and exclusively to my excellent manoeuvring.

As there is not now in Sasebo any other boat of the squadron but mine, we have to put up with the bother of continuous questioning. My person and my boat are looked upon as remarkable, and the crowd never tires of coming on board at all hours to see, touch, and even smell the flags taken from the Russians,

I am quite sure that if my lieutenant were not careful to calm the most excited, each visitor would take away a piece as a relic!

How can I answer so many questions? To tell the truth, I am bound to confess that I know nothing or next to nothing; that I have not got a clear idea of what we and the enemy have done or left undone. We do not pay much attention to the telegrams from the admiral, for one must remember that the greater part of them are destined for publication. I read the papers with anxiety, and by means of them learn many things which have happened during my stirring cruises.

The thing which worries me most is the question of mails. During the time that I have been away I have only received two letters, and those by chance, when I happened to be near the flagship; and now here in Sasebo I find a pile of letters, parcels, and papers—all old, dirty, and damaged.

Sasebo, March 15th.

My slight wound has healed—that is to say, that I am more lucky than my boat, which will have to be a long time in dockyard hands. So far I have received no order concerning her; and in the yard they tell me that, if absolutely necessary, she could go out in her present condition. The engines, boilers, and rudder are in a fit condition to go into action, and at a pinch in war time one can do without things which are considered essential in time of peace.

They have given us two new torpedo-tubes, a question of a few hours, as well as two new small-calibre guns, and if occasion arises I am ready to start. If this were peace time I should be anxious about the frail state of the hull, for it is certain that with bad weather and a heavy sea there would be a repetition of what happened when my damages had not been well repaired, and I could not return to Sasebo alone, but had to be towed. Now, naturally, I must hold my tongue, though should we experience bad weather we are likely to sink.

Sasebo, March 16th.

Now they do not want my boat to go out because, they say, she is not needed. On the other hand, there are several repairs to be done. The bottom requires cleaning again, some boiler-tubes which were leaking have to be changed, and I don't know how many other things.

They are quite right. But I do not like standing here with my arms folded, watching them repairing my boat. I have left no stone unturned to get them to give me another one. The worst one possible would be a God-send to me. But at present it is impossible.

Sasebo, March 18th.

The flagship has been here for one day only, and I repeated my petition for the hundredth time to the chief-of-staff.

The *Fuji*, the bird of ill omen of the squadron, is being repaired here, and has lost one of her officers. Tomorrow she sails, and I am glad to say I am to sail in her.

Sasebo, March 19th.

A ray of light in the darkness! I have just been to the *Fuji*, introduced myself to the captain, and have received an affectionate letter from the chief-of-staff in which he tells me that, thanks to my exceptional behaviour on the night of the 8th of February, they are going to give me command of my boat again—when she is ready—or of another like her. I do not owe any thanks to the commander of the *Fuji* for my appointment; I have been able to discover that. He is glad to have another officer, especially as some of his have had to be landed sick. But the commander is one of those men who look upon destroyer commanders as troublesome, presumptuous people. Moreover, it does not please him that I should be a bird of passage. Anyhow, I don't care what he thinks or does. Tomorrow we start, and I replace the sick officer who commanded the after battery.

Yellow Sea, March 20th.

What a difference one finds, when one goes from a destroyer to a large battleship! It seems strange to move so slowly when one is accustomed to go so fast.

All the officers are complaining of the admiral. They say, and I agree with them, that after the attack on the 8th, Togo ought to have sailed immediately with the whole of the squadron to the roadstead of Port Arthur, and when he had got as near as he could, to have opened fire. The Russians were not ready, and it is said that most of the officers were on shore. The first officer of the *Fuji* kept me with him all day to tell him the events of that night in detail without omitting anything.

Togo did not know how to take advantage of the situation; he ought to have sent out to the fight not only his battleships, but also his destroyers. What could have stopped him? No Russian ship could have offered serious resistance. They would all have been taken by surprise, unprepared for the conflict and incapable of manoeuvring.

Naturally we should not have taken Port Arthur, for we were not carrying men whom we could have landed, and we could not use the crews of the ships. But it is probable that we should have been able to destroy the battleships and cruisers which were in the roadstead.

What a glorious victory! Certainly it would have cost us dear. But why not? To win, in war, one must always risk something. A gunner

CRUISERS IN ACTION

of the *Fuji* remarked that the operation was impossible because of the coast batteries of Port Arthur. But neither the first officer nor I shared this opinion. As a matter of fact, on that night the coast fortifications would not have been ready or manned. It is probable that the greater part of the garrison was quietly asleep in the town. Moreover, the fight must have taken place in the inner roadstead and very far in, and I believe that the field of fire of the greater part of the land batteries is over the outer roadstead, and only a few have got the special function of defending the mouth of the harbour. It must be added, in our favour, that our ships being close to and mixed with the Russian vessels, it would have been a somewhat difficult problem for the gunners on shore to open fire, because they might just as easily have sunk their ships as ours.

It is to be hoped that the inactivity of the admiral that night will not be repeated. All naval history goes to prove, and the English in some measure also teach us, that only an attack delivered with energy and determination can be successful. I do not think that Nelson with his squadron would have remained inactive before Port Arthur, as Togo did.

It is no good getting angry about what is already done with, but it is certain that a chance like the one we had on the 8th of February will never come back again.

March 20th, night.

I have been very busy all day, for I have had to look into a number of things. The captain thinks that one of these days we shall bombard Port Arthur with the whole squadron, and there are many preparations to be made now that I have to direct the fire of a heavy gun, with which I have not only to shoot but also to hit. The crew is excellent, and a spirit that cannot be improved upon reigns among them, just as on board a destroyer.

All want to see the enemy as soon and as close as possible. A petty officer of my battery opines that long-distance bombardments are no use whatever, giving very plausible reasons for this; but the discussion is useless, as tomorrow is the day agreed upon. A quarter of an hour ago we came in sight of the squadron, and by means of wireless telegraphy received a long message giving us instructions.

The destroyers are to attack tonight, and at the first break of dawn we are to begin the bombardment.

The captain thinks that Togo's intention is to make the Russian squadron believe that a decisive attack is imminent, and thus compel them to remain where they are or in the roadstead, without letting any vessels go out. For these, if they made a sortie, might give trouble to our First Army, which tomorrow morning has to disembark at Chemulpo.

A couple of Russian cruisers or destroyers in these waters could, at the cost of their own lives, cause us considerable loss.

Yellow Sea, March 23rd and 24th.

The bombardment took place, and the poor Fuji has come out of it somewhat damaged. And she is not alone in this, for the *Asahi* and a small cruiser, whose name we do not know, were on the point of foundering. This is what happened.

As was to be expected, the destroyers which made an attack the night before met with no success; and this was not surprising, for, besides the *Retvisan*, which always remains at the entrance of the harbour, like an advanced battery, a patrolling service has been organised by means of cruisers and the coast batteries, which keep continually searching the roadstead with their searchlights; so what possible chance is there for a destroyer to be successful?

The *Retvisan*, the only objective of importance in the roadstead, cannot be approached, and there are no other ships to attack.

Does Admiral Togo by chance think that the destroyers ought to go through the channel and get into the interior of the harbour? Probably he does, for I believe that he has never commanded a destroyer.

After the destroyers had withdrawn to the proximity of the battleships, and had received orders to go to the island of Miaotao, the squadron advanced.

The *Fuji* and *Yashima* were ordered to leave the squadron and to get into position behind the promontory of Liautishan, whence they could open high-angle fire on the city and harbour. The admiral wanted to distract the Russian fire and bring the hostile batteries into a state of confusion.

Our ship and the *Yashima* anchored behind the Liautishan Cliffs, aiming very high, in fact as high as possible; and with the chart and our range tables we worked out how to hit our invisible target.

I felt as though I had gone back to the days of my childhood, when I used to throw pebbles over a house to hit some man whom I knew to be at work behind it.

We had not yet opened fire, for we had to anchor, when suddenly a heavy projectile came whistling through the air apparently some hundreds of metres away, and buried itself shrieking in the water. It did not burst as it would probably have done had it been direct fire, and we were able to make sure that the Russians were attacking us with high-angle fire, having seen that we were detaching ourselves from the main body of the squadron.

A few minutes later another projectile fell a little further off, and then we opened fire.

We and the *Yashima* fired alternately, and we had agreed to keep one section always under fire, taking those given on the plans and charts of the interior harbour, city, and forts of Port Arthur.

It must be remembered that ships' guns, and these in particular, are not made for high-angle fire, and in the long run cannot stand it.

At each round the shock was really colossal; and this was natural, for the higher the muzzle of the gun is, the more directly is the recoil transmitted downwards, to which must be added the force of gravity acting on a huge mass like a gun.

To our great surprise, after the second shot a telegraph clerk came up with the following telegram from the cruiser *Akashi*:

Shot No. 3, nearly 500 metres over, lateral direction apparently good.

This was an excellent idea, for now at any rate we knew how to aim, and could correct the mistakes we made. A brilliant idea on the part of Admiral Togo. To carry it out he had placed some cruisers a long way off, and in front of the roadstead of Port Arthur, to observe how our shells were falling, and to transmit the result to us by telegraph, so that we could correct our aim.

After a shot from the *Yashima* came a telegram saying:

Shot fell in the town; continue.

The *Yashima* at once telegraphed to us with what elevation she had fired and the exact lateral direction, and we at once opened a furious fire with guns of all sizes—the whole ship vibrated, and the crew worked away madly, sweating copiously, and so fast that the new rounds were ready before the guns had been fired.

Our only trouble was to stop the guns being loaded too quickly. I always had my guns sponged out after every shot, for sometimes remnants of gunpowder remain burning, and when the breech is opened the draught is capable of turning it into a large flame and causing a serious disaster. But the crew did not mind this, and would have liked, under the circumstances, to have shot faster and not to have taken these precautions. They all worked like slaves, their voices hoarse, their mouths dry, and their faces all covered with a grey coating of smoke and sweat.

I was thinking how lucky it was that no shot from Port Arthur had struck us, when a loud whistling rent the air, a terrible roar deafened me, thick yellow smoke swallowed me up completely, and a great flame rose up to the blue sky. I think I wanted to shout "To the shore!" but I cannot be certain if I really said it.

When I recovered consciousness I was in the sick bay, with ice on my head; the doctors told me that a shell had landed between the after turret and the middle line of the ship. I had no actual wound, but had been hurled against the mounting of a gun by the great rush of air, and had hurt my head slightly. I was soon well enough to get up, though I felt somewhat sick, and my head seemed to be spinning round.

The *Fuji* had weighed at once, for the shell had done a great deal of damage. The deck was torn up and in some places completely destroyed. Of twelve men who had been working on the lower deck, the greater number were blown to pieces by the explosion, and the remainder seriously wounded. Clots of blood and brains could be seen on the deck and bulkheads. Some bits of the shell went through the lower deck and penetrated into the interior of the ship, without apparently doing much harm. There was a large irregular hole in the deck, and part of the woodwork had caught fire. It was very lucky that the shell—which was one of 30.5 cms.—had not fallen on the barbette of my guns, otherwise the damage would have been greater. The barbettes, as on all battleships, are not made to resist a plunging fire, and there is no doubt that the armour would have been destroyed. Thus not only my gun crews and I, but also my guns would have been put out of action.

To put a finishing touch on our misfortunes, the ammunition which we had got ready for the guns had exploded. In spite of all this we ought to be thankful on the whole.

The captain telegraphed by means of the *Yashima* to Admiral Togo, who ordered us to suspend the bombardment at once and to rejoin the squadron. It seemed a long way to us. Our spirits were somewhat damped, for it was impossible to shut our eyes to the damage which we had sustained, the destruction of a few houses in Port Arthur being but poor compensation.

The poor mutilated corpses and limbs scattered about the deck were collected, sewn up in a sack with a sinker, and committed to the deep.

We felt infinite pity for those unfortunate men; but such is war! and Russia will have to pay us a hundredfold for our losses.

We soon came in sight of the squadron, which had a short time before suspended the bombardment and was making for the island of Miaotao.

One can hardly realise how long the foul gases produced by a shell-explosion linger in a confined space. For some hours afterwards it was impossible to remain below deck, in spite of water, liberal ventilation, and everything else that could be done to clear the atmosphere.

We were about five miles from the squadron, when the chief engineer rushed up to the captain with important news. The first officer was immediately called, and soon we all knew that we had sprung a serious leak. Some large fragments of shell, after having destroyed the central part of the ship between the upper and lower decks, had reached the side, and made a hole several feet in diameter below the water-line.

As it had not been noticed at first, the water had been pouring in for an hour, and it took some time to ascertain the exact extent of the damage. The water-tight doors had been hermetically closed before this happened, so that the extent of the inundation was of necessity limited. In spite of this the pumps could hardly lessen the amount of water, which poured in in torrents. The ship was in no serious danger, for all that happened was that she heeled over slightly to port and the stern sank. But misfortunes never come singly, and to justify this proverb, an order came from the admiral, as soon as he heard of the injuries sustained by the *Fuji*, telling us to make for Sasebo on the following day.

No sooner had we resumed our position in the squadron and received this order, than Admiral Togo, with his chief-of-staff and flag-lieutenant, came on board to see what damage had been done, and to hear a detailed account of the accident from the lips of the captain. Obviously Togo was not best pleased, but he could blame no one for what had happened, and his amiability even reached the point of telling us that on the whole the shooting had been good, but that he could not make out exactly what the effect of our fire had been. I had occasion to speak for a few moments to the chief-of-staff, and he told me that the accuracy with which the Russian ships had fired was marvellous. This no doubt was one of the results of the excellent commandership of Admiral Makharoff, for since his arrival we had noticed a greatly increased activity in the Russian squadron and general defence of the harbour. He seems to be a very capable man, and I hope and trust that a Japanese shell will very soon prevent him confirming his reputation for intelligence and initiative at our expense.

The chief-of-staff told me that the Russians had intercepted the messages which our cruisers were sending us, and this presumably by means of their wireless-telegraphy apparatus. At any rate Makharoff so arranged matters that his cruisers maintained a heavy fire on ours—a fire so intense that it compelled them to withdraw. This explained what had so puzzled us, *viz*. why the telegrams which at first had been so useful had ceased coming in later, at a time when we most needed them.

Togo never abandoned his idea of bottling up the harbour with steamers and thus being able to keep his ships as far as possible undamaged.

The chief-of-staff, to whom I spoke about this business, told me that it was a very good idea, because the probable duration of the war could not be predicted, and there was the danger for us that the Russians would mobilise the Baltic Squadron, which contained six or seven battleships, mostly of recent construction. So, as we possess no fleet in reserve, and our ships will not be any the better for being continually on the move with their engines and boilers under steam, we must shut the door in their faces.

While we were talking, a gunner came up in a great state of excitement, and asked me to be good enough to look at one of my guns. The chief-of-staff, who agrees with me that misfortunes never come singly, accompanied me.

In accordance with my orders the guns had just been cleaned, and so bright had they become that they looked like mirrors. But when drying them the gunner had noticed a long and jagged crack, which began close to the rear end of the gun and extended some way down the bore.

I saw at once that it was a matter of grave importance, for every precaution must be taken when these cracks appear. On further examination I could at once see that the crack was a very deep one.

The chief-of-staff, who had served in the artillery, merely glanced at it, and said, "One shot more and it bursts. The barrel of the gun is unserviceable; it must be changed." Here indeed was a real misfortune.

Although there are always spare guns in Sasebo, as it is well known that a heavy gun cannot fire more than 100 to 120 rounds, it is none the less a great nuisance to have to be the first to return to the dockyard, just at the moment when the Russian squadron is showing greater activity than ever, and we could be of use.

To resume, the *Fuji*, black bird of ill omen, will have to remain some weeks in the dockyard at Sasebo. I'm sick of it!

Island of Miaotao, March 25th.

Tomorrow the *Fuji* sails. The leaks have been temporarily stopped up with planks, tow, lead, and cement. They were not really serious, and the only reason that so much water came into the ship was that we discovered them too late.

There was a lot of hard work on board getting the gun ready for coming out. This is a very complicated job, for it is impossible to do much with the means which we have at our disposal. We had to limit ourselves to getting ready for the dockyard hands to commence operations.

The weather seems to be settled, the sea is calm, and these jobs were carried out with comparative ease. I have left the ship. When I approached the captain to say goodbye, he was not very amiable, and said that I was a guest who had brought bad luck to his ship. Although he meant this for a joke, I thought it a bad one, referring, as he was, to the fortunes of war, which I could not control. So I put on a not very friendly face, and asked him in a dry tone whether he had any fault to find with the way I had performed my duty, or whether there was any want of zeal on my part. He at once changed his tone, said that he was joking, and was very pleased with me. I should have liked to reply that this was not a suitable occasion for such a joke, especially as I was still suffering from the effects of the shell.

The crew of the *Fuji* was in the worst of tempers. They had before them fifteen days of absolute inactivity in the arsenal. What a difference there is between war at sea and war on *terra firma*. On land when half a battery or half a company is knocked out; the other half goes quietly on, and continues fighting as before. At sea, on the other hand, a whole ship is put out of action by one portion being damaged, although every one may be wanting to fight, and may have the opportunity. We depend too much on mechanism, and have become too technical. How much better was war in Nelson's time! Then every man could show what he was capable of, and ships remained stable and seaworthy even when riddled with holes. Guns could fire an infinite number of rounds without loss of accuracy, whereas nowadays one can hardly fire a hundred before they become unserviceable.

But all these reflections are inopportune and superfluous, for I had better congratulate myself on my good fortune in having received a fresh appointment, and one which far exceeds my dearest hopes.

Once again I am to change ships! If I go on like this it will realy be most extraordinary, and in a couple of months I shall have served in almost every vessel in the squadron.

The day after tomorrow the division of the Destroyer Flotilla to which I belong sails again to try and carry out the old experiment. They still want to try and close the entrance to Port Arthur with steamers, and have offered me command of one of them. Meanwhile my second in command, a lieutenant very near his promotion, will take command of my boat, though he is not best pleased at this. For the destroyers will not have much to do, their duty being only to accompany us for the purpose of collecting those of the living and dead that they can, and to attract the attention of the shore batteries so that the latter may make targets of them rather than of us.

As we shall probably not meet big battleships in the roadstead, it is not likely that by giving up the command of my destroyer I shall miss the chance of attacking.

I spent the whole day in getting my fire-ship, the *Chiyo Maru*, ready. She is very large, about 2,000 tons, and according to the details which I have got, nearly new. The crew is composed almost entirely of volunteers—twenty-five men all told, of whom eight are stokers and engineers.

What a splendid sight it is to see the number of men who have volunteered for such a dangerous duty! The time before, one imagined that ignorance of the risk they were running accounted for the number of volunteers; but now, after that first attempt, in which two-thirds of the crews perished, it is encouraging in the highest degree to see such eagerness for death.

Would the Russians have done the same?

No one can deny that when they have received an order, they carry it out without flinching, going whither they are told, perhaps to death; but their heart is not in it, and they do it like machines, for there is no doubt that the Russians do not and cannot understand our interpretation of the word "patriotism."

Our ships are provided with small-calibre guns, for the advisability of this was shown us by our former attempt. They are quick-firing guns, which though not of much use against the larger destroyers, as they cannot do more than kill some of the crew, yet are of the greatest service against the small boats which carry out the patrolling and reconnoitring duties at night. Besides, the great height of our steamers gives us the advantage of being able to fire down upon torpedo craft, and of concentrating our quick-firing guns on the enemy.

In spite of this I do not feel much confidence in the result of the expedition, nor do I feel very certain of coming out of it alive, though this is a matter of complete indifference to me. We are here to die for our country, so what is the use of talking about it, since we are all aware of the fact?

And just as the seamen and stokers struggle with each other in their anxiety to be admitted on board, so do I take command with joy and pride, and once again, with a smile on my face, I shall risk my life for the greatness of Japan.

There is such a huge quantity of ammunition and explosives on board that I feel as though I were commanding an enormous infernal machine. The hold is quite full of stones and cement, and on the top of this a great quantity of explosives manufactured and prepared in the arsenal.

These materials will float when the ship sinks, and will set fire to everything with which they come in contact. All this is on the assumption that the steamers are sunk in the manner we intend, and not at the will of the enemy.

As soon as we get to the exact spot where we are to sink them, I shall have the dynamite cartridges, which are at the bottom of the ship, exploded, some by electricity, and others by means of small fuses which will be lit by my men. Before this the valves at the bottom will have been opened, and then, *Sauve qui peut!*

By the tests and calculations which I have been making all day, I am certain that the ship will sink at once. There is enough explosive material on board to blow up a battleship. The whole thing seems to me easy of accomplishment, with the exception of the last item in the programme—the *Sauve qui peut!* part. I shall arrange for all my men to be dressed in bathing rig, and we shall tow a small boat. This will be our only hope of salvation unless our destroyers come to our help, as I did with the *Akasuki* on the occasion of the first attempts at closing the harbour.

Very early tomorrow we shall put to sea, four steamers and six destroyers, and a cruiser detached from the squadron will bring us detailed orders.

Undoubtedly Togo, when we have finished the task, will remain behind bombarding Port Arthur.

We have been given an accurate chart of the harbour, on which we are shown the exact spot to sink our boats. A very easy thing to do—on the chart!

Now I must put my diary in a safe place, for I do not want it to be lost if I perish. I shall give it to the commander of the *Miyako*, who will take it to Sasebo where he is going to coal, and there it will be looked after for me.

Sasebo, March 27th.

I am here once more! I must say I did not think I should ever open my poor old book again!

There is real satisfaction in having taken part in one of those adventures which seldom occur in a lifetime; and as goodness only knows where I shall be tomorrow, I had better tell the story today.

Before beginning I must point out that the command of a destroyer for a long period, especially in war time, and of a transport destined for sinking, are not very good for the health.

Yesterday I looked at myself in a mirror for a long time; and though I never had any pretensions to being a type of manly beauty, I was disagreeably surprised to see my face thin, full of wrinkles, and as old as though I were fifty. My clothes cover nothing but a skeleton, and my bones are full of rheumatism. If only we could have a little warm weather! I am not weak or delicate, nor are my crew, but life on a destroyer in winter, with bad food and no sort of comforts, would sap the powers of the strongest in the long run. Besides, this type of vessel is always more uncomfortable than the others, and rain, snow, and sea-water combine to make them damp; in fact, in bad weather there is not a dry spot where one can rest for a moment.

I have had the chance of experiencing this again on board the *Sadzanami*, where I was not very comfortably accommodated, although I owe her an eternal debt of gratitude for rescuing me at a time when I was running great risks of being drowned. Yet I must confess that there is a something in the damp and cold of life at sea which disagrees with everybody in the end.

Our ill-starred attempt took place as follows. I could not have narrated more than the part in which I was concerned, had it not been for what I heard from the commander of the *Sadzanami*.

On the afternoon of the 26th we put to sea. The destroyers were leading while we followed with our steamers, and in this formation we reached the roadstead of Port Arthur at about two o'clock in the morning of the 27th.

As rear-guard to us, and some way off, came the whole squadron, the cruisers first, and then battleships. In spite of the darkness of the night they intended, if possible, to open fire on the harbour and houses of Port Arthur, to call attention to themselves and thus enable us to carry out our plan without being noticed.

The roadstead was as dark as a wolf's den; not a light showed either in the harbour or town; the destroyers, acting according to orders, showed us the direction in which we had to go when inside the roadstead, and we went along, one behind the other, at seven knots.

I take the liberty of criticising the suitability of these arrangements. They ought to have left us alone to get to our objective as quickly as possible. As it was we made up a regular fleet, and if the enemy discovered the destroyers and opened fire on them, we should merely be in their way.

However, we managed to get, as far as we could judge, very near the entrance without being discovered.

It was about a quarter past two, when suddenly, just as on the former occasion, a terrific fire burst out. Probably gunboats, and not cruisers or destroyers, had been entrusted with the duty of guarding the harbour. One of these vessels, when she discovered us, flashed out her searchlights and fired as soon as the light flooded us.

At the same instant the shore batteries and a great many ships opened fire.

Nor were we behindhand, and opened fire with all our guns, while we pounded along as fast as our heavy cargoes permitted.

I had taken the helm, and my men, some below and others on deck, were ready to open the valves and make the electric contact which was to blow up the ship when I sounded the siren.

Then ensued some moments of incredible excitement, even greater than that of a torpedo attack, for on this occasion I had to keep all my wits at high tension, so as not to let the right moment for sinking the ship slip by, and we were now approaching the mouth of the harbour. I can frankly confess now that I never saw the entrance at all. It was likely, judging by our watches and maps, that we were at the appointed spot, but we could not tell for certain. The brilliant light of the searchlights, and the flash of the guns ahead and on all sides, excited my nerves to the highest pitch. I felt like a man who suddenly finds himself in a dark room, through the windows of which brilliant rays of light are flashing. Unable to make certain of his whereabouts, he moves along with his arms outstretched, expecting every moment to collide with a wall or piece of furniture.

Anyhow, this uncertainty could not last long, for the ship which preceded me slowed down, and no wonder, for, as I found out afterwards, she had been struck by a shell which disabled her engines and boilers. I turned slightly to starboard, ordered "full speed ahead," and moved on in front of my luckless companion, hoping that possibly the enemy's attention would be concentrated on her.

Although there was no ship in front of me to obstruct my vision, I could not distinguish any features or objects on shore which would enable me to calculate how far I was off, and whether the course I was steering was the right one for reaching the mouth of the channel. While I was occupied in scanning the horizon, a gunner belonging to the gun on the bridge touched me on the back and made me look to starboard, in which direction he was waving his arm. I thought he was calling my attention to the guns on that part of the shore, for, with that infernal noise going on, nothing could be heard.

But immediately afterwards I saw a destroyer dashing at my ship. She was lit up by a Russian cruiser, for they have not yet learned to work their searchlights properly.

She came along at full speed, throwing up mountains of foaming water.

What was to be done in this perplexing situation? Should I fly? Perhaps I could have done this successfully, but if I did I could not have carried out my orders. For it is quite certain that once I strayed from my course I should never find it again, whereas now I could not be more than two minutes away from the appointed spot.

These thoughts, which crossed my mind rapidly, came into conflict with others which urged me to go on towards the boat and try to sink it.

I decided not to alter my course, and at full speed, banging away with all my guns, I kept steadily on.

If, instead of the quick-firing guns, of an obsolete pattern, we had been provided with modern guns of seven or eight centimetres, affairs would have worn a different aspect. What a brilliant idea it was, to give us those useless old encumbrances!

Meanwhile the Russian destroyer kept coming nearer at full speed, and I noticed that she turned suddenly; she seemed to me to have only one tube in working order.

At the exact moment that she turned I stopped the engines, and then ordered "full speed astern," hoping that the torpedo would cross my bows.

Half a minute afterwards I found myself in the water and doing everything in my power to get out, for the temperature was not exactly tropical. I had miscalculated, and the Russian boat, it must be admitted, had made a capital shot.

If the ship had not stopped, the torpedo would have struck her between the engines and the boilers. As it was, it struck a little more forward; but my presence in the water gives one an idea, without any more explanation being necessary, of what had happened to my old ship. The torpedo must have struck some metres away from the engine-room and produced irreparable damage, which is not strange in view of the fact that the ship had not got a double bottom.

The shock knocked me down flat on the bridge, and at the same instant a deafening roar completely stunned me. There was no time to think, for the ship was sinking rapidly, heeling over to starboard and settling down by the bows. A few minutes later the bridge touched the surface of the water, and so did I.

I came to at once, and swam with all my might as far as possible away from the ship so as not to be sucked down by the backwash, for everyone knows the danger of this. As soon as I could breathe comfortably I tried to penetrate the darkness, and saw the boat which we were towing a short way off, half submerged, and leaning over to one side. Owing to the fact that she was attached by a very long rope, she had not yet been dragged down by the steamer.

I swam vigorously towards her and seized her with one hand, while with the other I cut the rope with the knife which, like all our sailors, I carried slung round my neck. The boat at once resumed her normal position. I went on swimming, holding on to the tow-rope with one hand.

At first I meditated climbing into her, but I thought this would be rather a risky proceeding, for I could see Russian destroyers and gunboats not far off.

The firing from the guns went on furiously, and it seemed to me that some of our destroyers were adding to the din. Afterwards I found out that this was the case. My situation began to be most unpleasant.

Now and again shells fell in my vicinity, and one fell so close that the splash from it hit me in the face. On all sides destroyers and gunboats were cruising about. Not only would it not have been strange, but it was the natural thing to expect that one of them would pass over me, and there is no doubt that not even our boats would have turned from their course for a floating object, and especially for an empty boat, for of course they could not see me.

I do not think that any of the other ships which followed me got any nearer the entrance; they evidently turned to starboard and port and there sank.

I had been about five minutes in the water when I noticed with surprise that the distance which separated me from the opposing vessels kept increasing, and soon I could make out the cause to which I owed my salvation. This was that the tide was ebbing, and so naturally I was leaving Port Arthur and going out to the open sea.

And now new troubles began for me. The current removed the danger of my being destroyed or drowned, but at the same time it diminished the probability of my being found and recognised by our ships or destroyers. I had to prepare for a wait of more or less long duration, and tried to climb into the boat.

Now, this seems a very easy thing to do, but, on the contrary, I cannot remember ever in my life having experienced such a struggle or such physical fatigue. The lower part of my body was almost stiff from the intense cold, in spite of my having done everything in my power to prevent this by means of constantly moving and rubbing my limbs. However, this saved me, for had I remained quiet all the time I should not have been able to make use of my muscles.

My bathing-dress kept out the cold fairly well, and even preserved something akin to warmth in the upper part of my body, in spite of my having been some twenty minutes in the water. This may be a slight exaggeration, for everyone knows that time always seems longer than it really is to a man who is waiting and counting the seconds.

Though I was not in as critical a situation as shipwrecked people are always supposed to be in, yet I had to struggle desperately to get into the boat. I tore my hands with the splinters and nails which stuck out everywhere, and which caught in the texture of my dress. This hindered me and added to the difficulties I experienced in getting out of the water. I had to make use of my knife again and cut away everything which hindered my movements. After this I was able to carry out my gymnastic exercises with greater success.

74

Without food, perished with cold, and yet sweating freely, my hands and face covered with scratches, I fell like a log into the bottom of the boat, my labours over.

The hardships and excitements of that night, added to those of the past week, left me in a state of stupor, in which countless intangible visions flashed through my mind. Now I thought I was on board my destroyer, now in my battery on board the *Fuji*, now in the dockyard at Sasebo. I gave orders, fired my guns, and heard the roar of the others.

A violent sensation of cold, which kept constantly increasing, brought me to my senses and I realised my actual situation. I had dragged myself along till I was nearly touching the foremost thwart, while the ice-cold water kept ceaselessly splashing over my face and body; the air was even colder than the sea, and though the latter was not very rough, yet it was quite sufficiently so to add to my discomfort.

Day was breaking, grey, cold, and gloomy. Far off I could make out the vague outlines of the coast, which showed that I was still fairly near the roadstead of Port Arthur. In contrast to the sky, which kept constantly growing brighter, the sea got darker every moment, and only here and there gleamed a small speck of foam. The tide continued to run out, which increased my hopes and comforted me, although I was so near the coast.

All the time I kept hoping that one of our destroyers would turn up, either one of those which had taken part in our mad escapade, or one of those which had been searching in the roadstead. For I knew that as soon as it got light, Admiral Togo would order them to look for us.

Every moment it got lighter. I took an oar and tossed it up, securing it to one of the thwarts, like a mast. Unfortunately, the mast alone was not sufficient to attract attention, and to the blade I fastened my bathing-dress, as a signal of distress. Of course I now felt the cold terribly; but it was better to shiver for a few hours than to die of hunger or thirst. And by this means I was almost certain to be found.

It was about five o'clock in the morning when I saw a great column of smoke on the horizon. This was evidently our squadron which was coming on to bombard the town, preceded by the cruisers. Soon afterwards, to my great delight, I made out eight or ten smaller columns of smoke, which indicated the presence of our destroyers.

As the ebbing tide had taken me out, following the direction of the roadstead, I had got near the promontory of Liautishan; so that the cruisers and destroyers in all probability would have to pass very near me.

I had to make the best of the opportunity and make myself as conspicuous as possible. I seized the mast with its improvised flag, stood upon the thwart, and began to wave my only hope of salvation from left to right and right to left, just as the shipwrecked mariner does in a novel.

I was glad to have something to do, for in that critical situation, while I waved my flag for help, I could think of nothing but the joy of being warm, and of eating and drinking once more.

Thus I forgot my adventure, and that under my orders two dozen good men and true had probably lost their lives. Such is war! One becomes insensible to the sufferings of others as well as to one's own.

One of the destroyers kept drawing nearer. Soon I was discovered, and to prove this fact to me and take me out of my abyss of despair, they began to hoist and dip their ensign. I, my heart bursting with joy at the prospect of once more being warm and procuring something to eat and drink, answered by hurling my mast with its flag into the water, which described a great curve in the air as they went. A few minutes later the *Sadzanami* came up, two seamen jumped into the boat, made her fast to the destroyer, and rescued me.

Then I realised that my powers of endurance were exhausted and my feet frozen, for unconsciously I had kept them in the water which lay in the bottom of the boat. The commander, my old friend Kurosi, marvelled not a little to see me thus, alone and in such a plight. I kept shivering, and stammered out an anxious appeal for something to eat and drink.

They took me to the cabin, where I was able to refresh myself. I soon felt much better, and began thoroughly to enjoy being on board a destroyer as a passenger. They had picked me up at the very moment when the destroyers had to retire.

Our battleships were some way off the roadstead, and now and again fired a shot with their guns of medium calibre.

The Russians, as has been their invariable custom since Makharoff has been in command, were in the roadstead in order of battle. I could count five battleships and a certain number of cruisers which came on at full speed. Our cruisers were their objective, and they ignored us humble destroyers.

Naturally we made haste to retire as quickly as possible, so as not to come under the fire of the Russian cruisers, which followed us as

RUSSIAN FLEET IN PORT ARTHUR

fast as they could; they were, as far as we could make out, the *Askold*, *Novik*, and *Bayan*.

As the distance which separated us was comparatively great, they could not have got nearer than 6,000 or 7,000 metres, in spite of getting the utmost out of their engines; besides which, our squadron had no real intention of accepting the challenge after the disaster of the night before, and shaped a south-easterly course.

When we were all out of sight of Port Arthur the flagship hoisted the signal "Re-assemble," and by means of wireless telegraphy transmitted a long signal to the squadron. This order was brought to the torpedo-boats, as they had no wireless-telegraphy apparatus.

The *Mikasa*, *Yashima*, three armoured cruisers, two small cruisers, and all the destroyers were ordered to proceed to Sasebo to coal and undergo necessary repairs. The rest of the fleet remained as usual on look-out duty before Port Arthur, two cruisers being detached as advanced look-outs. Perhaps some of the battleships may have to cover the disembarkation of troops near Chinampo.

During the voyage to Sasebo we had the opportunity of counting the destroyers, and it is strange, but none the less true, that none of them were sunk or disabled in our night operations; I suppose the Russians devoted their attention to the steamers, and they thus succeeded in sinking them before they got to the entrance, or anywhere near it. The destroyer which attacked my luckless vessel was the *Silny*, but our boats avenged me, for it appears they drove her on to a sandbank, and so prevented her being of any further use.

In the course of the voyage I transferred myself to my *Akasuki*, where most of my effects and baggage were. My lieutenant was delighted and very much surprised when he saw me coming from the destroyer which had rescued me.

He had come to the conclusion that I had gone down with my steamer, like my men, of whom, as far as I knew, not one had been saved; so this would not have been strange.

The *Akasuki* had not had many adventures, but as a matter of fact the lieutenant was not in a position to say what had happened. In the night three cases of ammunition, which had been carelessly secured, fell on to his head as he came out of the cabin to go on to the bridge, knocking him down and leaving him senseless all night long. The boatswain had to take command, so that my arrival on board was most opportune.

Once again we are at Sasebo. And now both officers and men have got to rest a little, for we are completely exhausted. Presumably the coming of spring will make these adventures at sea more pleasant; but it must be admitted now, that our strength and powers of resistance are worn out. In spite of every effort, our duty is not done as it used to be, and this is not from any want of will.

My sojourn in the water has not done me much good; the wound in my back has got worse; I am feverish, depressed, and feel very ill. I hope I shall be quite well again when operations are renewed.

Sasebo, April 6th.

I feel rather better, but fear that it is only a respite in my illness. However, I am able to take command again. I always feel as though my boat were a living being, like some proud and noble horse who guesses my intentions and even knows when I am not in full possession of my faculties.

It appears that in a few days we are going to put to sea: We suppose that Togo does not contemplate another attempt at closing the entrance, but he is sure to be devising some other ruse with the help of the chief-of-staff.

The doctor has just paid me a visit, and apparently is not very well satisfied with me; but I asked him to patch me up temporarily, even if he could only guarantee me for a couple of days. I do not want to miss the next operations, especially as there is not a single officer who can replace me in command of the *Akasuki*.

Sasebo, April 8th.

At last we possess a craft which we ought to have had since the beginning of the war—a minelayer, the *Koryo-Maru*. I have been able to go over her in detail. She was formerly a merchant vessel, and has now been transformed for the purpose of carrying and laying mines. It looks as though waging war with mines is Togo's new programme. Even we destroyers have to carry mines on board, and appliances to facilitate their management have been made in the dockyard.

The day before yesterday the battleships and cruisers set out to join the squadron. A small cruiser arrived two days ago, bringing orders from the admiral to get on with the repairs as fast as possible. The officers of the ship say that Admiral Makharoff puts to sea with his squadron nearly every day. A short time ago he was seen near the island of Miaotao; a few days later at the Elliott Islands; in fact the Russian fleet is constantly on the move, and is most careful not to be surprised outside the protection of Port Arthur.

Makharoff must have been informed by means of his cruisers that many of our ships left the squadron on March 27th, because he kept making sorties right out to sea all the time that our squadron was too weak to attack him.

All this gives us hopes for the future.

Has the time come at last when we are to have a real fight in which battleships will take part?

I am an enthusiastic admirer of torpedo-craft, but it is an undoubted fact that they cannot accomplish everything, and a decisive victory, except by some extraordinary chance, can only be won by large battleships.

To be quite truthful, which one can only be when confiding in one's diary, I must confess that up till now we have had incredible luck, and it all springs from a most simple fact—the unpreparedness and faulty organisation on the part of the Russians. This can be seen at once especially as regards their torpedo-craft. For what have the latter done up till now?—nothing. Yet there is no doubt that they could have done the same as we have, and compelled us to take more precautions and employ more of our forces to counteract theirs.

It can be seen now how things have changed since Makharoff took command of the squadron. For this reason, I feel sure that something decisive, some operations on a large scale, ought to be brought about, even at the risk of our meeting with defeat. For if the Russians are left in peace like this, they will become more daring, more skilful, and consequently more dangerous, every day.

Yellow Sea, April 10th.

Tomorrow night we have got to set out—six ships in all accompanying the *Koryo-Maru*—to lay mines in the roadstead of Port Arthur, and also in the place where the Russians form up in line of battle when they reply to our bombardment. In itself the idea is not bad, but what is bad is our lack of numbers. In place of a minelayer and six destroyers, we ought to have six mine-layers, because otherwise we cannot lay mines fast enough.

We shall see—the most important thing is to reach the roadstead and lay our mines without being observed. Today the weather is lovely, and I suppose it will remain so, but for this sort of work, bad weather is a great assistance.

Yellow Sea, April 11th.

The wishes I expressed yesterday have been realised, for it is raining and a strong wind is blowing.

In the roadstead the sea will be very choppy and the night very dark. A damp cold which penetrates to one's very bones prevails, and I fear that if I am alive tomorrow, I shall have to make a long stay in hospital to get thoroughly cured of my wound. Everything is ready for tonight; my men and I handle the mines as though we had done nothing else all our lives. I think we shall do well—better, anyhow, than the last time, when none of us knew anything about it.

Island of Miaotao, April 13th (on board the *Koryo-Maru*).

It went off splendidly. I must tell the story at length, not hurriedly and carelessly, for the benefit of my beloved relations who someday will read in this diary the principal deeds of the campaign.

The night, as I have said, was dark and wet. At about midnight we reached the roadstead in three divisions, with the *Koryo-Maru*.

As on the former occasion, we began in the centre, so as not to be nearer one shore than the other. In this way there was less probability of our being seen.

The staff had made out a plan by which each vessel was shown the number of mines she had to lay, and the exact spot in which to lay them.

As I have already said, our object was to lay a number of mines in the position where the Russians always formed up in line of battle to reply to our bombardment.

So as not to hinder each other in the dark, we separated at the very beginning, but still remained close enough together to be able to concentrate in case of necessity. With my lights carefully covered up, I went to my position at half speed.

Everything was quiet—I am referring to the enemy, for the sea was rough and weather threatening. At one moment I saw a dark shadow pass very near me, obviously a Russian destroyer; but we were not discovered, and went slowly on our way: a few seconds later, and she was swallowed up in the darkness.

The work of laying the mines, which at practice had seemed easy to me, turned out on the contrary to be difficult and tiring, owing to the bad weather and the care which had to be exercised. It was about two when I began the work, and at half-past four, or perhaps a little earlier, I prepared to leave the roadstead. Almost immediately day began to break. The *Koryo-Maru* had naturally finished some time before, and had filled a large part of the roadstead with mines.

I cannot say what the Russians were doing all night, for though the darkness was intense and the weather awful, with rain, snow, wind, and a high sea running, yet I cannot understand why they did not discover us. As a matter of fact, not one single destroyer was seen by the enemy.

In compliance with our instructions we proceeded out to sea to the place where the squadron, with cruisers thrown ahead as look-outs, had been awaiting us since dawn.

We now heard that some of our destroyers, *viz.* those of the Second Division, which had not been with us in the roadstead, had cut off and sunk a Russian destroyer which was running into the harbour.

I will try and explain in detail our position at eight o'clock that morning.

The Third Division of the squadron, composed of six fast cruisers and some divisions of torpedo-boats and destroyers, of which I was one, was in front of the roadstead of Port Arthur.

We saw a Russian destroyer trying to enter the harbour, and of course our boats started off in pursuit.

When Makharoff saw the danger which threatened his destroyer—I do not know for certain what her name was, but they say she was the *Strashny*—he sent to her assistance a powerful cruiser, the Bayan. Possibly she may have started off of her own accord, as she was outside the entrance to the harbour. Anyhow, she arrived too late; their destroyer was already lost, and our boats had withdrawn under cover of the big cruisers.

And now we noticed great activity on the part of the Russians. Three battleships, three or four cruisers, and a quantity of destroyers came out to meet us. We retired, drawing the Russians after us, till we reached a point about fifteen miles from Port Arthur.

Both we and the cruisers went at such a speed as to ensure our making a good offing and keeping out of range of the enemy. Notwithstanding, they, as well as our cruisers, fired constantly. Our ships, as I heard later, had informed the admiral by wireless telegraphy that Makharoff was pursuing us and had reached the abovementioned distance from the harbour.

Soon Togo turned up with his large battleships and the two new armoured cruisers, the *Kasuga* and the *Nisshin*. Of course the Russians did not want to fight far away from the protection of their forts with an enemy so superior in numbers, so they turned round and retired at full speed, succeeding in reaching the shelter of their land batteries before we could get within range.

We advanced all together, I with my usual audacity in front of every one, so as not to miss any detail of what was happening.

We all thought that the Russians would retire peacefully into the harbour, and little suspected what was about to occur.

I was watching the enemy with my glass. When they reached the roadstead, the *Petropavlovsk* made a signal, whereupon the squadron changed its formation: it seemed as though the ships were altering course and forming line abreast at the same time.

There, in that very spot where the Russian squadron was manoeuvring, were our mines. I saw all this distinctly, and must confess that never before have I felt my heart palpitate as on that occasion.

I followed each movement of the enemy's ships with feverish anxiety. They were seeking the shelter of their forts in expectation of our bombardment.

Suddenly I saw a cloud of smoke rise from under the bows of the leading vessel; first it was white, then yellow, and then turned into a huge red flame.

Instinctively I pointed my telescope to the mast-head, and by the admiral's flag saw that this was the *Petropavlovsk*. The following remark may seem extraordinary and out of place, but it is a fact that at the moment I could only think of the difference in the time taken by the flash and report of the explosion to reach us.

The flame and yellow smoke had nearly disappeared when the noise, or rather the dull echo of the explosion, followed by several others not so loud, came to our ears.

With my telescope I could see the ship settling down, first by the bows and then to one side.

It all took place with incredible rapidity.

I could see the screws and rudder out of the water. The masts inclined more and more; the hull kept sinking and getting smaller and smaller, and at last—disappeared.

Thus perished the *Petropavlovsk!* What a pity that we cannot find out who laid the mine which produced so good a result.

The rest of the ships all launched their boats and hurriedly did all in their power to rescue the victims of the disaster. They may possibly have been successful in this, though it is a matter of indifference to us, provided Makharoff was not among the rescued. His death is of the greatest importance.

What an extraordinary impression it makes on one to see a powerful battleship like this disappear for ever into the depths of the sea—

the whole thing happening in a few minutes from no visible cause. It seemed like a dream, not reality, and produced a cinematograph-like effect on us.

Owing to the distance, as I have already said, the sounds did not reach our ears soon enough for us to connect them with the events which our eyes saw. It is a sight that can never be blotted out of my memory. Every instant the stern rose higher, every instant the mast leaned over more, with the admiral's flag streaming from the mast-head; the yellow smoke, the red flame, the grey water, and far away the high coast line vaguely showing through the damp and rainy atmosphere. In spite of what Makharoff's death means to us, one cannot but deplore the death of so brave a man, falling as he did into a trap.

Everywhere appeared an infinite number of boats and launches, hardly visible to us, which dashed about and ceaselessly continued the search.

Another battleship, the second in the line, unless I am mistaken, must also have come in contact with a mine, for a second loud explosion could be heard, and I thought I saw her heel over to one side.

I cannot be certain, for the distance was too great for me to see clearly, but I imagined I noticed a good deal of confusion among the Russian ships. They adopted no particular formation, and apparently withdrew in great haste.

I thought that our admiral ought to have taken advantage of this confusion to bring on an action, but to my great regret he did not do so, and withdrew with the main body of the squadron, leaving the cruisers in their usual position watching the roadstead.

We destroyers received orders to come here to fill up with coal, and the *Koryo-Maru* is going to Sasebo to get more mines; I have been put on board of her, for I myself am forced to go into harbour for urgent repairs.

My wound will not heal, the edges are inflamed; I have fever constantly, and must really take myself in hand seriously. It is quite certain that in my present condition I cannot do duty or be of any use at all; and what is more, I should get worse if I attempted it.

I have just said goodbye to my crew and my old *Akasuki*. Shall I ever see her again? If I do, I hope that it will be before peace comes, and that I shall be able once more to sail in her to meet the foe... Even writing is hard work, but I wanted at all costs to finish this description of my last adventure now. I shall not be able to do it in hospital.

At Sea, May 13th.

I am completely restored to health, and have taken over command of a new destroyer. I know that this is a good thing for promotion, but the great thing is to get back and take part in the operations.

All through the month which I have spent in the military hospital, the navy has not had one single important fight, nor attained any decisive result.

After the death of Admiral Makharoff one battleship and two cruisers which had been slightly damaged returned to Sasebo. Admiral Togo knew perfectly well that once the Russians were deprived of an enterprising leader, who inspired confidence in his subordinates, he had nothing to fear from an attack. And so, although the damage could have been repaired at sea, he thought it better for the ships to go to the dockyard.

My brother officers told me that on April 22nd the Battleship Division approached Port Arthur and discharged about a hundred and fifty 30.5-cm. shells at the forts. The land batteries replied without doing any harm.

On the 25th the First Destroyer Flotilla made a detailed reconnaissance along the eastern shores of Kuan-Tung, and got within two kilometres of Dalny.

They wanted to find out whether the Russians had mounted guns all along the coast. For this reason, they bombarded the villages along the coast from some way off.

Their fire was only answered from Ta-ten-nan. Rather more to the northward they discovered activity among the soldiers, but not a single gun replied to the fire from our ships.

On April 29th a cruiser division commanded by Admiral Uriu, consisting of six big ships and two destroyer flotillas, the Fourth and the Fifth, convoyed twenty-two large transports to Pitsevo. Each of these transports carried about 3,000 infantry. These 70,000 men composed the Second Japanese Army, the command of which was entrusted to General Oku.

The disembarkation operations began with a furious cannonade by the destroyers and cruisers.

Then the transports came on, and began to launch boats, which were filled with soldiers, who in the meantime got their weapons ready.

General Matsumura, one of the cleverest men in the Japanese Army, put himself at the head of the expedition and unfurled the banner of the Rising Sun which belonged to the Fourteenth Regiment. Barely fifteen minutes elapsed before the general leaped on shore and planted our country's flag in the square of Pitsevo, while a loud "*Banzai!*" burst out like a peal of thunder.

A detachment of Russians, seeing that resistance was futile, fired a few shots and retired hurriedly to the interior of the peninsula.

Two hours later General Oku's whole army had disembarked on the Kuan-Tung peninsula.

This disembarkation was to decide the fate of Port Arthur.

On the 4th of May Destroyer Flotilla No. 1 made a preliminary reconnaissance of the coast to the west of the Yalu River, as far as the promontory of Takuchán,

This is all I know about the naval operations which took place during my stay in hospital.

Yesterday at ten in the morning we started from Nagasaki, our course being SSE.

We were escorting thirty-one large transports, filled to overflowing with troops of all arms.

In the first twenty were the infantry regiments, and in the eleven others the field artillery, two batteries of 12-cm. guns, cavalry, and engineers. The staff of General Nodzu, who was the commander of the Fourth Japanese Army, was on board a cruiser commanded by Captain Oputo. We had to escort the expeditionary troops as far as Takuchán, the point selected for General Nodzu's disembarkation. We spent all yesterday and today peacefully steaming along the coast, and searching for this place.

At Sea, May 14th.

We are just finishing the disembarkation. Admiral Uriu, who commands the expedition, is sending me to Port Arthur so as to give Admiral Togo an account of our voyage.

The *Osiva* has got under way, and Takuchán is soon left behind. Thus, coasting along as far as the Cape of Liautishan, we shape our course for Port Arthur.

At daybreak we saw the outlines of the big cruisers, which keep constantly cruising about before the Russian harbour to prevent the squadron escaping.

I went up to the *Mikasa*, which signalled to me to close, and was received by Admiral Togo.

His appearance has not changed in the least since I saw him towards the end of January. Neither the incidents of the campaign nor his moral victory over the enemy have banished the benevolent smile which seems to be always on his face.

He asked me pleasantly about our expedition, showed satisfaction at hearing that the whole of the Fourth Army had landed without accident, and wanted to know what state the other destroyers were in.

He asked me at the same time whether General Nodzu was pleased with the sailors, and when I answered in the affirmative, remarked that he was delighted, because the general is one of the most estimable and esteemed leaders of the Japanese Army, and a man whose opinion must always be respected. He allowed me to have a talk with the officers, who told me that they hoped that very soon fighting would be renewed at Port Arthur, for that the admiral who had succeeded Makharoff was doubtless anxious to have a fight on his own account, whether for the purpose of trying his luck or of seeing whether he could escape from the harbour where he was condemned to inactivity.

As from the moment I stepped on board the *Mikasa* I was under his command, I asked Togo what orders there were for the *Osiva*. He told me to go and join my division, without giving me any message for the divisional commander.

Sasebo, May 19th.

Destroyers are without doubt magnificent fighting vessels, but they cannot stand bad weather. After we had started for the coast of Japan the *Osiva's* two boats were washed away, and the heavy sea damaged the funnel to such an extent that we had to repair it. Tomorrow I believe we start again.

My orders are to join Admiral Kamimura's squadron, which is going to attack the Vladivostock cruisers.

At Sea, May 20th.

We have now started in search of the Vladivostock ships, which now and again dash out to chase merchant vessels and look for defenceless harbours to bombard.

The division consists of five armoured cruisers, three protected cruisers, and twenty-two destroyers and torpedo-boats.

We cruised about for four days in the Vladivostock waters; but we did not manage to see even the ghost of one of those phantom cruisers which are so daring when they fight with merchant vessels, yet are unwilling to risk the fury of our ships.

We fired a few shots at the forts as an invitation to Admiral Yessen

THE JAPANES BATTLESHIP MIKASA

to come out and give battle. The forts answered, but there was no sign of the Russian cruisers.

On the 23rd we shaped course to the southward and left Vladivostock, as it was inadvisable to have our fleet split up for long.

Our enemies, who have never been remarkable for their foresight and knowledge of the whereabouts of our ships, will keep quiet for some days yet. They are unwilling to venture out of their lair, for they fear a surprise which may cost them dear.

Evidently Admiral Kamimura has had orders, ever since the beginning of the war, not to leave Admiral Togo's squadron for any length of time, for the five armoured cruisers may be wanted at any moment to fight the Port Arthur squadron.

Sasebo, May 25th.
We reached here at 11 a.m., went on shore, and sought out the chief Admiralty official. Commanders of ships gave him an account of their cruise, and we then had a talk with the other officers and asked them for news of the war.

From them and the newspapers we heard that General Kuroki continues to hammer the Russian troops and is advancing rapidly northwards, after occupying Feng-huan-chang.

General Oku also has had a tremendous battle on the isthmus of Kinchou, capturing all the Russian positions at Nanshan, and sixty-two heavy guns. The capture of the isthmus is a mortal blow to the defenders of Port Arthur. For after this the investment was seriously begun, and unless General Kuropatkin succeeds in defeating Marshal Oyama, the fortress must fall sooner or later.

This news filled us with joy, for there is no doubt now that the campaign looks well for us.

Sasebo seems extraordinarily animated. No one would think that we are at war. The liners which ply between here and China come and go as though we were living in the most peaceful times; some of the ships even, who are engaged in coasting trade with ports in the north, have not stopped running, in spite of the danger of the Vladivostock squadron.

The population is engaged in peaceful occupations. Trade seems to be flourishing, and foreigners are more numerous than before. No one could possibly believe that Kuropatkin is coming, at the head of half a million *Cossacks*, to dictate terms of peace to us, in accordance with his boast.

Only one thing reminds one that war has broken out—the constant movements of troops. Also now and again bands of little boys can be seen armed with broomsticks and poles marching about and shouting in stentorian tones, "*Heiran, heiran!*" ("War, war!")

Captain Nashima, who is on General Oku's staff and is an intimate friend of my brother the artillery colonel, tells me that in his opinion the war will last a long time. The Russians are making formidable preparations. The Trans-Siberian Railway is bringing quantities of soldiers, and they say that every man who reaches the plains of Manchuria comes determined to avenge the reverses which his brothers have sustained by land and sea.

Without meaning to boast, I must say that I do not think that the Russians will get their own back at sea. Their squadron is demoralised by the reverses it has sustained, and by the death of Makharoff, besides which it is now weaker than ours.

It must also be remembered that the Russian leaders, ever since the outbreak of the war, have failed to show the determination which might have been expected from them.

Instead of fighting, their one idea seems to be to preserve their ships from all possible danger; and when all is said and done they possess six first-class battleships while we have only five. They could take the offensive, and yet they do not. Their tactics do not, apparently, produce the best results. They resemble those of Persano rather than Tegethoff, Villeneuve rather than Nelson.

Sasebo, May 27th.

The *Kincho-Maru* and *Heiden-Maru* arrived today with about seven hundred wounded from the First Army. Amongst them were a colonel and five captains.

I had a talk with one of them. He was wounded at Ka-lien-tsé, when the Imperial Guard crossed the Yalu to carry out the turning movement which proved so disastrous for the Russians.

He says that their clothes are bad, their artillery much worse than ours, and that they seem to fight without the slightest enthusiasm, and merely from a sense of duty.

He is sure that before two months have elapsed Oyama will have defeated the Russian commander-in-chief, and that the war will finish with a series of Japanese victories.

At the same time some small guns taken from the *Variag* arrived. The corrosive action of the water has rusted them to such an extent

THE *POLTAVA* AND *RETVISAN* FROM THE *PERESVIET.*

that they are unserviceable.

One of them, which was struck by a large fragment of one of our shells, has had part of its breech blown away.

They are the first trophies of our victories, and a huge crowd is collecting in the dockyard to see them.

Tomorrow the Russian prisoners taken at the Yalu are due to arrive.

Sasebo, May 28th.

The *Asahi-Maru* has brought the prisoners.

They disembarked at midday—about four hundred all told. Only a few especially favoured people have been allowed into the dockyard.

The prisoners are mostly rough and athletic-looking Siberians, and form a great contrast to our little men. They seem to be indifferent, and not very unhappy. They talk and laugh among themselves, and look with the greatest curiosity at our uniforms, guns, and the houses which can be seen in the distance.

The lovely park of Simonoseki, which is next to the dockyard, with its flowerbeds and magnificent vegetation, seems to astound them. Evidently they have never seen anything like it. As I look at them I think of the strange fortunes of war. These men, who were tilling their fields a short time ago, who have no reason to hate us, have been forced to fight against us for their lives, and are now prisoners—perhaps for a long time—in a country which they do not know, and whose customs are a source of constant wonder to them.

As soon as the bottom has been cleaned, I shall take the *Osiva* to the Elliott Islands, to rejoin the divisions under the command of Admiral Togo.

At Sea, June 2nd.

Two other destroyers, the *Okubo* and the *Yamato*, joined me in the duty of escorting the *Kava-Maru* to the Elliott Islands.

This vessel carried several foreign correspondents on board who were *en route* to join the staff of the Second Army, so as to follow the operations of war.

At a point twenty miles away from the islands, at three in the morning, a fast despatch boat, the *Kanavara*, stopped us.

An officer boarded the destroyers, and ordered the captain of the merchant vessel to change his course to the south-east so as to prevent those on board from seeing the exact position and numbers of the warships.

We went on at half speed to the anchorage originally intended. To the left we could see the dark and formidable-looking shapes of the battleships and cruisers. The sea dashed against their iron hulls and the waves burst furiously over them, yet they remained motionless. Two destroyers cruised constantly up and down in front of these floating forts, like sentinels guarding the slumbers of a band of monsters.

All the same, everyone on board the big ships was not asleep. Our eyes, used as they were to see great distances in the dark, perceived that the funnels were smoking. Everything was ready for a start at a moment's notice.

It is true that the Russian squadron might have come out of the harbour and slipped away before we could stop them, but the superior speed of our ships would permit of our coming up with the enemy at sea, and giving battle under conditions favourable to ourselves. It must be admitted now that the European newspapers have been very wrong ever since the beginning of the war—in declaring that the Russian squadron in the Far East is as powerful as ours. At first sight it looks as though it might be so, for they have the advantage over us in battleships; but actually we are far stronger, owing to the fact that we possessed six magnificent armoured cruisers before the arrival of the *Nisshin* and *Kasuga*, whilst they have only got two, the *Bayan* and *Gromoboi*.

Our battleships are superior to theirs in tonnage, weight of guns, and speed, whilst we possess an enormous advantage over them in torpedo-boats and destroyers.

Had this not been so there is no doubt that Makharoff would have tried to bring on an action. He was enterprising and capable enough to do it, but for the very reason that he was so capable, he wanted to reserve his squadron until the Baltic Squadron should arrive and join the Vladivostock cruisers, which, in an evil hour for the Russians, Alexeieff had detached from the main body.

The Italian critics, too, who declared that if Russia had had all its squadrons in the Far East, war would not have broken out, were absolutely wrong. In the first place the ships of the Baltic Squadron could not have sailed for the East for the simplest of reasons: they were not ready.

In the second place, had those ships weighed anchor, war would have broken out all the sooner. We had the most accurate information of what was happening in Russia, and it was quite impossible for us to be caught napping. Our government knew that sooner or later war was inevitable, and had made the most complete preparations.

One other thing must be mentioned to explain the tremendous effect produced by our shells. The greater number of the actual shells came from England and Germany, but an important item is manufactured in Japan. This is the burster, which is made in our arsenals; and the Chitose powder is better than any which other nations are using at present. The foreign attaches have been able to convince themselves of this fact during the war.

To sum up, we had a better navy than the Russians at the outbreak of hostilities, and the loss of the *Variag* and the damage done by our destroyers to the *Retvisan* and *Czarevitch* at the very beginning of the struggle, accentuated the inferiority of our adversaries.

I do not know what fate awaits our beautiful vessels, but everything combines to make me believe that if a real action takes place they will gain a glorious victory. When will that fight for which we are all so anxious take place? Probably when, the assaults by land having made the position in Port Arthur untenable, the enemy's squadron tries to cut its way out. The bravery of our soldiers, and the formidable weapons on which they rely, lead one to suppose that this battle will come off at the end of July, for it is probable that by then the fortress will have ceased to exist. (Like all his countrymen, the author was wrong about this).

If fortune smiles on us then, we shall be absolute masters of the sea, for I do not think we have much to fear from the Baltic Fleet, even supposing that it succeeds in reaching the Far East.

Dalny, June 5th.

The *Iwate*, the *Idsumo*, the *Kasuga*, two protected cruisers, five destroyers, including mine, and twenty torpedo-boats have the honour of escorting General Nogi to Dalny.

A soldier who fought like a hero in the Chino-Japanese War, where he commanded a brigade in General Oyama's army, Japanese to the backbone, clever, yet modest to a fault, he is going to take command of the forces which will shortly invest the town of Port Arthur.

The general and his staff are on board the *Iwate*; his chief-of-staff is General Tchigin, from the corps of engineers. Twelve large transports, which are carrying some 35,000 men and a complete siege train, will discharge their burdens at Dalny at the same time as the general. With the 30,000 men detached from Oku's army and 10,000 more who are due to arrive tomorrow in other transports, General Nogi will have in all an army of 75,000 combatants, all picked men. Most of the officers and sergeants took part in the Chinese campaign and were present at the entry into Port Arthur when it capitulated to Marshal Oyama.

A colonel, to whom I talked when I was at the Elliott Islands, told me that 7,000 veterans were arriving shortly, every one of whom had volunteered so as to assist in the taking of the town.

We reached Dalny at six in the morning. The day is lovely, but the sea rather rough. The disembarkation is rather a difficult matter, for the Russians behaved like Vandals before abandoning Dalny. There is not a single undamaged wharf, and, such as they are, they possibly shelter fixed or floating mines; so we avoid them with the greatest care.

General Kodama is already in the town. He is the chief of the general staff, and the real director of all the operations.

I went on shore, when the soldiers had been safely landed, and entered the town of Dalny. Quite half the houses have been reduced to smoking ruins.

The Russians, in the spirit of revenge, have burned the Chinese quarter, which now presents the most miserable appearance. As a fair reprisal, the Chinese have set fire to, sacked, and gutted the European houses. Somewhere or other they found a quantity of dynamite, with which they have committed every kind of atrocity, as though they wanted to wreak on the white stones the vengeance which should have been the lot of the white men.

The house in which General Kodama has installed himself is one of the few which have been preserved almost intact in the general destruction.

The commander of the army of investment had a long talk with General Kodama, then mounted a black horse and went off to the harbour, where the troops had remained. He gave some orders. Unusual bustle was noticeable at once: shrill bugle calls rang out; some regiments started off, and others remained where they were, waiting to be told their destination.

General Matsumura, the youngest general in our army, is at the head of the troops who are going at once to Port Arthur.

He has spent two years in Germany and one in Russia, and understands the fiendish language of the Muscovites.

Those who know him well say that he is very clever, and brave to a fault.

Dalny, June 6th.

Tonight we put to sea in the direction of Port Arthur, for the enemy might make a sortie and seize the transports which are due to arrive tomorrow laden with troops. A sortie *en masse* by the Russian ships is not probable, but the *Bayan* and *Novik* might come out, and these two ships by themselves could easily do a lot of damage.

The weather had got worse, and the south wind was raising a nasty sea which made it dangerous for small vessels to put to sea. When I first felt the ship moving I trembled for the *Osiva*. I called to my lieutenant, Nimoto, and we both watched the boat attentively to see how she would behave.

Unlike the *Akasuki*, which had the defect of getting her stern swept by the waves, the *Osiva* stood the seas perfectly, and buried her nose in them without any worse result than a good wetting to those of the crew who were on deck.

Although she certainly dives into the waves, she rises again quickly and buoyantly. Reassured about the stability of my boat, I devoted myself to searching the horizon. The *Osiva* was on scouting duty, and in rear, at a distance of three miles, came the main body of the fleet with destroyers and torpedo-boats on either beam. Two first-class gunboats formed the rear-guard.

When we had gone about twenty-three miles to the south, we altered course slightly to the westward. After proceeding in this direction for about half an hour, we saw a ship which seemed to be Japanese. We made the usual signals, and the ship, which was the *Yadana*, came nearer and told us that everything was quiet in Port Arthur, and that there were no signs that the enemy contemplated a sortie. I communicated what they told me to the captain of the *Iwate*, and the admiral ordered us to alter course to ESE. In this direction we continued all night, and when daylight dawned we were still steering the same course.

Soon after the sun came out we saw the transports coming along, six in number. They were very big ships and very heavily laden. Some of the ships were carrying heavy guns, and there was no means of accelerating their speed, as they were nearly all very old.

If the Russians had possessed a good Intelligence Department, they could, by merely going out five miles from Port Arthur, have inflicted a terrible disaster upon us.

Our forces were insufficient for defence, and, while we could have got away with whole skins to the protection of the main fleet, I do not know what the merchant vessels, filled as they were with troops and guns, would have done. A couple of 20-cm. shells would be enough to sink them, if they struck in a vital spot. Luckily nothing of the kind happened, and next day we were once again at Dalny, where great animation prevailed. Some engineers who had landed the evening before were temporarily repairing one of the piers, both for the purpose of accelerating the landing of troops and preventing any of the soldiers falling into the sea. I watched the disembarkation from the bridge of my boat, and it was delightful to see the joy that the men felt reflected upon their faces.

They were leaving their country, many of them were going to their death at a time when their strength and age seemed to promise them a long life yet they were laughing and singing.

The first men who came off the *Yeden-Maru* collected near a little stone house, now in ruins, which the Russian customs officers must have used, and one of them bringing out a *yesiván*, the instrument used by the *gheishas*, played a tune which was very popular in the Yoshiwara. Many of the soldiers who had arrived the day before drew near to listen to the music, and without any warning the full and pleasing tenor voice of the musician sang:

Madunagta nika Kura
Otovara masiné.

Then came a roar of applause, in which I joined. I was much moved by these reminders of my native land, of that enchanting country where I spent the first years of my existence, where I learned to love and to weep.

I could not help feeling the warmest sympathy for that soldier who had been born in the same country as myself, and who, like me, was risking his life for his fatherland.

The music stopped for a moment, and then, accompanying himself on the instrument, he sang the hymn of the *Samurai* in a strong and manly voice:

Sutsumé! Sutsumea sotovara:
Sutsumé! Kara kiri namaja!

Then a vast chorus, which must have consisted of more than two thousand voices, took up the refrain, vibrating sonorously over the water.

Suddenly there was a commotion among the crowd, then silence.

General Nogi, smiling, and accompanied by his two sons, was passing through the soldiers. The latter became silent from respect; but

97

the general, going up to the singer, said, "Yes, yes; *sutsumé*, my sons; *sutsumé* for Nippon."

Loud cheers greeted the veteran soldier's words, for he inspired an absolutely blind confidence in his subordinates.

Dalny, June 8th.

The admiral, who is giving a farewell banquet to Generals Nogi and Kodama, has invited all of us commanders to it. At half-past twelve exactly the National Anthem was played by one of the military bands on the quay.

The two generals were going on board. I never get tired of looking at General Nogi. He must be about fifty-six years of age, but he looks much older.

His hair and beard are grey; only his eyebrows are black, and under them his eyes, which are small, very dark and very alert, glitter, sometimes with indescribable fire. He is the exact type of a Japanese without a drop of Chinese blood.

His body is short and thin, but muscular and lithe. The expression of his face is always benevolent, and very kindly is the smile which never leaves his lips.

But his prominent brow and clearly defined lower jaw show that he is a man of great determination. He looks impulsive rather than cold, and one realises the activity of his mind when one sees the rapidity with which he glances from side to side, noticing all that goes on around him.

Before sitting down, perhaps because he noticed that I was looking at him so attentively, he took two steps towards me, and said with a smile:

"Are you of our party, or are you going north with Kamimura?"

"I cannot answer that question, general. I shall go where I am ordered, confident that I am working for Japan."

"Well said, commander!" he replied cheerily. We sat down. The first few minutes were rather stiff and ceremonious.

Gradually the atmosphere thawed. We talked with greater freedom and liveliness; Kodama explained some technical details of the ship to Nogi, who knew hardly anything about warships.

The admiral, when the time for toasts came, rose and said:

"I drink to General Nogi, General Kodama, and all those who are taking part in their glorious enterprise."

He touched the general's glass with his own, and the former re-

GENERAL BARON NOGI

plied:

"I drink to the navy, General Kodama, and my soldiers."

General Kodama smiled, and did not respond, but said in a low voice to General Tchigin at his side:

"To the rapid fall of Port Arthur! "

One of the English *attachés* could not restrain himself, and exclaimed "Japan for ever!" We all laughed but did not applaud, out of respect for our superiors. Will Port Arthur fall as soon as we think?

At Sea, June 8th;

At six in the afternoon I started off in the *Osiva* towards the harbour of Port Arthur. I am sure to be under the orders of Admiral Togo. I am glad of this, for I shall be able to witness a big sea-fight. The Russian squadron will have to give battle so as to avoid falling either into the hands of Nogi's troops or into ours.

But I must confess that while we are waiting for the day of battle, the duty which we have to do before Port Arthur is very wearisome.

Our orders are to cruise about continuously about six miles from the forts.

This is a standing order, and if no disaster happens to us, it must be due to the fact that the Russians do not want to waste ammunition or to reveal their exact gun-positions.

This is too silly for words, in view of the fact that for more than eight months all the commanders of vessels have been in possession of a detailed plan of all the batteries which can fire on us from the shore.

We know for certain that since the outbreak of hostilities the Russians have not mounted any new guns.

They could if they liked fire on us with impunity, and amuse themselves by chasing us about, secure in the knowledge that we cannot answer them. Another danger for us is the presence of the *Retvisan*, which continues, as ever, to block up the entrance to the harbour like a powerful floating battery.

Her searchlights are always lit. But for this she would have sustained a serious disaster, for we have been given orders to attack her at the slightest sign of relaxation on her part, and see if we cannot once more damage her.

The duty is wearisome, for besides the two fast cruisers which do duty like ourselves, there are only four destroyers to watch an area of thirty-two, miles.

This means that every twelve hours we have to go to the cruisers to get coal.

We are on duty a whole week at a time from Saturday to Saturday.

On board each boat we have wireless-telegraphy apparatus to communicate amongst ourselves and with the flagship *Mikasa*.

About midnight the wind, which was blowing from the west, brought us the sounds of a furious cannonade on shore. It lasted about an hour and a half, and from the briskness of it there was evidently an important fight going on between the besiegers and those who will soon be besieged.

This plan of fighting at night is a capital one for troops who are well acquainted with the ground on which they have to fight.

From what I was told by one of the Russian prisoners with whom I had a talk in Sasebo, the attacks which Kuroki's army delivered on the nights of the 29th and 30th of April completely disconcerted the Russians.

The latter, blinded by the light from the searchlights which every company carried, did not know how to defend themselves, nor in what direction to direct their rifle fire. In night attacks the searchlights are placed at a distance of at least 1,000 metres from the troops to which they belong; and as they are constantly put in different positions, sometimes show to the left and sometimes to the right.

The cannonade stopped long before dawn, but burst out again a few hours later, when the first rays of the sun appeared.

At Sea, June 11th.

Although Admiral Togo declared the blockade of the whole Kuan-Tung peninsula, there is no lack of ships which try to run the blockade.

Last night, at half-past ten, when the *Osiva* had reached the extreme limit of her usual cruise, the officer of the watch awoke me.

A merchant vessel was in sight and was making straight for the harbour, hoping to get in unseen.

I warned my companions by telegraph, and dashed resolutely at her without showing my searchlight. When I got within range I turned on my searchlight and fired a shot by way of warning.

The ship changed her course and seemed to be making for Niu-chang, but a few moments later, increasing her speed, she turned her bows southwards in the direction of Chefu. Had it not been for her first change of course she might have escaped; but the time lost by this proved fatal to her. I started in pursuit at full speed, and in a quarter of an hour, having made certain that I could capture or sink her, fired another blank round. The ship did not stop, so then I ordered my men to load with shell and open a rapid fire.

The third shot smashed one of her funnels, and then, seeing that I meant business and that I should sink her when I got within torpedo range, she hove to and waited for me. I launched a boat, and my lieutenant, with ten men, took possession of the ship. She proved to be German, the *Blume*, of 3,500 tons. The cargo consisted of corn and forage.

She was coming from Chefu, and could not deny that she was trying to carry provisions to the Russians. After informing the commander of the division, and getting his permission, I set off for the Elliott Islands with my prize, well satisfied with my exploit.

On the following day I was received by Admiral Togo. I gave him an account of my capture, with exact details as to cargo, the locality in which the prize was taken, the hour of its capture, and all the other details which are usual in these cases.

The admiral listened to me kindly, and told me that I and my crew were relieved from duty for that week.

In my presence he gave orders for another destroyer to go out and take up the position before Port Arthur which the *Osiva* had vacated.

I landed on one of the islands where there was a large number of seamen and officers who were off duty, and who were lodging in the houses of the Chinamen, who in these parts are engaged in fishing.

Following the example of my companions, I had a meal in a Chinese inn and started talking with the proprietor, who understood a little Japanese.

He told me that the Russians had committed the most dreadful atrocities in Manchuria, slaying and looting as though in a conquered country.

He added that the Chinese were very glad to see that we had defeated them; but in spite of his reticence on this point, the worthy being evidently did not rely much on the triumph either of our navy or our army. Our conversation was much as follows:

"Port Arthur is very strong, and has a large garrison, your honour. Besides, in a short time the Russians will come from the north to relieve it."

"Well, let them come," I answered.

"Does not your honour know how powerful the white men are?"

"They did not show it at the Yalu; we took seven hundred prisoners from them there, besides thirty-two guns and a stand of colours, and they ran like hares."

The innkeeper scratched his head and looked at me in a way which showed that he did not believe a word of what I was saying.

Obviously the Russians have so terrorised the wretched Chinese that the latter think they are invincible, and the mere apparition of an ugly-looking *Cossack*, threatening every kind of evil, is enough to paralyse a whole Chinese village with terror and make them ready to do anything the man may want.

In the evening I had supper with some brother officers, amongst whom was the captain of the battleship *Fuji*, a veteran of the Chino-Japanese War. We talked of our future naval operations, and the captain said that in his opinion the war was a lost cause for the Russians— anyhow at sea.

Their two best battleships, which we torpedoed during the night of the 8th and 9th of February, are not yet fit for active service, and although we have lost the *Hatsuse*, (May 15th it ran into a mine and foundered), we are far stronger than they. Our torpedo-boats and destroyers would suffice to give us the victory. Even though we lose twenty or thirty of them it does not much matter, for in our dockyards at Osaka, Sasebo, Nagasaki, and Simonoseki are fifteen destroyers and forty seagoing torpedo-boats under construction.

In three or four months we shall have completely routed the Port Arthur squadron, and then, if it should be necessary, we shall be quite capable of meeting the Baltic Squadron, in spite of any losses.

"And what do you think the Vladivostock cruisers will do?" I said.

"We have nothing to fear from them. They may commit a few atrocities in their cruises along the coast, but as soon as Kamimura sets his eyes on them they are lost, as they are not in a fit condition to compete with our cruisers."

We then spoke about the land operations, and we all agreed as to the superiority of our weapons, and that the *élan* of our brave children would give us a decisive victory over the Russians.

After this we strolled about on the beach, enjoying the fresh evening air, and a little before eight o'clock we all got into our boats to go on board.

At Sea, June 24th.

Absolute tranquillity has reigned during the last few days. Our brother officers who come from Dalny and the Elliott Islands say that Nogi is going on methodically, driving the Russians from their positions on the Kuan-Tung peninsula. He will continue attacking the troops commanded by Generals Kondratenko and Fock till the moment arrives for the blockade to become a regular siege, and it will not be long before this happens.

Today we have had bad news. The Vladivostock cruisers, with remarkable daring, shaped their course for the Yellow Sea, eluded the vigilance of Admiral Kamimura, and having sunk a transport laden with troops and heavy guns, fled northwards; thanks to a fog, our cruisers saw no signs of them.

At Sea, July 3rd.

In company with many other warships I have been convoying twenty steamers laden with troops to the Liao-Tung peninsula.

Marshal Oyama, who is going out as commander-in-chief of the four Japanese armies, was in command of them.

The voyage went off without a hitch. The marshal landed at Dalny and put up in General Kodama's house.

Most of the soldiers landed at Pitsevo, and only 12,000 men are left to reinforce General Nogi's troops when it becomes necessary.

The soldiers say that there are loud outcries in Japan against what they call the bungling of Admiral Kamimura, and that everyone is demanding his recall.

To us who know the character and intelligence of the young admiral, the disasters that keep on occurring seem most extraordinary. They tell me that he has sailed with his squadron of cruisers for Vladivostock, determined to give battle to the enemy, and to take him by surprise if he ventures out of the harbour again.

At Sea, July 17th.

The weeks go by with hopeless monotony. Decidedly the Russians are not so fear-inspiring a foe as we imagined before war broke out. All the foreign papers declare that the damage on board the battleships and cruisers is now repaired; but in spite of this we cannot tempt them from their base. Admiral Witheft, who has taken over the supreme command since the death of Makharoff, does not seem to be of the same temperament as his predecessor, for days and weeks go by without his putting to sea.

These last days we have twice bombarded some Russian positions in Pigeon Bay. At first the enemy's batteries answered; but the *Kasuga* and *Iwate* advanced fearlessly, and in fifteen minutes succeeded in dismounting most of the guns and silencing the rest.

The *Kasuga* got a 12-cm. shell into one of her turrets, which destroyed it completely, killing three men and wounding five; she then went to Dalny, where her injuries will be repaired.

As time goes on the situation of the Russian squadron gets more critical, and although it is hard to believe, it is said that they will very soon make a desperate sortie.

They have no hope now of help coming. General Oku has three times routed the Russian Army which came to the relief of Port Arthur, it is retiring in confusion to Liao-Yang, after losing many guns and prisoners and more than 9,000 dead and wounded.

The Japanese Army has already occupied Niuchang and Inkeu, and the garrison and squadron of Port Arthur are in dire straits.

As regards the Baltic Squadron, we hear that it is not yet ready to put to sea. However, it would not be strange if Admiral Witheft made a sortie, if only to meet his end like a brave man: fighting with his back to the wall.

At Sea, July 24th.

At six o'clock this morning eight large ships from our squadron were sighted steaming full speed. They approached to within about twelve miles of the entrance to the harbour, made signals to one of the cruisers on look-out duty, the *Akagi*, to close and receive orders.

The latter took up a position which enabled her to see the interior of the harbour, and then the five big battleships and three cruisers advanced to a point about nine miles from Port Arthur and began a terrific bombardment of the enemy's ships, the fire of course being indirect.

The cruiser signalled the result of each shot. Some of the shells hit the mark. The Russian ships, surprised by this attack, immediately opened fire, and kept under way to render aim more difficult. When each ship had fired fifteen shots, and it was evident that the enemy did not intend fighting, Admiral Togo retired to the eastward, and soon his huge battleships were lost to view.

Then the *Bayan* and *Novik* came out as far as the entrance to the harbour, and; out of bravado, fired several shots in our direction without touching us.

We retired by the orders of our commander, to try and entice them out to sea; but they guessed our intentions, and did not venture any further.

At Sea, August 2nd.

A wind has sprung up which revives us. Yesterday one of my gallant seamen died from congestion of the brain produced by the heat. As we could not leave our post of duty he received a sailor's burial, and sank to the bottom of that sea which has devoured so many human lives. He was a man of the north, from Hakodate; and an excellent sailor.

Fortunate being! for he has given his life for his country.

At Sea, August 6th.

This morning General Nogi's army began a general bombardment of the town. As the firing began our cruisers appeared and joined in the operations as well. The din could be heard from Chefu; it was absolutely terrific. When four or five heavy guns fired together, the whole peninsula seemed to shake.

The firing lasted five hours; then the Russian battleships, finding they were none too safe in the harbour, came out to the outer road-stead. What a magnificent opportunity for firing a few torpedoes at them!

But the flagship made no signals, and although we were burning to do so, we did not attack them.

The opportunity seemed to me to be excellent. By sacrificing four or five torpedo-boats we could have put a couple of the enemy's battleships out of action, and thus victory in the end would be assured to us.

With the main body, between the battleship and cruiser divisions, came thirty torpedo-boats and eight destroyers. Admiral Togo evidently did not think this a suitable opportunity for an attack, so at two in the afternoon we left the neighbourhood of Port Arthur for our anchorage in the Elliott Islands.

At Sea, August 11th.

At last we have had our battle. The Russian squadron has been vanquished, just as China was at the Battle of the Yalu. Japan is absolute mistress of the sea!

I write these lines while the *Osiva* is running to the southward at full speed in pursuit of the *Novik*.

The battle took place yesterday. Before day dawned our look-out ships noticed unusual activity in the harbour.

The whole of Admiral Witheft's squadron was preparing for sea, either to seek a neutral port or to give battle. When we commanders of vessels heard this, we were delighted, and Admiral Togo was informed.

At half-past five, one after the other, the six Russian battleships steamed out of the harbour, the first being the *Czarevitch,* flying the admiral's flag.

Then followed the *Retvisan, Pobieda, Sevastopol, Peresviet,* and *Poltava,* in the order stated; and finally the *Bayan, Askold, Diana, Pallada,* and *Novik.* A few torpedo-boats came out last, following five destroyers.

We were drawn up in inverse order; that is to say, the smaller ships were in front.

We six torpedo divisions formed three arcs of a circle, at a distance of eleven miles from the coast.

Filling the gaps, and five miles further from the coast, were the armoured and protected cruisers.

Three miles still further to the southward—so as to block the enemy's road to Wei-hai-Wei and Chefu, loomed the enormous shapes of the *Mikasa, Shikishima, Asahi, Fuji,* and *Yashima.*

The enemy's squadron got under way at half-past seven in order of battle.

The *Czarevitch,* flanked by the *Retvisan* and *Pobieda,* advanced towards us and fired the first shot at nine minutes past eight.

The battle had begun.

Our cruisers replied, and our torpedo divisions began to manoeuvre so as to get between the enemy's big ships. Our battleships came on at half speed, and the *Mikasa* discharged her big guns at the *Czarevitch,* which replied, but without stopping.

Now began a tremendous duel between the guns of the three Russian battleships and our five.

The other three, the *Sevastopol, Peresviet,* and *Poltava,* had difficulty in defending themselves from our attacks, and instead of joining their companions, remained a long way off.

The fire from our battleships became more accurate every moment. The *Retvisan* and *Czarevitch* were on fire. At a signal from the admiral we ran up to the battleships and discharged our first torpedoes at them.

Our armoured and protected cruisers had pushed themselves like a wedge between the Russian divisions, separating them.

Thus the enemy's line of battle was broken. The *Bayan* and *Pallada* withdrew, at about ten o'clock, towards the harbour.

Our battleships drew nearer the Russians, and for fifteen minutes kept up a furious fire with all their larger guns.

Admiral Togo, who saw signs of weakening in the enemy's squadron, despatched three divisions of destroyers (among which was the

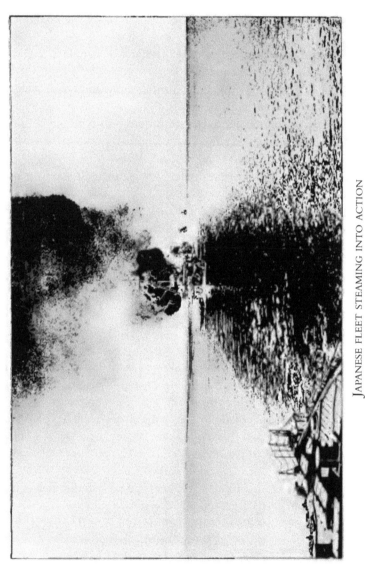

JAPANESE FLEET STEAMING INTO ACTION

Osiva), to get behind them and prevent the Russian ships retiring to the harbour.

Suddenly an important change in formation took place in the enemy's squadron. The ships exchanged signals amongst themselves, and while *the Czarevitch, Askold, Diana,* and *Novik* continued to advance in different directions, the torpedo-boats and destroyers withdrew towards Port Arthur. On their way they attacked our three destroyer divisions, so as to leave a clear passage for the five battleships, which, tired of fighting, were returning towards the harbour hotly pursued by the *Iwate, Yakumo, Azuma, Asama,* and six of the protected cruisers.

One of these, the *Hiroya,* showed such daring that she got close enough to the *Retvisan* to discharge her small guns, killing many of the crew.

The latter, however, fired the large guns which she carried aft, and a 32-cm. shell tore up the deck of the *Hiroya* near the bows, and started a big fire on board.

I took advantage of this *mêlée* to approach unseen, under cover of the *Hiroya,* and attacked the *Retvisan.*

My first torpedo missed the mark. The second struck fairly on the keel of the monster, which quivered and shook in her tracks. I thought I had dealt her a mortal blow, but it was not so; the double bottom had saved her, and she continued her journey towards the harbour, though more slowly than before.

To get away from the *Retvisan's* guns, which had killed three men on board my boat and wounded eight, I steamed off in an easterly direction. Suddenly, to my astonishment, I saw another Russian battleship, which was steaming towards the harbour and approaching me. It was the *Peresviet.* The *Kasuto* and *Osiva* dashed towards her and fired three torpedoes. Two of these hit their mark, and we were about to put an end to her when a hail of shells falling round our boats warned us that we were under fire from the Russian batteries on Golden Hill.

We received the signal to retire. The battle had proved a complete victory for us, and the Russians, routed and battered, were returning to their doomed harbour without any hope of ever quitting it again.

From the bridge of the *Osiva* I watched the *Retvisan* and *Peresviet* entering the harbour, both damaged by our torpedoes.

The crews of all our vessels burst into enthusiastic cheers when they saw the last of the enemy's ships disappearing behind Golden Hill.

It was evident, to us who had watched the retirement, that three of the enemy's largest ships and two or three smaller ones had been unable to follow the rest and were in a very critical position. Although we scanned the horizon, we could not see the slightest trace of either the main body of our squadron or of the enemy's ships, and not even distant firing could be heard.

Had the enemy's ships been sunk, or had they succeeded in eluding our pursuit and taken refuge in some neutral harbour? At four o'clock in the afternoon I got orders to go at full speed to Sasebo.

Ten other torpedo-boats and all the destroyers came with me.

The commander of our division said that at Sasebo we should get orders.

Probably we are going to guard the straits, for possibly the Vladivostock squadron may have co-operated with the Port Arthur squadron to try and re-unite. The weather is lovely though the sea is somewhat rough, which makes me sorry for my poor wounded men, twelve in number, who will get no rest till they reach the hospital at Sasebo.

If on board all the ships of our squadron the results of the battle are as serious as on board mine, the number of dead and wounded must be very great.

I have lost nearly one-third of my crew, and the *Osiva* has been struck in the bows by a shell which has damaged her port torpedo-tube.

In half an hour we shall reach Sasebo, when I shall land my wounded and bury my three dead men.

At Sea, August 13th.

At Sasebo I heard that the *Czarevitch* and *Askold* have run into the German harbour of Kiau-chau, and the *Diana* into Saigon. Meanwhile the *Novik* escaped northwards, to join the Vladivostock ships.

The first three will have to be disarmed in accordance with the laws of neutrality, and are lost to Russia till the end of the war.

Two of our small cruisers, which are as fast as she, are pursuing the *Novik*, and will not let her escape unless she succeeds in joining the Vladivostock ships.

In Sasebo there are great illuminations in the streets, and great rejoicings over our victory. At dusk we left harbour and, as I had anticipated, proceeded to watch the straits, with standing orders to dispute the passage of Admiral Yessen's cruisers, even though we should lose all our boats.

Admiral Kamimura has started off to look for these ships, and presumably if he finds them he will compel them to fight.

I have now repaired the damage to my torpedo-tube, and my boat is again ready to fight.

We cruised about all night in the straits without seeing even the ghost of the Russian squadron, and continued peacefully cruising in the same place all the morning.

At mid-day the despatch boat *Hiroda* came up with orders from Admiral Togo for us to return to the Elliott Islands and rejoin the main body.

At Sea, August 20th.

The day before yesterday we heard that Admiral Kamimura's squadron has gained a decisive victory over the Vladivostock cruisers, which are now reduced to complete impotence.

The *Rurik* has been sunk; the *Gromoboi* and *Rossia* have been so damaged, and have lost so many of their crew, that they will be unable to put to sea for at least three months. That phantom squadron which has committed so many atrocities on defenceless ships has been unable to withstand the first serious blow from our armoured cruisers. The poor *Novik* has also been sunk, near Korsakova. Her captain, who was one of the cleverest and bravest men in the Russian Navy, deserved a better fate.

All the same his ship met with a heroic end; she fought till the last moment, and then sank. The two blows which the Russian Navy has received within the space of five days have left it practically helpless.

On the other hand, we have only sustained losses of slight importance—the *Hatsuse*, *Yoshino*, and three destroyers.

The Russians have lost two big battleships, one armoured cruiser, three protected cruisers, two destroyers, the *Novik*, and two gunboats, besides seven torpedo-boats put out of action.

Our general opinion is that Port Arthur will surrender in a couple of months, for Nogi has already begun assaulting the advanced works; and as the place has no hopes of reinforcements, presumably it will not offer much resistance.

We are absolute masters of the sea; we hold in our grasp that "sea power" which, according to the English, is a definite proof of our victory. The Port Arthur squadron must surrender or perish in a sortie.

To us the behaviour of the Russian sailors seems most extraordinary. They seem to be far more anxious to preserve their ships from harm than to fight. In none of our encounters has there been one act of daring on their part.

Why did they not, with their five battleships and four cruisers, fight a duel to the death with our larger vessels, to avenge the loss of Admiral Witheft? (Killed by explosion of shell in conning-tower of *Czarevitch* during action of 10th August).

Had they done this it might have cost them the loss of one of their fighting units; but, fighting in desperation, they would have done us serious damage.

Is it true, as the English maintain, that there is not a single good sailor in Russia?

Some of our officers, chiefly the younger ones, also think it strange that Admiral Togo did not turn the last battle to better account, for he might have captured some of the enemy's ships.

Quite true; but to effect this he would have to risk losing some of his battleships or cruisers, and this would not have suited him at all.

Japan has no reserve squadron, and must preserve the one which she possesses intact, in the event of the Russians trying, with their Baltic Squadron, to avenge the misfortunes sustained in the Yellow Sea. With the destroyers and torpedo-boats our commander has sufficient forces to deal with the battleships and cruisers which the Russians have left, and there is no necessity to expose the larger and more costly fighting units to danger.

At Sea, August 27th.

As the siege of Port Arthur by land becomes more vigorous, the attempts to run the blockade which we have established by sea become more frequent.

Though the Russians say that they "have provisions enough for a year," the fact remains that every day we capture Chinese *junks* trying to bring provisions into the town.

Altogether seventeen vessels are patrolling near the harbour.

We are disposed in such a way, out of effective range of the land batteries, that it is very difficult for any ship to elude our vigilance at night. By day it is absolutely impossible.

Yesterday there was a heavy bombardment on land. Judging by the way the reports followed each other, at least two hundred guns were taking part in the cannonade.

They say that one of these days a general assault on the town will take place.

Tomorrow, when my tour of patrolling finishes, I shall go to the Elliott Islands and get news of the war.

As regards the Baltic Squadron, we now hear that it has been decided not to despatch it for the present, as all the battleships are still in a very backward condition.

At Sea, September 10th.

Once more I am on duty before Port Arthur. The general assault has cost us many lives, and not produced much of a result.

They say that more than fifteen thousand Japanese have been killed or wounded. But if as yet we have not triumphed at Port Arthur, we have at any rate won a great victory in Manchuria. The entrenched camp of Liao-Yang, which, according to the Russians, was impregnable, has fallen into the hands of our troops after a week's fighting.

The losses on both sides were enormous. But the Japanese Army has demonstrated its superiority over the Russians, and shown that it can fight as well on a plain as in a mountainous country.

If Kuroki had had fifty thousand men more, he would have captured several large bodies of the enemy.

At Sea, September 13th.

This morning two battleships and six big cruisers arrived. For five hours they bombarded some batteries and trenches which the Russians have constructed to the east of Liautishan, which is in the western section of the Port Arthur defences.

As the *Osiva* is patrolling in that neighbourhood, I was able to see that the defences became untenable, and that General Nogi's troops were establishing themselves on the shore, thus cutting off the Russians' last chance of communication by land.

The enemy's ships show no signs of life. Now and again one of the battleships comes out into the outer roadstead, wastes some ammunition, and then returns to the harbour once more.

The Japanese batteries continually bombard the whole place. In the daytime they fire at the forts; nearly every night they bombard the town, causing many fires. Yesterday a store of Russian ammunition blew up; it made a terrific explosion.

Those of our ships which bombarded the coast are now, as I write these fines, firing on the town. Their fire is indirect, but is evidently effective, for the Russian battleships have got under way. Only the *Peresviet* lies motionless, listed to port, probably repairing the damage inflicted by my torpedo.

Dalny, September 17th.

We have returned to Dalny, escorting a force which started from

JAPANESE HEAVY GUN AMMUNITION.

Nagasaki the day before yesterday.

It was composed of 17,000 soldiers and 100 mortars of a new pattern, 11 inches in diameter. They are enormously powerful pieces. In a short time, they will be in position on Wolf Hill, and then the town will be in a far worse plight than before.

Everyone thinks that the forts will be unable to withstand the shells thrown by these monsters; but as they weigh no tons each, their transport and erection will take a long time—at least a month.

Since I was in Dalny last, the city has changed in appearance. All traces of the vandal-like destruction committed by the Russians and Chinamen are gradually disappearing.

Many shopkeepers have come from Japan and set up here, and as the sea is now absolutely safe, there is a large amount of traffic between this port and Japan.

The articles of comfort and luxury which were wanting at the beginning of the campaign are now abundant both here and in Niuchang. Trade with China is now more flourishing than before the outbreak of war, and large numbers of Chinese have come here with their families in the certainty that our army will come off victorious.

The commander of the division has given me good news. In a couple of weeks, I shall be promoted to the rank of commander, and given command of a third-class cruiser.

At Sea, September 20th.

This morning, before sunrise, a furious bombardment of Port Arthur from all four points of the compass awoke me. I at once went on to the bridge, and saw that the large battleships and cruiser division, at a distance of eight miles from Port Arthur, were firing their heavy guns. The forts on shore were answering, although their projectiles seldom reached the line of our vessels.

At the same time General Nogi's army, which has already taken many of the positions which dominate the line of Russian forts, was employing all its guns against the town and forts.

It was the most gorgeous sight I have ever witnessed in my life.

Dense clouds of smoke marked the discharge of each gun, and as I looked towards the town through my glasses, I could see masses of far thicker smoke which now and again burst into terrible conflagrations.

After an hour and a half of this fiendish din, which filled one's imagination with a vivid picture of this world during the volcanic period, we heard the deafening roar of a terrible explosion. A huge sheet of flame breaking through a dense, black bank of smoke marked the position of the catastrophe.

I asked one of my comrades what had happened, and with the plan of the town before us, we made out that one of the powder magazines in the arsenal had exploded. Minutes and hours went by, yet the intensity of the fixe never flagged; most of the time more than thirty heavy projectiles a minute were falling into the besieged city.

All her forts kept firing their heavy guns, which made a quite distinct sound from the detonations of the Japanese artillery.

All our ships are continually under way, steaming at half speed, manoeuvring, now turning their stem and now their bows towards the harbour, so as to fire their heavy guns alternately.

We destroyers cannot take part in this fiendish symphony because of the short range of our guns, but we also keep continually moving to avoid being struck by any of the enemy's shells.

We are all struck by the fact that the Russian battleships have not gone out to the outer roadstead to take part in the fray. However, it looks as though Admiral Togo had foreseen this, as we destroyers have been given no orders respecting the Russian battleships. We are all longing for them to come out, for then we can attack them in our turn, and be participators in a fight of which up to the present we have been merely spectators. As I have said before, the Russian projectiles hardly ever reach us, but a little before one o'clock in the afternoon an enormous shell, which must have been at least 28 centimetres in diameter, fell about two hundred metres from my boat and sank into the sea with an ugly hiss.

A few metres more and the *Osiva*, my crew and myself, would have ceased to belong to the Japanese Navy.

The noise is really awful. We are all half stupefied, and the air vibrates in the most extraordinary way.

The atmospheric commotion produced by the artillery fire is so great that at a quarter past two an absolute hurricane arose, accompanied by a fall of rain such as one only expects to see in the tropics.

At three in the afternoon punctually the fire of the ships suddenly stops, and they retire out to sea in two large divisions, one composed of battleships and the other of cruisers. But the bombardment by land goes on uninterruptedly, and with implacable determination, as though the besiegers were imbued with the desire to demolish once and for all the immovable blocks of granite cut out of the living rock which form the walls of the forts.

There can be no doubt that a serious attack on the besieged town is in course of preparation, and we all entertain hopes that our army will gain a decisive victory, strong though the defences of Port Arthur may be.

Night draws on, yet the firing continues. At nine o'clock, when it is completely dark, the Japanese ships once more draw near and open fire, whilst the land forts, from Liautishan to Golden Hill; answer them.

It is now evident that the troops are getting ready for an assault, and Admiral Togo wants to prevent the gunners in the forts which face the sea from helping their companions who are struggling with the Japanese infantry.

The sight is twice as magnificent now as it was by day. Enormous searchlights flash in the darkness, momentarily illuminating the black masses of the ships and forts, while the heavy guns belch out sheets of flame several yards in length, which die away with startling suddenness.

Meanwhile the searchlights dart their beams of light in all directions, powerful and blinding; they cross and clash in space with the most marvellous effect, or fall on to the sea like flaming swords which mow down all opposition.

With good field-glasses we can see the effect produced by the fire of our soldiers on land. There also the brilliant lights are flashing, and searching the uttermost parts of the hills. They climb to the summits, dive into the torrents, descend into the valleys, and from my position, which is to the extreme west of the peninsula, I can see their white radiance illuminating dense masses of men who are hurling themselves forward in the assault of the defences.

Suddenly the fire of the ships and the land batteries ceases. Complete silence reigns, broken now and again by a few shots from the enemy.

We go a little nearer the shore, and while I am manoeuvring to get to a convenient distance for seeing, without being in the way, we hear a deafening uproar familiar to all Japanese ears—It is the "*Banzai!*" of the attack. The rattle of musketry sounds fiercely and continuously, whilst other noises die down. Then come the shouts of our soldiers, "*Sutsumé! sutsumé!*" ("Forward!") as they dash on to death or victory.

The searchlights intensify that scene of awful slaughter. Our soldiers are climbing the slopes of five hills, crowned with a triple line of flaming light, which flares ceaselessly, darting about, quivering, increasing in intensity, and waning.

We can see the lines of Russian trenches, from which the enemy are firing on our men.

At times we hear a distinct noise which dominates the sound of musketry: it is the voice of the machine-guns, as they mow down whole companies who fall never to rise again.

Ten, eleven, twelve o'clock strikes; yet the slaughter continues.

Now and again we hear a distant clamour which seems to show that the Russians or Japanese have taken some position or have gained a partial victory over their enemies.

At one in the morning, approximately, we hear a tremendous up-roar, and by the light of the thousands of guns which are firing we see, fluttering on a little hill which faces the fort of Sun-ti-chau, the banner of the Rising Sun.

My crew and I give vent to a resounding *"Banzai!"* which only the night and the fishes can hear. Once again the Japanese have con-quered.

That hill was crowned, like the others, with a triple tier of trenches defended by Russian soldiers. These have met their death, and my brothers, victorious, spurn their bodies under foot.

The battle goes on till half-past two. Then suddenly all the search-lights die out, all the rifles are silent. A moment later large beacon-fires illumine all the Japanese positions, and a terrible roar rends the air.

All the guns once more open on the Russians for ten minutes.

Then once again a deep silence reigns. The fight is finished—to-morrow we shall know who has won.

At Sea, September 26th.

As I write these lines the *Osiva* is convoying a fresh force of sol-diers, who are going to Dalny from the Elliott Islands.

I heard afterwards that the attack on the 20th was indecisive.

The Japanese lost heavily, and only captured the two redoubts on the hill where I saw our banner waving.

We know that the besiegers did all in their power, and made super-human efforts not to be beaten in their first assault.

Now we are landing twelve thousand soldiers more, who come from the North of Japan, from the division in the island of Formosa. The force includes nine heavy pieces of artillery, which will increase the havoc wrought by the recent bombardment.

Dalny has already resumed its normal appearance, except that in-stead of Russians, Germans, and Siberians pervading the streets and occupying the houses, Chinese and Japanese are *en évidence* everywhere. So sure is every one of our ultimate victory that even women and children abound.

The wharves have been repaired, all the mines, floating and fixed, removed, and ships can enter and leave the harbour with impunity.

Tomorrow, when we have taken a fresh supply of ammunition on board, we—that is the Torpedo Flotilla and squadron of protected cruisers—shall sail once again for the waters of Port Arthur.

At Sea, October 5th.

We have heard that a great battle will soon take place in Manchuria, and we hope that if the result is favourable to our arms, Port Arthur will shortly have to surrender. It is said, too, that the Baltic Squadron is on the point of sailing from Cronstadt to come to the assistance of the ships which are imprisoned in the Muscovite stronghold.

Though our strength and powers of endurance are sufficient to fight the two squadrons combined, yet I think that it would be a great advantage to us to be completely quit of the battleships which are in Port Arthur before the Baltic vessels reach the Yellow Sea.

One of these days another general assault on the defences will be delivered, and probably the navy will take its share in this with a vigorous bombardment.

★★★★★★

As I write these lines the uproar and turmoil of a fight which we had a few hours ago are just dying away.

Thinking doubtless to take advantage of the absence of the larger vessels of our squadron, the *Pallada* came out to the outer roadstead and opened fire on our protected cruisers.

At the same time, two sea-going torpedo-boats, proceeding at full speed, tried to break through our fines, no doubt with the intention of going to Chefu.

The *Kioto, Osiva*, and the cruiser *Akagi* disputed their passage, and brought them to action.

By means of a dexterous manoeuvre they succeeded in passing between the cruiser and our two destroyers, but then we, getting every ounce out of our engines, riddled them with projectiles for two hours and a half. The big guns of the *Akagi* had a most destructive effect on the Russian vessels. The latter gradually ceased firing, and the *Batrackzi*, one of the best and newest torpedo-boats in the Russian Navy, blew up without it being possible to save any of her crew. The other torpedo-boat, recognising the impossibility of continuing the struggle, altered her course. We ran alongside as she stopped momentarily, having been struck by two shells from the *Osiva*.

We approached to capture her, but she fired the two small guns which she carried aft, and started off again, hoping to gain some haven of refuge.

Our other torpedo-boats, however, which had been watching the incidents of the fight from afar, came up now, and the poor *Borinsky* had to haul down her flag. Of the sixty-two men who had composed her crew when she started from Port Arthur, only twenty-eight remained alive. The captain and his lieutenant were dead. I am to have the honour of taking this new prize to the Elliott Islands, and of handing her over to Admiral Togo.

No man who is not a naval officer can realise the immense satisfaction which I feel on these occasions, and the emotion which seizes me at the thought that Admiral Togo will be congratulating me in a few hours' time.

On board the Katzumo, October 8th.

I am now commanding a cruiser. She is one of the newest in the Japanese Navy: is called the *Katzumo*, was launched in January, 1903, has a displacement of 2,400 tons, carries two 12-cm. and eight 6-cm. guns, one torpedo-tube, and five machine-guns. The day before yesterday, when I got to the Elliott Islands, Admiral Togo received me most cordially and congratulated me before all my comrades on my behaviour in the fight of the 4th of the month. Then, with a smile, he gave me the brevet of a commander, and said to me formally:

In the name of the Mikado, I give you command of the cruiser *Katzumo*.

Continue to do your duty as you have done up till now, and remember always that only determination, and the conscientious fulfilment of the orders given by your superiors, lead to victory.

I answered that my dearest wish was to go on fighting for my country, and that my one prayer was for an opportunity of dying for her or of taking part in a decisive victory over the Russians. My comrades congratulated me. I handed over command of the *Osiva* to an officer who was pointed out to me, and hastened to take possession of my splendid new vessel. In her I sailed this afternoon for the waters of Port Arthur, where I shall shortly arrive. In spite of what my superior officers say, I have but slender hopes of a fight in the immediate future, for the Russian squadron seems determined to let itself be captured in its lair, instead of perishing in mortal combat.

It is, however, true that if they were to attempt a sortie now, their ships would probably all perish before they could reach a neutral port. A few days ago eleven new destroyers from the dockyards of Simonoseki and Osaka arrived to join the Japanese squadron.

These destroyers, with those which are now on duty, are more than enough to destroy the battleships and the few cruisers which the Russians possess.

Their one hope now is that the Baltic Squadron may arrive before the surrender of the forts, and then to make a desperate sortie, at the same moment that the new fleet is engaging us.

But all this is still a long way off, especially as the enemy's ships are not at the moment on their way to the Far East.

At Sea, October 12th.

Yesterday I captured a German steamer, the *Rundsçhau*, which was making for Port Arthur with a cargo of corn and food-stuffs. At 11 p.m. I thought I heard a suspicious noise to port, which sounded like a ship some distance off, going along at full speed.

I tried in vain to penetrate the darkness, but could see nothing. Not a spark came from the funnel of that invisible ship, but I ordered my furnaces to be looked to and turned my bows in a direction where, guided by the noise, I thought I should hit off the line of the ship.

For a long time I searched the sea all round me with the aid of my magnificent searchlights.

After firing a gun to warn the other ships on guard, I went on towards Port Arthur, at the risk of being fired on by the forts. Suddenly my torpedo lieutenant called out to me that he thought he could see a ship on the starboard hand and about two miles north of us. I ordered the foremost guns to be loaded with shell, and fired another blank charge as a signal for the steamer to heave to.

Two minutes later, as she did not obey, I fired with shell. The fifth shot struck her, and the ship hove to. I sent an officer and fifteen men in a cutter to board her, altered my course, and steamed away at full speed with my prize from the danger zone in which I found myself, for the forts were working their searchlights and I ran the risk of getting a shell on board the *Katzumo*. I reported myself to the commander of my division and awaited orders, which were, as I had expected, to take the steamer to the Elliott Islands.

This second capture, coming so soon after I had assumed command of my new ship, gave me great importance in my own eyes, and I was sure of earning the goodwill of the admiral.

The latter smiled when he saw me, and congratulated me cordially on my new prize, saying that if all the sailors of Japan were as lucky as I, there would soon be no room in her harbours for the quantity of Russian prizes.

He made me return to my post at once, and said that we should soon find ourselves in the harbour of Port Arthur, as a fresh general assault on the defences was contemplated.

At Sea, October 22nd.

At ten o'clock this morning the whole of the Japanese squadron assembled before Port Arthur and began a general bombardment of the town and forts. The batteries of Nogi's army are also firing, as they did on that famous day in September.

The Russians answer with less vigour than on that occasion, and the bombardment lasts without a pause till one o'clock in the afternoon. An officer on board one of the destroyers which come from the Elliott Islands tells me that we have won a great victory in Manchuria, the Russian casualties being over forty thousand.

It is to be hoped that in the assault, which they intend making this afternoon or evening, Nogi's soldiers will be as fortunate as those of Oku and Nodzu. A squadron of destroyers and three cruisers, among which is the *Katzumo*, have been bombarding some batteries which the Russians have established on the lower slopes of Liautishan, and which have been troubling the attacking force.

Our guns enfilade these batteries, and have done great damage to them, but one battery of the principal fort opened fire on us, and we had to withdraw to avoid the risk of a catastrophe.

We succeeded in our object without losing a man or being damaged in the least, and are delighted with ourselves.

The bombardment lasted till four o'clock without a pause. Now and again the guns give a sharp report, as though they were splitting, or bursting into a thousand pieces.

This is caused by using too heavy charges, which has a deleterious effect on the guns. But the impression of these discordant notes only lasts a moment, and soon the hellish concert, which deafens all who hear it, begins again.

At seven o'clock in the evening a thick fog arose, which shows that there have been floods of rain in Manchuria.

When that impenetrable curtain got too thick, the Japanese batteries suddenly became silent, and only the Russians continued firing, but as they did not know exactly where to aim, they also eventually ceased firing. The assault is about to be delivered, or has already begun.

Our large battleships do not stir from their look-out positions. Possibly when our soldiers have occupied some of the forts, the Russian ships may try their luck and make an effort to escape in the fog. They may try, but they will not do it without a fight.

All the destroyers excepting the 4th and 5th Divisions, which are patrolling in rear of the fleet, keep cruising round the outer roadstead; and so small is the interval between the ships that any vessel which tries to pass through them will be discovered instantly.

We protected cruisers are on the lookout as well, patrolling the space between the destroyers and battleships at half speed. And as the latter and the large cruisers form a huge animated semicircle in addition, which moves incessantly up and down, the Russian squadron will have to pass through three lines which are watching and hemming it in.

Fifteen minutes after the cessation of the artillery fire, the land breeze brought us the sounds of a battle which was taking place round Port Arthur: a faint, distant noise, mingled now and again with confused shouts.

The rattle of musketry and of the machineguns sounded like a train in motion when the brakes are applied on a slope. The shouts of the soldiers made me think of the fragments of applause which come from a crowded theatre, penetrating far into the stillness of the night.

The fight lasted till one in the morning, then suddenly stopped. The men, weary of dealing death, were resting. Which side had been beaten?

Six or seven dull detonations come to our ears from Port Arthur. As the wind has freshened, and is blowing from the south, we cannot gauge the extent of these explosions. My lieutenant, who is very keen and much given to exaggerating, tells me that he is certain that our soldiers have captured the outer line of forts and that the Russians have blown up their ships, not wishing to have to hand them over when the place surrenders.

I point out that there is a far simpler means of destroying the Russian battleships and cruisers: namely, to send them out to us and engage in a desperate fight, in which, though they may possibly not come off victorious, they may do us infinite harm.

I cannot pull him off his hobby-horse. He declares that the Russian sailors will not die fighting, and that they will do no more than destroy their ships. This ought to please us.

At Sea, October 27th.

Yesterday we carried a fresh contingent of 8,000 men to Dalny.

They are going to reinforce General Nogi's ranks, which suffered great losses in the unsuccessful attack the other night.

All the same, our soldiers captured the two redoubts which form part of the advanced works of the forts of Ehrlung and Keikwan.

It seems a very small result compared with the blood which was shed in attaining it. But in reality it enables us to sap the approaches of both forts.

Port Arthur begins to be in a very critical situation.

At Sea, October 29th.

This morning my old destroyer the *Osiva*, in conjunction with the *Katimatsu*, captured ten Chinese ships laden with provisions, which were going to Port Arthur from Chefu, hoping to pass us unnoticed in the fog.

It is a useful capture. The cargo consists of corn, fresh meat, vegetables, and green forage. The Russians would have feasted and gorged themselves with a vengeance, but decidedly fortune does not favour them.

The value of the captured goods amounts to more than 200,000 *roubles*, at current rates. But they must have cost the Russians more than a million, owing to the liberal rewards they have to give to the Chinese sailors for running the risk of so dangerous an undertaking.

Though the admiral would be quite within his rights if he punished the crews of these blockade-running ships, he never does it. He contents himself with confiscating ship and cargo and leaving the sailors at liberty. This is a judicious proceeding. If he hanged the Chinamen, they would offer more resistance than they do now before allowing themselves to be captured. As it is, they profit by these temperate measures, and, unwilling to risk their lives if discovered, surrender on the first summons.

At Sea, November 8th.

Snow, fog, and gales of wind are our daily portion. We are beginning to feel the cold, especially on night duty.

The admiral impressed on us yesterday the necessity for the most strenuous vigilance, for it looks as though the end of the siege of Port Arthur were approaching, and this means that the squadron will attempt a desperate sortie.

The *Katzumo* behaves wonderfully. The truth is that the crew do their duty like trumps. What a pity that I cannot have a fight as soon as I want, though according to all accounts we shall not have to wait long.

The Baltic Squadron is coming, determined to fight and see whether it can possibly liberate the five Russian battleships from their prison.

All the same, I think that when it arrives in the waters of the Yellow Sea, if it ever does, it will have to rely solely on its own powers to regain the command of the sea.

They tell me that tomorrow they are going to bombard the defences with the monstrous mortars of which I spoke a few days ago. Those who have seen the performances of these weapons on our ranges say that no fortress exists which can withstand their projectiles. We shall see.

At Sea, November 14th.

The batteries of mortars have begun a serious bombardment of the forts of Ehrlung and Keikwan. The reports from them are more powerful than those of naval guns, and where their shells fall the damage is awful.

It looks as though there had been a volcanic eruption, judging by the havoc.

Yesterday a Russian destroyer came out of the besieged harbour.

She took advantage of the first hours of darkness, and passed between two of our destroyers in the first line, without taking the precaution of hiding her fires.

My cruiser and two others went to meet her; but she did not stop for an instant nor change her course in the slightest, and in spite of being struck by some of our projectiles, would not pause to reply, but continued on her course towards Chefu like a rocket.

We pursued, but she rapidly gained on us. Her funnels belched live flame, as though they were burning oil to increase the combustion. Such was her speed that we thought her boilers would blow up. However, nothing of the kind happened, and the boat reached Chefu safe and sound. Her commander has done his duty like a man.

At Sea, November 29th.

The squadron remains invisible. There is no way of compelling it to come out of the harbour. I hear that most of the ships are damaged, that they have landed their heavy guns and are short of ammunition.

We do not believe one word of this. When the defences are on the point of falling, it is certain that the ships will come out, doomed to sink like the *Petropavlovsk* and so many others, but making us pay dearly for our victory.

Three days ago a desperate fight between the besieging troops and the besieged began. It is not a question of a general assault, but of taking at all costs a hill which dominates with its fire the interior and exterior roadsteads of Port Arthur, a hill which has on its summit none of those formidable forts which crown the other heights.

If Nogi succeeds in capturing it. Port Arthur may be considered ours.

Besides the damage that can be done to the other forts from here, the squadron can be destroyed with impunity, and will have no alternative but to allow itself to be destroyed or give battle to us.

The assault has been going on for the last three nights. Yesterday I was able to observe some of its vicissitudes from sea.

When the attack of our battalions began, the whole hill, which they call "203-Metre Hill," was lit up, and glittered.

The searchlights threw their brilliant beams on to the assaulting columns. Thousands of rifle and machine-gun bullets, hand grenades, etc., anything, in fact, which could stop the assailants and thin their ranks, rent the air.

But our men never faltered, and, overcoming all obstacles, despising all dangers, they took trench after trench, and reached the summit without stopping to count their dead, without attending to those who fell wounded. Only with daylight every morning did the slaughter stop.

At Sea, December 5th.

We are approaching the *dénoûment*. 203-Metre Hill fell into the hands of the Japanese the day before yesterday at two in the morning.

A tremendous uproar announced the capture of the hill, and by the light of the rockets which for a few seconds lit up the town, the forts, the roadstead, and the open sea, we could see the banner of the Rising Sun waving on the heights which have cost us so much blood.

At half-past three the Russians made a furious counter-attack, coming on in dense columns from Liautishan; but they were defeated.

DECK OF THE *PERESVIET*.

With our glasses we see that they are beginning the work of establishing the terrible batteries of mortars on the summit of the hill.

Port Arthur is vanquished.

When the 11-inch shells begin to rain on the forts, the town, and the battleships, these will all be destroyed. Surely the time for a sortie approaches. The whole squadron has come from the Elliott Islands, and is near the harbour. Togo does not want one single ship to escape the general destruction.

At Sea, December 15th.

The Russian squadron has now ceased to exist. The magnificent battleships, which sailed from Russia to terrorise Japan nearly two years ago, are useless hulks, and the splendid cruisers can no longer float. Ten or twelve projectiles fell on their decks and completed the work of destruction. The *Retvisan* lies with her bows in the air, as though imploring supreme aid from the heavens to which her ram is pointing. The stern is sunk, battered out of shape and covered with water.

The *Peresviet* is almost entirely submerged; only her superstructure stands out from the sea.

The *Pobieda*, who has not done credit to her name of victory, is listed to starboard, and exposes enormous holes in one side and in the bows.

The *Poltava* has disappeared

The *Sevastopol* is the only one which made any attempt at defence.

She came out to the exterior roadstead, and, to shelter herself from Nogi's terrible projectiles, got as near as she could to Golden Hill.

But she reckoned without our torpedo-boats. When once night had fallen, five torpedo-boats and two destroyers, ignoring the fire of the coast batteries, attacked her.

She defended herself well, but was struck under the keel by two torpedoes, which prevented her moving.

If there were a greater depth of water in that spot, the *Sevastopol* would now be totally submerged; as it is she is balanced on some rocks which support her, though they are tearing her keel off. Anyhow, she is as useless as the rest of her comrades.

Now the Baltic Squadron can come when it likes, for we are prepared for the fray.

At Sea, December 17th.

One might think that after the enemy's squadron had been destroyed, or reduced to such terrible straits, our fleet would have finished its task. Unfortunately, this is not so. I say unfortunately, for now we have no enemies to fight and our duties become most wearisome. Nevertheless, they are of great importance; the entrance to the harbour must be watched, if possible, with greater care than before. It would not do for the besieged to be supplied with ammunition or victuals, which would tend to prolong a resistance that has already lasted too long.

The commander of my division was telling me no later than yesterday, before I went on duty with my ship, that the Chinese *junks* are become more enterprising than ever, in the belief that we have relaxed our vigilance since the squadron which has served under so many admirals has sunk into the depths of the sea. Of all the Russian admirals not one gave the squadron the chance of a good fight nor took the ships out of the prison to which we consigned them at the outbreak of hostilities.

My chief's words did not pass unheeded, for scarcely two hours ago—at this moment it is 8 p.m.—I had to fire on two ships, which, hugging the cliffs of the coast, were trying to enter Port Arthur. The fog which has prevailed since dusk saved them from certain capture.

As they were so close to the shore I was unable to get near them for fear of the rocks, and in a short time they were lost in the dense curtain of fog which enfolds us.

For some days now intense cold has prevailed. The wind which blows from shore is icy. My crew have had to don their sheepskin coats and the fur caps which cover their heads and necks and protect their ears.

We officers wear coats which were issued to us at the beginning of the campaign. They have silk linings, are stuffed with eider-down, and are much lighter than those worn by the men, though they protect us equally well. Our gloves are of doeskin, lined with wool, and reach halfway up our arms. By these means we avoid direct contact with the metal-work, which inflicts a sensation as painful as a burn if touched with the bare hand.

The Russians must be very short of ammunition, for the forts do not reply to the shots which we fire now and again by order.

This order is issued in the desire to see if they will waste ammunition in salvos as they used to do during the first days of the siege.

One cannot help thinking, in view of this want of ammunition, that the defences will not be able to hold out many days more.

They say that General Kondratenko died a week ago in one of the advanced land forts. He was, as I heard from one of General Kodama's *aides-de-camp* some time ago, the real defender of Port Arthur, an intelligent, active, and brave man, in whom his soldiers had the blindest confidence, and who always produced from his fertile brain devices for prolonging the resistance, for reinforcing threatened points and for encouraging those whose spirit flagged.

The loss of General Kondratenko will be far more felt by the Russians than the loss of their commander-in-chief would be.

I hear that no general capable of replacing him is left, for Stöessel, who ever since the beginning of the war has been represented as being a hero, is far from being a great general.

The second in command of the *Shikishima*, who knew him in Port Arthur long before war broke out, says that all this is on the surface only. Very likely he has the physical courage which faces death without fear, but he lacks education and the gift of commanding others.

The qualities which he possesses are—insisting on obedience to orders and maintenance of discipline; but no more than this is to be expected from him. Nevertheless, it is probable that it is his name which will be connected with the history of the siege, and not that of General Kondratenko, which is the name that should really become famous. Smirnov and Fock are two excellent subordinate leaders, very zealous, very brave, but they do not show that they have sufficient initiative at the moments when it is required. We are all waiting with curiosity and anxiety to see the end of this protracted siege, which has cost us so much blood.

It is quite clear that the garrison will not perish to a man, as they declared would be the case ever since the commencement of the siege.

But what will the generals and admirals do who are inside?

They cannot attempt a desperate sortie, as the opportunity for this has gone by, nor is it probable that they wish to face the consequences of a general attack, which would result in horrible slaughter.

One of my companions, an officer of the *Asahi*, who watched the taking of 203-Metre Hill from the Japanese camp, told me a couple of nights ago that the Russians fought admirably, also that all the valour of our soldiers and all the skill of our leaders were called into play to overcome their resistance.

A point which undoubtedly contributes very much to the success of the undertaking is the indisputable superiority of our artillery over that of the enemy. While the latter cannot reach our batteries with their shells, ours do tremendous damage to the Russian batteries, and the moral effect produced is far greater and more demoralising than that caused by the projectiles.

Another factor which, since the beginning of winter, has greatly affected the resisting powers of the Russians is that most of the soldiers are without overcoats in this intense cold.

This, combined with the fact that they do not have enough to eat, is sufficient to destroy the energy and dash of the best intentioned. Our soldiers, on the other hand, have not been without overcoats or complete rations since the beginning of the campaign.

Our military administration has given proofs of admirable organisation, and the Ministers of War and Marine, both present and past, can boast of a foresight seldom surpassed.

The supply of ammunition and food has left nothing to be desired as regards both quantity and punctuality.

It has been said that during the Chinese War there were public officials and contractors who committed absolute iniquities: scandalous defalcations occurred which reflected discredit on the army. Certainly two staff officers and three merchants committed suicide without any apparent motive two days after a commission was opened to inquire into the acts alleged.

However, their punishment proved effective, for this time absolutely no one has failed in the performance of his duty, and all the papers go into ecstasies over the excellence of the auxiliary services. The Marconi wireless-telegraphy apparatus, which was installed on all our ships three months before mobilisation began, has done excellent work.

While I write these lines I can hear the distant sound of guns, which never stops by night or day and keeps the garrison of Port Arthur in a constant state of alarm.

I, who am far from the scene of action, quietly writing in my cabin, well protected from the cold which outside gets more and more intense, cannot help thinking of the anger, the horror which those everlasting gunshots must evoke in the breasts of the besieged.

When all Nature is at rest, when men forget their troubles and sorrows in sleep, and refresh their powers, exhausted during the day; when the darkness and silence of the night seem to establish for a few hours a reign of peace; when all activity has ceased, man, the most intelligent of earthly beings, moved by hatred, an insane, unreasoning passion, rests not, but with ceaseless roar of artillery reminds his fellow creatures that he is burning to accomplish their ruin, and to bring death amongst them. Nor is the grand stillness of the night potent enough to disarm his rage, to quench his destructive passions. Those who have fought, and those who are fighting now—we do not know each other, we do not hate each other.

But the law which governs the human race ordains it, and we must bow to the inevitable.

I see that unconsciously I have embarked in reflections which have nothing to do with a nautical diary.

But the winter nights are very long, and now and again I cannot refrain from remembering that I am a man, first, before being a naval officer, and from thinking as such. These thoughts would certainly not come to me in summer, when one can combat *ennui* by a stroll on deck, while one contemplates that sight which seems ever new and lovely, a star-lit night at sea.

The waves which gently lap the sides of the ship or which strike her with terrible fury, the breeze which blows ever fresh, the scintillations of the stars reflected in the water, clear as a mirror, all these give me a deep and ineffable sensation of pleasure.

But now in mid-winter, shut into a cabin, feeling a shiver at the slightest movement, knowing that outside it is freezing or snowing, that the stars are hidden by a thick fog which not even the moonlight can pierce, and that the breeze which caressed us in summer now cuts like a knife and penetrates through the best of overcoats to the fur underneath, even one's thoughts feel the depressing influence of the cold.

For cold is the inseparable companion of the death which for months has brooded over Port Arthur, over the camp of our army, over the waters which have engulfed so many bodies since the night of the 9th of February.

Dalny, December 19th.

We have come here to coal, and tomorrow shall return to our look-out post.

I cannot express the delight I feel at the news which I heard here in course of conversation with some of the officers of the army.

Port Arthur is in its death-throes, but its agony will be much more brief than is generally thought.

While the bombardment from the heavy mortars executes havoc on all the fortifications, the sap-works are proceeding to such an extent that in a few days several forts will be blown up.

Then the fines of defence will have lost much of their efficacy, and the town must surrender or suffer the horrors of an assault without quarter.

In this case all the smaller ships would certainly take part in the fray, and would land their crews near the forts which defend the harbour.

It would be a magnificent sight, but I do not think we shall have to go to these lengths.

The garrison of Port Arthur is far more numerous than we thought at the beginning of the siege. A Russian officer, taken prisoner during the capture of 203-Metre Hill, who speaks English perfectly, told me that when the siege began at the end of June, there were 47,000 soldiers in Port Arthur. He also thought that it would still take us a long time and cost us much loss of life before the town was taken.

I did not want to make him more unhappy than he was already, by telling him that we knew for certain that ammunition and food were, failing, and that lack of these and not of men would compel the Russians to surrender.

He spoke of General Kondratenko, and of his contempt for death, and sang his praises loudly, saying that he was one of the best generals in the Russian Army, and would be a difficult customer for the Japanese to tackle.

When I told him of the general's death he seemed much impressed.

Several hours later I had a talk with some other prisoners, private soldiers, who said that Russia had put her head into a wasps' nest when she made war with Japan. They think that in the end they will lose not only this campaign but the whole war, and are delighted at it, strange though this may seem, for they say that now they will not have to serve in regions as inhospitable as those in which they have been fighting up till the present. The truth of the matter is that Russia was guilty of an act of madness in compelling us to fight.

In the first place she was not ready to meet our forces, and secondly all her soldiers went unwillingly to a war the object of which they cannot understand.

How can they possibly be victorious when they are without enthusiasm and without adequate preparation?

We, on the contrary, have these advantages, whilst all the Russian prisoners realise that they lack them both.

An officer of the general staff told me that in a short time there will be a great battle in Manchuria, as the Japanese are determined to inflict a decisive defeat on Kuropatkin's army.

A strange fact is that the Russians, who, according to the French newspapers and their own, have more men than ourselves in the neighbourhood of Mukden, do not try and make use of this advantage; for when Port Arthur has surrendered they will have more difficulty in taking the offensive against our army. To conclude, I hope that in a short time there will be great doings.

At Sea, December 20th.

When I came in sight of Port Arthur I heard a furious cannonade going on. So terrible was the noise that I thought our soldiers were delivering the final assault; but I soon made out that it was only an energetic bombardment, which possibly had no other object than to disguise a partial attack.

It was about nine o'clock in the evening. The darkness was profound, and only now and again, as I looked towards Port Arthur, did I see flames shoot up.

The forts were replying to the fire of our army. Suddenly out of the darkness arose the form of a ship dashing along at full speed, vomiting smoke and flames from her four funnels.

There could be no doubt that she was a Russian vessel, probably one of the destroyers which had escaped from the bombardment of Nogi's army undamaged.

I tried to cut her off; but her crew, in blind despair, paid not the slightest attention to my cruiser.

I am sure that had I not changed my course she would have struck me fair and square and we should both have gone to the bottom.

But while I gave orders to let her pass, I got my guns ready for action and began to fire on her.

The first shots cannot have struck her, for she did not reply to them, but soon afterwards she fired her after guns, without ceasing to run on at a speed far greater than mine.

One of her shells fell near our bows. For a long time, I continued the fire and pursuit, but my ship was losing ground.

The hostile boat must have been the *Boriastock*, one of the swiftest and most modern destroyers which the Russian fleet possessed, and also heavily armed.

Her guns never stopped answering ours, perhaps because this was to be the last fight in which a ship from the Port Arthur squadron would take part; or possibly because the destroyer was carrying all the admirals on board.

They were now out of range and could have reached Chefu without molestation, when, doubtless from bravado, they slackened speed, and as I increased mine we were soon within easy range.

She now fired her two stern guns, set off again at full speed, and, turning to starboard, got broadside on and fired two more rounds.

Observing that she had made a good shot, and that one of her shells had opened a hole near my water-line, close to the engine-room, she got bolder, and for two minutes steamed along parallel to me, firing her starboard guns.

Another shell smashed one of my funnels, yet my fire never touched the cursed boat; she seemed to be invulnerable. A very good sailor must have been in command, judging by her manoeuvring.

My second in command was in as deep despair as myself at not being able to damage the Russian boat. The latter again dashed off at full speed, and was nearly lost to view, when suddenly a torpedo-man and two gunners uttered shouts of joy

One of our last shots had smashed two of her funnels, and another projectile had made a great hole in the stern.

For a moment she seemed to lose speed; but in a few minutes she disappeared completely into the darkness. Was she going to Chefu? Was she going to Kiau-chau? In any case her crew could consider themselves saved. The officer who commanded the boat must have been delighted with the way they behaved.

If the commanders of the large battleships which are lying at the bottom of the roadstead of Port Arthur had been capable of manoeuvring, defending themselves, and attacking as that destroyer has just done, our magnificent squadron would probably have lost some of its fighting units, and many vessels would have had to undergo repairs in the dockyards. The pursuit lasted some minutes; but realising that it was absolutely impossible for me to keep up with my enemy, I turned round and returned towards Port Arthur. On the way I repaired the damage done by the enemy's fire as best I could, and subsequently gave an account of my fight to the commander of my division.

It hurt me deeply to have to confess that the destroyer had escaped, but in view of her superiority over my ship in point of speed, it was not at all strange.

At Sea, December 21st.

We hear that the destroyer which escaped yesterday, leaving a record of her powers in the hull of my *Katzumo*, was commanded by the former captain of the *Bayan*, now a vice-admiral, having been promoted for the purpose of preventing Prince Uktomski from taking command at the last. Truly Virenius's selection was an admirable one—yesterday's sortie proved it.

What a pity that he was only given command of the squadron when matters were hopeless! When he took command of the battleships there was not a gun, not a case of ammunition on board, and the engines were almost entirely destroyed—so the bluejackets whom we captured on the 14th say.

All the guns have been mounted in the forts so as to contribute to their defence—a lamentable error which cost the Russians dear.

From the first moment of the siege, Alexeieff, Kuropatkin, and Stöessel ought to have realised that the most important thing to be saved was not the stronghold, for this must have succumbed sooner or later, unless it were relieved, but the squadron: that squadron which, in conjunction with the one from the Baltic Sea, could have inflicted such damage upon us as would almost have amounted to a disaster.

Instead of this the ships have been sacrificed in the defence of the stronghold, the squadron has been destroyed. Port Arthur is on the verge of capitulation, and the command of the sea is lost to Russia without hope of being regained.

At Sea, December 22nd.

An hour ago we weighed and proceeded to Sasebo. Some of the others are going to Nagasaki and Osaka. We are going to clean the bottoms of our vessels and repair the damage done in this long campaign, which, although not very bloody, has never allowed us a moment's rest.

Admiral Togo ought to be well pleased. He has succeeded in destroying a fleet as powerful as his own without losing more than a battleship and a second-class cruiser.

The enemy, on the other hand, have lost seven battleships, two armoured and eight protected cruisers, twenty torpedo-boats, four destroyers, two mine-layers, two gunboats, and a quantity of less important craft, both mercantile and belonging to the navy.

Truth to tell, most of the blame for these huge losses lies at the door of these same Russian sailors, who have never tried to fight, but only to preserve their ships from harm.

With what object? No one can conceive, when we look at their

WRECK OF THE *PERESVIET*

disastrous end.

Did we not know that the Russians fight well when the opportunity occurs, it might be thought that it is fear which has inspired such strange behaviour on the part of our adversaries.

Perhaps it is an absolute want of skill, a complete lack of preparation, an inconceivable ignorance of the complicated machinery in their charge, which have lost the command of the sea to the Russians, have permitted us to gain it, and left u& force sufficient to maintain it.

How terrible must be the position of the surviving admirals! What bitterness they must feel! I fear that many of the officers will commit suicide when they see that it is impossible to leave Port Arthur except as prisoners.

One of our naval officers, poor Katavara, who fell into the hands of the Russians during the second attempt at closing the harbour, when he found himself in prison dashed his head against the wall of his cell, and made a great gash in his skull which stretched him senseless.

They took him to hospital, and when he recovered consciousness he absolutely refused to eat. The doctors fed him against his will, but he was anxious for death, and he died.

The attendant relaxed his vigilance for a moment, and Katavara hurled himself headlong from the second floor to the courtyard.

He died because he did not want to survive the shame of having been taken prisoner, in spite of the fact that he had done his duty like a hero.

★★★★★★

How I long to hold my dear ones in my arms! My father awaits me at Sasebo, and I shall be granted leave to go and embrace my mother and brothers. My Uncle Kato, who is also going to Sasebo on board the *Iwate*, has already announced my arrival.

How glad my relations will be to see me, and with what pride shall I show them the badges of my new rank!

Sasebo, December 24th.

It is unlikely that we shall have to return to Port Arthur. Torpedoboats and destroyers are doing all the blockade duty. A division composed of four large armoured cruisers remains in reserve at the Elliott Islands.

It appears that the Chinamen, who up till now have felt confident that Port Arthur would be relieved, have given up all hopes, and therefore da not try to bring in provisions.

Besides the heavy price at which they could sell their goods, the blockade runners hoped that if the Russians came off victorious their services would be rewarded. Now they see that they have made a mistake, and do not want to risk their lives uselessly.

There is good news of the war. Marshal Oyama will not allow Kuropatkin's army to take one step forward, and he has men enough at his disposal now to compel the latter to retire towards Siberia.

This morning a colonel of the staff who has just arrived from the line of the Sha-ho had luncheon with me, and told me that as soon as Port Arthur and Mukden have fallen into our hands, the Russians will be compelled to make peace, unless they are possessed of a suicidal mania.

In this city the animation which one sees in the dockyard and all the State offices is extraordinary. Troops keep constantly coming from the interior, perfectly equipped and clothed for the rigorous cold which prevails in central Manchuria.

The civil population seems most contented, and most hopeful now that it sees the war has not stopped commercial transactions, and that all the industries show greater vitality than before the outbreak of hostilities.

Nagasaki, December 28th.

I have come to this place to do some commissions which are connected with the navy, but which need not be gone into here.

In this town, like every other in Japan, one notices great enthusiasm, and also the confidence which the masses feel that our army will emerge victorious from the protracted struggle.

Many of the business houses have subscribed largely to the Interior Loans, and this probably not from motives of patriotism, but because they realise that they are investing their money well, and that their expenditure will be reproductive.

A great naval contractor said to me:

Remember what happened in Prussia and Germany during the Franco-Prussian War. Many timorous patriots said that though Prussia would be victorious in the war she had undertaken, her situation would be very precarious, for the expenditure involved by the war and the efforts she had to make would cripple her for many years to come.

Those who thought thus were utterly wrong. Prussia developed her industry and commerce in the most wonderful man-

139

ner, due entirely to the fact of having conquered by her arms a nation which was considered the most powerful in Europe.

The war indemnity permitted her to offer premiums to ship-builders, and five years after the victories of Sedan and Paris, Prussia, or Germany, call her what one will, became one of the first commercial nations in the world.

The English began to fear the articles 'made in Germany' which flooded her markets; Russia inaugurated the era of protectionist tariffs, and the whole world was compelled to recognise that the work of Bismarck, Moltke, and Von Roon had produced better results than anyone had ever expected.

The same thing will happen in Japan if our army conquers the Russians decisively. As Japanese commerce is among the most important in the world, there is no doubt that in the future our rulers will be able to ratify a commercial treaty with China, and obtain most important concessions.

Many other Asiatic nations which up till now have only been exploited by Europeans, will also be our clients, and then Osa-ka, Yokomuro, and Yokohama will become ports of the first importance.

I must say I think the worthy merchant spoke to the point, and that the consequences of Japan's victory over Russia will in the future be far greater than the prophets have made out, especially the Russian and French prophets.

When Japan has succeeded in completely taming Russia's pride, all the Asiatic peoples will recognise her supremacy, and the peaceful conquerors who go to China, Indo-china, India, and the Philippines will gain laurels in abundance; in other words, they will do a thriving trade. I do not think that our government contemplates a Pan-Japaneseism which will make most of Asia ours. I do not think that the Emperor of Germany, who lays down the law on all subjects without knowing anything really, gets anywhere near the mark when he talks of the "Yellow Peril"; but there is no doubt that our victory will produce good results in the field of commerce as well as in that of politics.

Touching the subject of the Yellow Peril, I must say now, while I have the time, that I have been more than two years in China, that I know the language and customs well, and there is nothing, absolutely nothing, which warrants the supposition that the Chinese will soon follow in the path which the Japanese have trodden, compelled thereto by the rapacity of the Europeans. For the latter tried to do in Japan what they have done in China and all the countries which, because they have not armed themselves in the Western manner nor adopted the uses and customs of Europe and America, appear in European and American eyes to be moribund countries, or rather societies in course of decay, which can only be kept awake under the brutal lash of the white races.

No. China labours under conditions very distinct from those of Japan.

The Chinese utterly abhor the profession of arms, whilst in our country it has always been the most honourable that a man can adopt.

They are and always have been more civilised than ourselves, and for this reason dislike individualism more.

China will never be a nation of centralisers, but rather a society in which the autonomy of small groups of beings will always be respected, esteemed, and defended with all the energy and tenacity of which the Chinese are capable. This is a doctrine which is beginning to spread amongst all the cultivated races in the world.

A great revolution or an iron rule would be necessary to impose on the Chinese customs diametrically opposed to those which they now possess. Perhaps if the Russian rule in Manchuria had continued for several years, as well as the assaults by the French, Germans, and English on the Chinese coasts, anger might have produced the same effect as foresight, and the Chinese would have armed themselves and inflicted a terrible blow on the European nations, who take that which does not belong to them so freely, and proclaim the superiority of their race over others of whose good qualities they are completely ignorant.

If the Yellow Peril is to be feared someday, if it materialises and brings harm to the Europeans, I do not think that it will be us Japanese who will provoke it. For it would not profit us in any way. An armed and powerful China is not a neighbour who would suit us. What we desire is to so manage that the Chinese continue as up to the present, peaceful and quiet.

The most we shall do is to try and free them from the aggressions of the Europeans, who, after the lesson we have given Russia, will behave with greater caution and treat the "Yellow Race" as enemies to be reckoned with—the Yellow Race who have made the proudest whites in Europe, the home of the white men, turn their faces to the wall. If China adopts the Occidental civilisation, it will probably not be owing to any encouragement from us, but because the Chinese, made wise by the number of evils they have endured, realise that their integrity will only be respected on the day that they are in a condition to hound those who treat them with insolence from their country.

The reason I have been discussing the Yellow danger is that I see it has become the fashion in the European papers to do so, and it appears to me that it is advisable for all, white and yellow, to dissipate an error and drive away a bugbear which can only take form in a diseased imagination.

Matsumotu, December 29th.

Now I am at home! All my relations and friends have come to congratulate me.

Even many of the neighbours whom I used to annoy with my pranks when I was a boy are delighted that a young man whom they have known ever since he was fed on pap should have been through the whole campaign against the Russians, should have been commended by his superiors, and promoted. Without any exaggeration, I think I must have told the story of the disaster to the *Petropavlovsk*, my fights with the Russian destroyers, and the battle of August 10th three hundred times.

The papers today have the news of the taking of the forts of Keikwan and Ehrlung. It does not surprise me.

Once 203-Metre Hill was taken, Port Arthur was vanquished.

And now that these two forts have fallen into our hands, very soon we shall be masters of the situation.

For the very reason that modern forts support each other so effectively, when one falls the rest are in a very critical position.

Anyhow Port Arthur has offered more resistance than I thought possible; but I think that now it is only a question of days before we hear the news of its surrender.

Sasebo, January 4th, 1905.

The first part of the campaign is finished. Japan's victory is complete—Port Arthur capitulated three days ago. The year is beginning well for our arms.

Stöessel, thirty thousand soldiers, sailors, and officers have surrendered, unwilling to face the horrors of an assault without quarter.

They do not want to follow the example of bygone days, but prefer to follow modern customs!

They are wise in this; but why say, as Stöessel did, that it would kill him if he had to surrender?

They say that the Baltic Squadron is approaching. The *Katzumo* is ready to put to sea. I have got orders from Admiral Togo, and sail with my ship tonight. Whither? if the war continues, and a new campaign takes place in which I do not perish, perhaps someday I shall tell the tale.

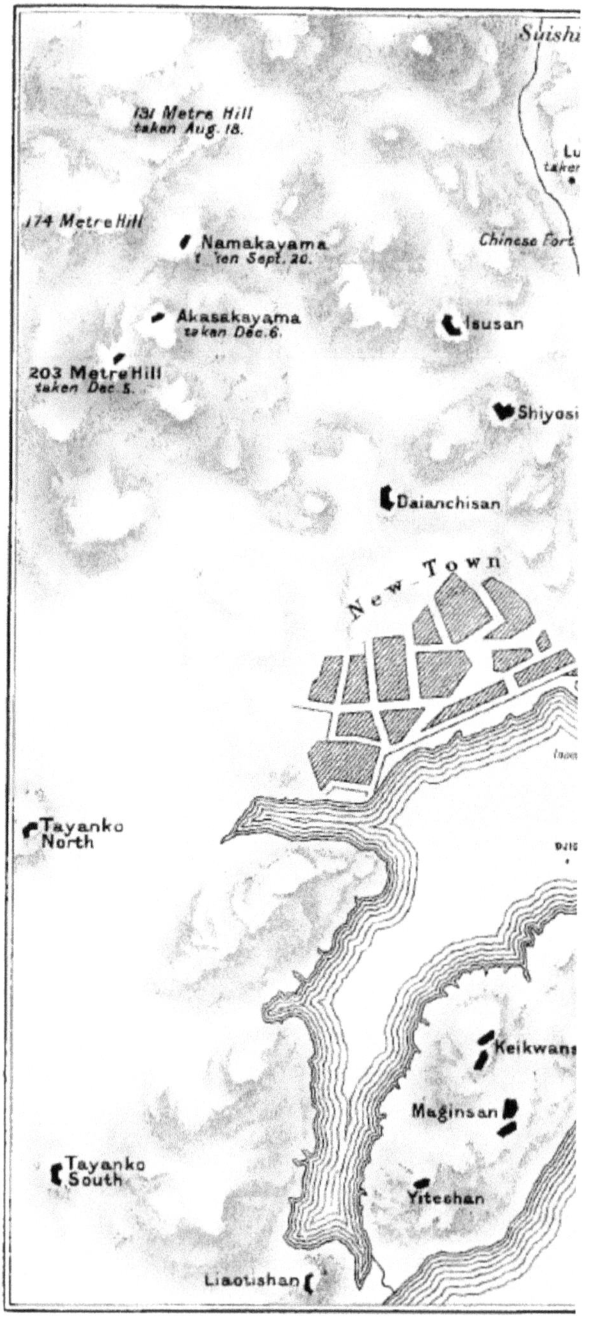

Suishi

131 Metre Hill
taken Aug. 18.

Lu
taken

174 Metre Hill

Namakayama
taken Sept. 20.

Chinese Fort

Akasakayama
taken Dec. 6.

Isusan

203 Metre Hill
taken Dec. 5.

Shiyosi

Daianchisan

New Town

Tayanko
North

Keikwans

Maginsan

Tayanko
South

Yiteshan

Liaotishan

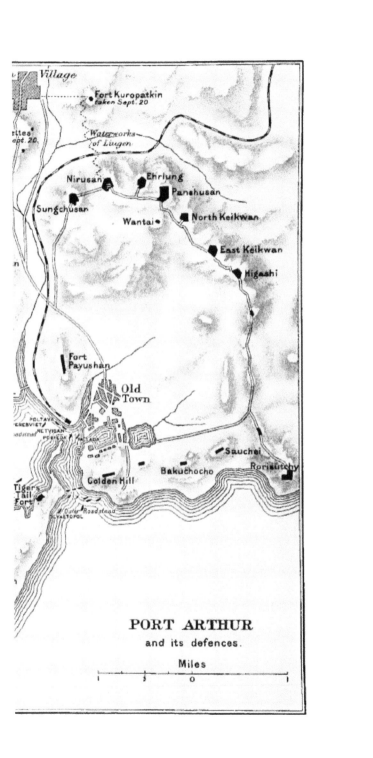

PORT ARTHUR

and its defences.

Miles

With Togo

Togo 1903

Contents

Yours truly

Seppings Wright

To Admiral Togo

and

The gallant Officers and Men of the
Japanese Navy

this book is dedicated

in token of the author's gratitude for the many kind-
nesses he

received at their hands, during his period of Service

under the Flag of the Rising Sun

With Togo on his flag ship

Preface

So many books dealing with the war in the Far East have been published during the past year, that an addition to the list will, no doubt, be thought by many to be unnecessary. But although the public has been provided with many war books, these have all chronicled the operations of the armies, and have given little or no information regarding the naval side of the war.

The Japanese authorities were not easily persuaded to let correspondents join the armies in the field, but for a correspondent to obtain permission to go aboard the warships and sail with the fleet seemed an impossibility. It was my good fortune to achieve the apparently impossible, for I served on one or other of Admiral Togo's ships from August, 1904, until last February. It was a privilege that was extended to no other correspondent, and, indeed, to no other foreigner save the British naval attaches, who were the only representatives of foreign powers so privileged.

The Japanese sailors, from Admiral Togo himself down to the youngest seaman, treated me with the greatest kindness and did all in their power to make my sojourn among them a pleasant and happy one, and, in addition, I was given every facility for witnessing the operations and studying the details of that marvellous system of naval organisation which has contributed so largely towards Japan's maritime success.

And it was not only the naval operations that I witnessed, for, by the kindness of Admiral Togo, my tent was taken ashore and pitched on the summit of a mountain within six miles of the Russian batteries, where, during my five weeks' stay, I was able to watch the fighting on land and sea at one and the same time.

It was, however, the naval operations (in which, as one of my ship's complement, I took part) that occupied most of my time, and it is the record of what I saw of Japan's navy on active service that forms the bulk of this volume.

S. W.

Havant, June, 1905.

Chapter 1

Off to Japan

On March 5th, 1904, I left England on a journey to Japan to try and see something of that navy which has since become world-renowned. The task before me was not easy, and I was told by everyone that it would be impossible for a foreigner to obtain permission to go aboard the Japanese warships. To the war correspondent, however, the word "impossible" is unknown. I carried in my pocket-book letters from Sir W. Armstrong, Noble & Co., of the far-famed Elswick works, to the Minister of Marine at Tokyo, and other influential officials, so that I was in possession of credentials that would, at least, be helpful to me, and, notwithstanding the pessimistic utterances of my friends, I was hopeful of success.

One journey is much the same as another, and the trip to Japan has been written and talked about *ad nauseam*, so that I will not weary my readers with a long description of the voyage and journey across Canada. At Vancouver I was delayed one day, waiting for a mail, and the Canadian Pacific Company's ship *Empress of India* carried me the remainder of the journey to Japan. Notwithstanding severe weather and cold, the trip was delightful, and cricket, deckbilliards, and even bowls, tended to relieve the monotony of the voyage, and keep the digestion fit to enjoy the ample and luxurious bill of fare provided by the company. Among my fellow passengers were several British officers and their families, a few diplomats and a number of Japanese officers—the first I had met. Amongst these Japanese was a prince and several officers and attaches from the different capitals of the world, some of whom were sailors. Among the latter was Captain Sakai, one of the ancient *Daimios*, on his way home from St. Petersburg, where he had been stationed. He was a quiet, somewhat reserved man, and seemed really sorry that the war had broken out.

"I have so many friends in St. Petersburg," he said, "and only recently I said 'goodbye' to Admiral Makarof, who," he added, with rather a sad smile, "hopes to meet me in the Far East."

By the way, there is a story told about Makarof, who, as most people are aware, was one of the signatories at the Treaty of Shimonoseki, after the China War. During the discussion of the terms of the treaty the Japanese suggested that they should retain Port Arthur and occupy the Liaotung Peninsula. Makarof sprang to his feet and, laying his sword across that part of the map, cried vehemently, "Never!"

The first thing that struck me about the Japanese was that they look 'thorough-bred,' and my subsequent experience of them confirms my early opinion. Only a few of these spoke English, but they all could speak German and French fluently. On some of our fair passengers expressing fear at the possibility of being captured by the Vladivostock Squadron, they smiled and shrugged their shoulders. Their Intelligence Department, which is one of the most wonderful branches of their perfect organisation, was apparently well informed on this point, but it struck me at the time that the Rooskis could have made a valuable bag had they come our way. The Russian cruisers, however, stayed at home, and we made Japan safely. We were piloted over the mine fields which protected Tokyo Bay and anchored in the fine, spacious harbour of Yokohama on April 5th. The boat was instantly boarded by a number of Japanese families, who came off in the curious sharp-nosed boats to greet their kinsfolk. I landed at 5 o'clock and put up at the Oriental Hotel for the night.

The following morning, I proceeded to Tokyo to present my credentials, which occupied the greater part of the day, and in the evening I went to the Metropole Hotel, which I made my headquarters, the Imperial being already overcrowded. There are plenty of Japanese hotels in Tokyo, but only a very limited number of "foreign" ones. The Imperial, of course, is the most important of the latter, and it has the advantage of being much nearer to the embassies and public offices, and consequently is the best for correspondents.

I had the honour of being made a member of the Tokyo Club on my arrival, an honour that is specially gratifying to a correspondent, for telegrams and war news are received at the club earlier than anywhere else in the town. There, too, one meets most of the Japanese politicians and officials, who are as fine-looking and well-tailored a lot of gentlemen as it is possible to see anywhere. Their hospitality is unbounded, and their kindness to strangers within their gates proverbial.

I confess that I felt drawn towards these charmers of Tokyo, if such an expression can be applied to the sterner sex, and everyone who knows them will bear me out in saying what delightful people they are.

Finding myself established in Tokyo, I set to work at once. First I sought out Captain Boyle, an Elswick man, and one of the British officers who brought out the two cruisers *Nishin* and *Kasuga*, which have since done such splendid service. (These are Elswick ships and the name of the greatest firm of shipbuilders has not suffered from their performances.) My object was soon explained, whereat he shook his head.

"They won't let you go near their dockyards or arsenals, much less allow you to go on any of their ships. Why!" he said, "they won't even let the foreign naval *attachés* see anything."

This was a "facer," but the interests of the firm required me not to let such an opinion as this deter me, so I set to work at once to write to various officials so as to get the ball started. Also there were the agents to be consulted. Mr. Bell, the hospitable representative of Jardine Matheson, lived at Yokohama, so to Yokohama we went, where I was introduced to him. On hearing my wishes, he looked surprised and expressed great doubts about the Admiralty even entertaining such a proposition.

"We can but get a refusal," I persisted.

We then discussed the matter earnestly, and a line of action was decided upon. I need not enter into the various details, but I may say that I was fortunate in securing the interest of Mr. Takata, a Japanese merchant, and one of the best known and most influential men in Tokyo; and also of Mr. Kondo, another rising young man. The result was a direct application to the Minister of Marine, and I could do nothing then but wait and hope, although my case was of very little importance compared with the great issues and events which the government had on hand. I passed the time visiting my colleagues of the newspapers, studying the Japanese, and thoroughly appreciating and enjoying the many beauties of quaint Tokyo. There are numerous public parks and gardens to be visited, *fêtes*, theatres, and other places of interest and amusement.

Japanese thoroughness is noticeable everywhere in Tokyo, and even to looking after the trees. These are most carefully pruned and protected from the ravages of time and the weather. If a big limb is cut off, the stump is preserved by a large cap not unlike a big fer-rule, fitting tightly on the stump which prevents the rain from rotting the branch. Unsightly gaps in old trunks are stopped with cement as carefully as a dentist might fill one's teeth, and it keeps the trees in a healthy condition.

The bazaars, huge emporiums wherein all the curios and wonders of Nippon may be seen and purchased, are an unfailing source of delight to the European, with their elaborate system of gates to keep the crowd always moving in the same direction and passing by the stalls in regular succession. This excellent system prevents crushing. The salesmen never bother anyone to buy, and they always look bright and happy. If you buy there is a profusion of thanks; if you do not, there are pleasant looks.

To some of these bazaars are attached gardens where the world-famed dwarf trees are exhibited in pots for sale, and there are also ponds where sluggish goldfish of the multi-tailed species sleep and dream all day in the clear water, rarely disturbing themselves except when the dip-net splashes down amongst them. Nearly every Jappy boy possesses a goldfish. He tends and cherishes it, trying to keep it alive and healthy as long as possible, and comparing it with the finny favourites of other boys. This and their love for flowers constitute the chief charms of Nippon's children, and they always seem so kind and considerate one to another, that I do not think one can really find a bad boy in the whole country. It is the result of the national training. Everyone is obedient: the child to the parents, little children to their elder brothers and sisters, and the girls and the women to their husbands and brothers.

Old people are always treated with respect and tenderness amounting to reverence. The workhouse system is unknown in Japan and would be resented as a national disgrace. Every child supports his aged parents as a matter of duty, and, consequently, one sees everywhere happy old age, and merry youth. How long, I wonder, will it be ere iron-hearted commercialism, which is gradually sapping the best feelings of the people, blights and destroys the generous, human characteristics which today are so strong in this delightful race? Let Nippon beware of its insidious advance and try to sustain the old, high principles in the age of golden prosperity which is now dawning.

They take their time at most government offices, and Tokyo is no exception to the rule, but with the anxieties of the present conflict there is every excuse for them. At last I received a letter from the War Minister, informing me that my application must be forwarded through the British Minister. I called and saw Sir Claude Macdonald, and he listened to my wishes with a kindly smile and promised to use his best endeavours on my behalf.

"You are not the only one," he added, and he spoke of the heart-breaking difficulties of the correspondents and attaches. I returned to my hotel, wrote my official application, and then there was nothing for me to do but wait.

Tokyo was undergoing a transformation. The much, and justly, lauded cherry blossom was just bursting into bloom. The Japanese are very proud of their beautiful national emblem, and with good reason. Cherry blossom season is the sweetest in the year, for Spring is just beginning, the winter sky is softening into a fresh, bright, joyous tint, and the sunlight vibrates, quickening tender buds into life. In the morning when one awakes, the country is covered as though with a soft pink snow, birds carol merrily and all Japan turns out to admire and contemplate the beauties of nature.

Up the river is the place to see the trees at their best. As you drift along in the *sampan*, the blue sky with a sea of pink blossom beneath, both reflected in the warm yellow of river, form a colour picture quaint, rare and beautiful. Along the banks throngs of gaily dressed Jappy girls chatter and laugh in the fullness of their joy, and the very fragrance of the cherry flower seems exhilarating. The scene is charming and picturesque, the only discordant note being the European black umbrella which many of the Japanese carry, using it as a parasol. Imagine a *kimono* with this common-looking utility of the West! And their native sunshade so dainty and graceful. In the gardens the scene was the same—all flowers and dainty maidens wildly happy. It made me feel young again looking at them.

The days passed, very little news of the war ever coming through, although the *Gogei*, or special edition man, ran shouting through the streets to the accompaniment of the bell stuck in his girdle. The correspondents had a weary time awaiting orders, but in the circumstances one could hardly expect much. My first bit of cheering intelligence came from Mr. Takata, who rang me up on the telephone one day to inform me that he had heard, unofficially, that my name was down for a trip to Port Arthur in the *Manchu Maru*. The trip was to be a sort of government picnic on a large scale, although the numbers were to be strictly limited to members of parliament, foreign *attachés*, and a few correspondents.

Apparently I was to be one of the favoured few special visitors. Takata told me not to speak of it, and in due course he would let me

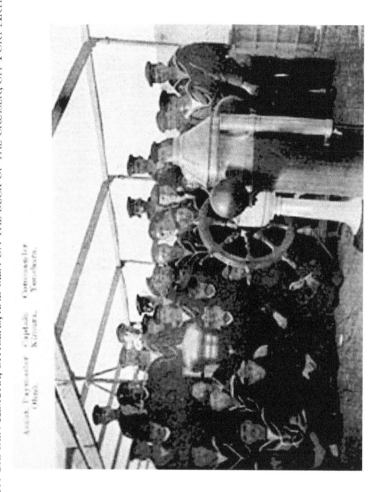

GROUP: CAPTAIN KIMURA, OFFICERS, AND MEN ON THE DECK OF THE CRUISER, OFF PORT ARTHUR.

A RUSSIAN FIELD CEMETERY,
PORT ARTHUR

IN THE DOCKYARD, PORT ARTHUR,
SHOWING THE DAMAGE
DONE BY A SHELL.

know the date and place of departure. In the meantime, the blocking of Port Arthur was in progress, and public funerals of the heroes took place in Tokyo every few days. Most impressive were the ceremonial rites at the burial of Commander Hirose's remains. This gallant officer succeeded in beaching his ship close under the batteries of Port Arthur, losing his life in the act. The Russians found his remains, which they sent to the Japanese lines, to be forwarded to Tokyo.

I now became a pretty constant visitor at the Admiralty, although I went to see and chat with my friends, not to bother them with my affairs. Admiral Saito, the vice-minister, is a good specimen of a Japanese sailor, big and burly and with a kindly face. He might easily have been mistaken for a sun-tanned British admiral. I was introduced by him to Vice-Admiral Ijuin, who looked not unlike the great Prussian General Von Moltke. Admiral Ijuin presented me to an admiral with a head like Bismarck—Vice-Admiral Count Ito, of Chinese war fame. Arima came next, and he strongly resembled America's General Grant. These resemblances are remarkable, and I was very much struck by them. I was also introduced to Admiral Sason, and by the kind manner with which I was treated by all I felt sure that, when the time came, I should get my passports.

CHAPTER 2

Invited to join the "Manchu Maru"

My invitation to join the *Manchu Maru* duly arrived, and on June 12th I entered the *Shinbashi* (Tokyo railway station), where a special train was waiting to convey the party to Yokosuka, where the *Manchu Maru* was lying. Amidst the confusion and crowd (for we had a great "send-off") I soon picked out the foreign contingent, some of whom were showing the most desperate anxiety about their baggage. There is not much need for this in Japan, for if you leave things alone your Jappy henchman will bring you, and all your belongings, to your appointed seat in the train. At last we all got settled, and with a tremendous *"Banzai"* from crowds of well-wishers, we steamed slowly out of the station. At Shinegawa, the first stop, we met more enthusiastic friends, and the train made a long wait to permit our making our final *adieux*. Jocular sallies as to the possibility of our being captured by the Russians caused shouts of laughter. Our merry detainers released us at last, and at Yokohama we picked up some more guests, who were heartily greeted by their Japanese hosts.

At 1 p.m. we drew up at a siding at Yokosuka, where the Japanese officers and bluejackets took charge of us and our baggage. Steam launches conveyed us to the *Manchu Maru*, which looked like a steam yacht as she lay at anchor a short distance from the dockyard. We were received on board by Captain Yamaguchi, the Commander, Captain Takarabe, who had accompanied us, having charge of our party. We soon settled down on board, and after a substantial lunch the siren sounded and the privileged few who had been allowed aboard to see the last of us left the ship. During lunch a steamer with the naval band, discoursing sweet music, cruised slowly round the ship. In the harbour two ships of the Japanese navy lay moored—a "mother ship," the *Toyo Maru*, and a cruiser of the second class, which had been built in the

163

Yokosuka dockyards and had just completed her trial trips.

At 2 p.m. we weighed anchor and, preceded by the government pilot, steamed through the mine fields. The strains of *"Auld Lang Syne"* was the last we heard of the band steamer, now shrouded in the mist. The afternoon turned out rainy, but as the wet season had begun we could hardly have expected anything else. But a wet day at sea is never pleasant. The horizon is contracted, and dry deck space limited. Some of us smoked, others looked to the stowing of their baggage in the cabins. The ship was crowded, each cabin being full, but I was fortunate in having only one "stable companion"—a young Oxford man. I was surprised to see that all the notices posted up in the ship were printed in Russian.

Viscount Inouye was leaning over the rail, so I asked him the reason, and he told me the story of the ship. She had been a Russian, and belonged to a line of steamers, built in 1900, to carry passengers from Dalny and Port Arthur to Japan, in connection with the Siberian railway. At the outbreak of hostilities, she was on the repairing slip at Nagasaki, was seized by the government, and was the first of a very useful fleet of steamers, now running into three figures, which have been captured at various times since the beginning of the war. The Russian captain either destroyed or threw overboard the ship's papers, so that there is no authoritative information as to her tonnage and one or two minor details. It is thought, however, that she is about 3,500 tons. The decorations are very handsome, and the saloons are panelled with pictures in a mosaic of various coloured woods.

Our party numbered 55. The run to Kobe was without incident, although a magnificent rainbow glorified the ship as with a halo, which was an omen of a happy voyage. We remained at Kobe for the night, some of us going ashore to see the celebrated waterfall and the mineral springs at Tokiwa. Lighted by the beams of the rising sun we entered the narrow channel of the Inland Sea, Japan's crowning beauty and, indeed, the loveliest piece of water in the world. It is a glorious panorama of sea and land and mountain, the blue water flecked with the white sails of innumerable golden-hued fishing boats. The custom of scrubbing the wood-work of these boats instead of painting gives them this beautiful harmonious colouring. Schooners and *junks* floated by as our gallant steamer steered slowly (for the benefit of the party) through the waters.

The mountains looked curiously patched and mottled, an effect that is caused by the sand, a great belt of which runs through that part of the country. From an artistic point of view the dusky blue and gold of the mountains was singularly beautiful, although a practical American correspondent compared them with a mangy-backed mule!

On the day following, in the afternoon, we rounded the lovely Miyajima Island, sacred to the sea, where numbers of stone lanterns line the shore. Arrangements had been made for our party to land and visit the different show places. The chief "sight" is the Water Temple, which is built over the water in a tiny bay sheltered from the winds. The *Torii*, or Gate, stands by itself, majestic in its simplicity, and during the *fêtes* processions of boats file through it, bearing pilgrims to the shrine. I climbed the mountain with my friend Lieut. Matsumura, one of the heroes of the early days, who had been severely wounded by a shell splinter on the *Mikassa*.

The ascent was steep, especially towards the top, and the last few yards were a flight of stone stairs hoary with age. The cedars near the temple were particularly fine, and the sacred groves sheltered numerous deer, which were very tame. We dined at the Maple tea-house, which is a unique hostel—a fairyland of tiny houses in sheltered nooks and leafy retreats, which span the bright, clear stream and form ideal little dining-rooms. The place is lighted with electric light. We were shewn into one of the little houses over the stream, and were not kept waiting long ere our dinner was brought. It consisted of the usual soup, fish, rice and stewed beef and vegetables—an improvement on *boeuf à la mode*.

The *Geisha* girls were in attendance to pour out our *saké* and while away the evening with their singing and dancing. They are a picturesque addition to a dinner, for their position is something between hostess and waitress. Many of them are beautiful, and all are charming. They flit about, like great moths, in their picturesque parti-coloured *kimonos*, doing the honours with an elegance and grace which is peculiar to them. But we could not remain long in this fairyland, for we were to make an early start and visit Etajima, the Naval Training School, and see Kure, one of the arsenals.

The training school was most interesting and instructive. We anchored in the charming bay of Etajima, which is nearly land-locked and sheltered by high mountains. The tide flows gently in this protected haven, and boating and bathing are perfectly safe. An old gun-boat and a bathing raft were moored about a hundred yards from the jetty, and the college boats hung from davits along the sea wall ready for lowering. A small dock or basin runs into the grounds, and there

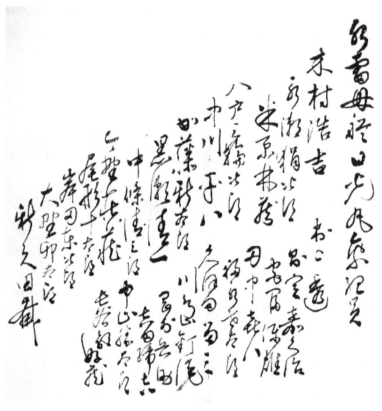

A Japanese Compliment

Names of my messmates on another Japanese cruiser,
Port Arthur, written on a handkerchief.

lay the boat which brought back the crews from one of the steamers at the first blocking of Port Arthur. We were received by Admiral Tomaoka and the officials, and were conducted through the college buildings, which, well designed and beautifully decorated, are situated in grounds that are half gardens and half park.

The main building is a long two-storied structure, and we entered the hall and walked straight through to a passage at the back (which runs the whole length of the building), and first looked in at the dormitories. In each were two rows of beds, with bedding folded, and mosquito curtains of green with a red border. The pillows were stuffed with tea leaves, which is said to be a specific for headache. Along the walls were rows of middies' chests, one of which was opened for our inspection. It was fitted with three tills, or trays, which when lifted up showed the kit neatly folded beneath. The Board room, or Council Chamber, was immediately over the hall, and its walls were decorated with framed photographs of various admirals.

The space between the two windows was, however, reserved to the pictures of the emperor and the royal family, from each of which two purple tassels hung. The most interesting ornament in the room was a perfect model of a war junk, about ten feet long. This beautiful, though clumsy-looking, ship was fully rigged, one big sail hanging from the yards in lengths of silk, laced together instead of being sewn, and every detail was reproduced faithfully, even to the anchors and the ancient lanterns and streamers and pennants which hung from the masts. The temple, or shrine, graced the stern, while a row of pavilions or little cabooses with silken hangings filled the centre. These ranged between the fore and main masts, and were evidently the officers' quarters. The model of a modern battleship, nearby, formed a striking contrast to this obsolete war vessel.

At Etajima the memory of heroic deeds is kept alive, for the blood-stained chart which we saw hanging on the wall was the identical chart which Captain Sakamoto was studying when he received his death wound from a Chinese shell at the Battle of the Yalu, in 1895.

Below the dormitories are large airy classrooms, in which cadets, neatly dressed in white duck, are instructed, in English, in various subjects. It is worthy of note that as the long procession of visitors streamed past the open window, not one of all the hundreds of youngsters raised his eyes or took the least notice of the foreign invasion, so absorbed were they all in their tasks. The silence of the room suggested a convent at devotions rather than a college for naval cadets.

From the class-rooms we passed to a gallery containing some working drawings of engines, guns and field pieces, drawn by the students. Considering that they have only one hour a week allotted for this class of work we marvelled to see what had been done. In the model rooms, which we next visited, we saw working models of every engine in use on a battleship, and we were shewn a working model of an Elswick 6-inch gun, mounted and fitted with improved gear for running the gun in. As far as I could see in the short time allowed for inspection, the T beam for the runner was the same in every respect, but the pulley rope was attached to the trunnion, the running in being effected by means of a steel pulley instead of the chain.

In the next room we visited we saw a fine model of a battleship, complete in every detail, and then we entered the gymnasium, where we witnessed the far-famed *Ju-Ju-si*. The Japanese rightly attach the greatest importance to the study of this science—for it is nothing less. It consists of using the weak points in your opponent's attack to make him throw himself. To such perfection have some of these *Ju-Ju-si* wrestlers attained that they can, with ease, throw their opponents completely over the head. The scene in the gymnasium when we entered beggars description. There were some hundreds of human beings flying about in all directions, heads and limbs alternately appearing and disappearing. The noise of the falls, although the floor was matted, prevented us from hearing one another speak. Squatting around the large hall were many more cadets resting until the professor should summon them to take their places on the floor again. We also were shewn the fencing with large two-handed single-sticks of bamboo. Masks and leather armour was worn, also padded gloves, but the arms were bare to the biceps. The cadets showed great skill in the use of this ancient weapon, and even now the Japanese use the two-handed sword with effect when charging the Russian trenches.

We next witnessed the big gun drill in a long shed constructed on the plan of a battle-deck, with 6-inch guns on the broadside and a 9-inch in bow. We saw some very smart work, for the loading and firing was done in the record time of eight seconds. The final performance was something quite out of the common, and Viscount Inouye explained its object to me by saying that the last aim of all *Ju-Ju-si* is to train to *fight*. Two goal-posts were planted, some 200 yards apart, and sides were picked. One half of each side defended its post, and the others made a dash for the opposite post. With a roar they attacked the enemies' post, and round these rallying points a scrum occurred to which ordinary Rugby football is child's play. They fought with fists—anything to capture the post. Some of them got badly mauled, but not a sound or complaint escaped them. It was, in fact, a mimic battle, fought in the best of tempers, although black eyes, bloody noses and torn clothing testified to the roughness of the sport.

The official photographer grouped us around the muzzle of the 9-inch gun for a "snapshot," and an excellent light lunch closed our visit to the training college.

We steamed away for Miyajima at 4 p.m., and once more the beautiful *Torii*, reflected in the glorious sea, hove in sight, blazing like a golden gate in the rays of the setting sun.

There was great excitement aboard the *Manchu Maru* on June 17th, for it was on that day that we first heard of the attack upon the transports by the Russian cruisers off the island of Okishima. It appeared that if we had kept to our programme we should have run into the arms of the Russians, and, no doubt, included Vladivostock in our trip.

About 4 p.m. on the day we received this startling news we arrived and anchored in the roadstead of Matsuyami. There, in a drenching downpour of rain, we landed to visit the Russian prisoners, confined in various parts of the town. Matsuyami is beautifully situated at the base of a high wooded hill, on which stands the castle of the ancient *Daimio*. This castle was, at the time of our visit, occupied by soldiers, and, in consequence, we were not allowed to go over it. It was a great disappointment to many of us, as it is one of the finest specimens of ancient Japanese architecture.

The following day we left for the Straits of Shimonosaki, and on arriving at Moji we heard the good news that the *Sado Maru,* one of the transports attacked by the enemy, had kept afloat and been towed in by *junks*. One thousand were saved and were then in the town. We passed her where she lay beached, with two steamers in attendance ready to refloat her.

On Sunday, June 19th, about noon, we entered the danger zone. The smoke of two steamers, hull down, gave us an unpleasant reminder of the scene which had taken place there some two or three days before, when the Vladivostock cruisers sunk the transports. One gentleman went so far as to produce his passport and explain that he was an American citizen. The exact spot where the disaster occurred was between Okishima, Oroshuna, and another island, the three forming an irregular oblique triangle, with the now historic island of Tusuma visible in the distance. Tusuma lies between Japan and Corea, and a

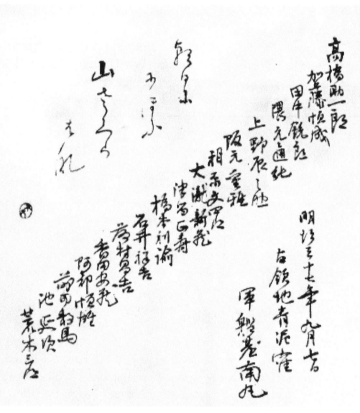

NAMES OF MY MESSMATES ON THE CRUISER.
WRITTEN ON POCKET HANDKERCHIEF.

strong naval base has been established there.

We continued our journey to Sasebo at 3 p.m., and were met by the picket torpedo-boat from that place, which escorted us to harbour. Admiral Superintendent Samijima invited us to sup with him and his staff; the invitation was accepted, and we enjoyed a memorable evening. It was a glorious moonlight night, and the keen air was warmed by huge bonfires in iron crates and the scene illuminated by electric light. It was a "stand-up" supper, and the food was both European and Japanese. The wine was handed round by bluejackets, and a novelty, even in that land of surprises, was given by the band, who left the stand and marched round the assembled guests. The latter, in groups, joined in until a never-ending ring of people followed round and round until the last "*Banzai*" was shouted.

Coaling ship began next day at 10.30, and Captain Yamaguchi informed us that lunch would be provided on shore, and steam launches were at the side to take us off at 11 a.m. Through the numerous transports that blocked the harbour we made our way and passed the torpedo "mother" in her official coat of dark grey, looming large among the shipping. The hospital ship, painted white with the broad green ribbon, sat lightly on the water, looking, as one of the officers said, "like a harmless dove." *Junks* and *sampans* swept past as we steamed to the entrance of the bay, and a long arm opened out into another haven, where half-a-dozen captured ships lay quietly moored awaiting the decision of the prize court.

On a fir-clad point jutting into the sea, known as "the watering station of the navy," stood marquees decorated with flags of all nations, and under the green canopy a very good lunch was served. Servants from the ship waited, all knowing the peculiar tastes of each guest. We spent the rest of the day inspecting the dockyards and arsenals, where the usual feverish work was going on, the workmen earning 60 *sen* (about 1s.) a day and grumbling, not for more pay but for more work. These people all work for their country. From end to end of the dockyards we tramped, hot and dusty, and saw the fine spacious docks in course of construction. We passed on to the store sheds where the food to keep the navy going was stowed in small quantities to ensure freshness. Each day 5,000 lbs. of bread is baked; each loaf weighs 1 lb. and is carefully wrapped in paper and packed in semi-circular baskets. The clothes of the bluejackets at the front are also sent here to be mended, which work is done by women. In another department, clothing was being cut out by tailors, and captured stores of tea and beef filled other huge go-downs to the roof.

Our next visit was to the hospital, where were about 300 patients, wounded and sick, from the front. It is a naval hospital, but if the military require its services they are freely given. Many of the patients were suffering from burns and shell wounds, being mostly men who had taken part in the blocking operations off Port Arthur. The arsenal was much the same as at Kure—casting, founding and repairing proceeding with feverish energy—but by far the most interesting sight was a quantity of very serviceable guns and munitions taken from the Russians, amongst them those recovered from the *Variag*. Guns, rifles, cartridges, shot, shell—every article in this collection of loot was carefully ticketed.

The long tramp was very tiring but quite repaid us, for this dockyard will soon compare with any in the world. There is plenty of land and shallow water that can be reclaimed, and although Kure is the principal building yard, this will be the chief repairing station where ships of the fleet will rest and refit.

The next day I went ashore with Captain Takarabe to make a picture and interview the commander-in-chief, Admiral Samijima. Samijima is a grand old man, with a fine head and very strongly-marked features; the mouth and chin are powerful and determined, but the kindly twinkle in his bright eyes told me that he possessed the sense of humour. Everyone echoed my sentiment that the best thing we saw at Sasebo was the admiral himself. He was not trained in England, being one of Japan's homemade admirals, but he spoke of England, which he visited just eleven years ago, and also of France, to which he once made a hurried trip to see how a cruiser ordered by his government was progressing.

"How do you like Japanese food?" he asked me.

"Very much," I replied. "It has cured me of indigestion. Give me a pair of chopsticks and I'll show you how I can handle them."

The necessary implements not being procurable at the moment, I had recourse to a pair of penholders, with which I performed in a manner that surprised him and met his approval. Cigarettes were produced, and tea—the usual beverage—very weak, but most refreshing. Weak tea is the best, and it would be a fine addition to the ration list of both our army and navy. Men do more on it than they possibly can on spirits. I sketched Samijima, smoking his cigarette by the side of the brazier which forms part of the furniture of every office, and afterwards he kindly took me off to the *Manchu Maru* in his barge, where, after mutual compliments and expressions of good-will, he left and we proceeded to sea. A government tug with the commander in chief's band played us out of harbour, and we were escorted by two torpedo boats, who remained with us for twenty miles on our way to Chemulpo in Corea.

Fan painting is a Japanese accomplishment. I tried my hand, painting one for the Marquis Kuroda, the emperor's representative on board the *Manchu Maru*. It turned out quite a success, giving great satisfaction, and in consequence I had plenty of demands on my time. On the way from Sasebo to Chemulpo, another interesting event occurred. I was the recipient of a present from Nabeshima. The present was a bottle of *"Banzai"* whisky!

On the 24th we arrived off the Corean coast, and the beautiful saffron sky with the delicate mauve of the rocks and islands were a picture never to be forgotten. Fishermen, with long hair done up like Japanese wrestlers, in picturesque boats—something between a *junk* and a *sampan*—gave life to the scene. The distant horizon was swathed with the smoke of numerous transports all bound Dalny way. Our ship was making good speed (sixteen knots) and we took the outside channel, giving a wide berth to the numberless rocks and shoals of this second inland sea. It was very dangerous in the dark, being unlighted, for there are only two lighthouses along the coast, and both are at Chemulpo.

After breakfast the next morning I sketched the members of the upper house, but I was interrupted by the stewards announcing that the doctors were vaccinating in the saloon and ready to operate on anyone so desiring. It was an interesting scene, nearly all the Japanese and the British *attaché*, Captain Jackson, submitting to the operation, although most of us made excuses. It was, nevertheless, a wise precaution, as smallpox was raging in Corea and in fact over the whole territory occupied by our troops.

The same afternoon we passed a number of islands, a small archipelago, inhabited chiefly by fishermen. The biggest island is about six acres in extent and has three or four houses each with a little patch of barley, cultivated by the tenant. The summit of this island is capped by a small wood, from which the people get their fuel.

A good deal of amusement was caused by reading out from the pool the guesses as to the date of the fall of Port Arthur. The consensus of opinion placed the fall about the 30th of August. We had no moments of *ennui*, for Captain Takarabe did everything possible for the

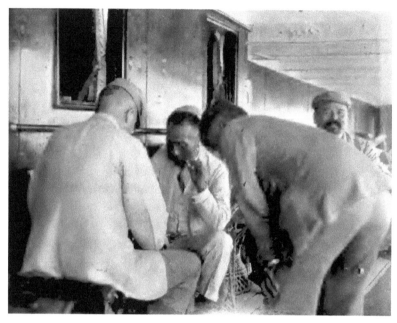

The game of "go bang" on the *Manchu Maru*.

amusement of his guests. We had a lost property office, which was simply a hook in the bulkhead where the notice board hangs. Any articles found, such as pipes, pens, fans, etc., were hung up there until claimed. The fan always forms a part of the Jap outfit, and a very necessary one it is, as most of us discovered. The heat and flies rendered it indispensable. The difficulty of catering for the variety of tastes on board the *Manchu Maru* may be imagined, for among the fifty-five guests there were no less than ten different nationalities. The food was, however, mostly European and there were wines and cigars, so that we got along very well, although in conversation politics were strictly barred.

We passed a singular group of islands a little later, which is really an ancient crater with nothing but the broken lip projecting from the water. The tide there rushes about seven miles an hour, not unlike the race of Portland. The sea was a delicate blue-green, murky shades marking the shoals. A solitary cube stands out of the sea like a sentinel, in advance of the main group. After lunch, when on the spot where the first naval action of the present war was fought, we grouped for a photograph.

The Corean fishermen objected strongly to our back wash, gesticulating wildly as we passed them, and swearing violently. A big shark, the biggest I have seen, was busy at the carcase of a dead bullock, and flocks of screaming gulls hovered over him. A few minutes before Captain Jackson, the naval *attaché*, spoke of taking a morning dip!

Chemulpo, with its long water front, lay before us creeping up the hill sides. The harbour was fairly full of shipping, and Britain, America and Italy were represented by men-of-war. The *Variag* was being raised from her watery bed, and the workers, like ants in number and industry, gave us a *"Banzai"* as we passed. Two other ships were peacefully settled in the mud. They rather interfere with the navigation of the harbour, and will shortly be raised or blown up. The steam launches from the British and Italian warships came alongside as we anchored to look up their respective *attachés*.

A tug boat had been engaged to take us ashore, and at 7.00 we landed for a couple of hours, wandering in the semi-darkness and smells. Many of the inhabitants were inclined to be hostile, but for what reason I do not know. Some of us went to the Chinese hotel, where we met Colquhoun, who had been in the *Haimoon*. He was correspondent for *The Times*, and was looking in good form after his arduous services. We tried to get hold of some news, but without success, and we left at 10.30 after getting a few stores that would be useful

CHINESE SHRINE ON THE ISLAND
OF KOJO-TAU,
GULF OF PECHELI.

SOME OF THE BLOCKING
TORPEDO BOATS ALONGSIDE
THE "MOTHER" IN A CERTAIN
HARBOUR.

LAST OF THE BOATSWAIN

MUSTERED FOR LOOK-OUT
DUTY.

later on when we were thrown upon our own resources. The captain of the tug seemed uncertain as to the time he would get off. He had been ordered to start at 10.00, and it was then 10.30.

After a hurried debate as to whether we should take a boat or wait, it was unanimously decided to hire a *sampan*, in which we put off at once, the lusty crew sculling us to the encouraging song of "*Sara ha! Sara heigh! Sara ha!*" the frail vessel wobbling along at a good pace. The tides at Chemulpo are the worst dangers of the harbour, and as we passed the spot where a boat belonging to a British man-of-war foundered with all hands a few years ago, we thought of their fate, but bright moon-light flecked the wavelets, the tide swished gently, and we met with no mishap. The night was so still that we could hear the chiming of the ships' bells, far out in the roadsteads, and the harmonious chant of the working gangs on the sunken Russian cruiser. We made good way against the tide, fetching our ship as the bell was striking eleven.

The programme of our future movements was handed round, the most important item being a visit to Seoul, the capital of Corea. We also heard the good news that the Russians had been badly beaten again in the last fight, losing two torpedo boats by mines, and we learnt that, for the future, troopships were to be convoyed to guard against such misfortunes as befell the *Sado Maru* and her consort in the Corean Straits. The following day we were to attend the mayor's reception, top hats and frock coats being *de rigeur,* and we were to leave the same evening, by special train, for Seoul. We left the ship at eleven, with our baggage, and it was an amusing sight to watch the frantic efforts of the foreigner to hang on to his property.

The excitement was put to an end by leaving matters entirely in the hands of our hosts. Landing at Chemulpo is rather a difficult matter, for the harbour is so shallow, and our boat, although it only drew two feet of water, was obliged to anchor, and we were transferred to *sampans.* Although only a few yards separated us from the broken jetty, it was nearly half-an-hour's work for our *sampan* to scull through the crowd of boats. M. Tomaiso headed a small deputation to welcome us, and very courteously he filled the office. The arrangements for our convenience and comfort were excellent, and our baggage was consigned to the Japanese Consulate, which saved us from all the worries of the Custom House.

We followed our polite guides to the banqueting hall in the tea-house or hotel, which stood on a high bluff from which a magnificent view of the whole harbour was obtained. We were fortunate, too, in the fact that the tide was in, so that our noses were spared the fore-shore smells. A large roofed verandah shaded the front of the hotel; here a few tables and chairs were placed for the foreign contingent. The floor of the huge hall was matted, and about 200 small cushions were arranged with great exactness, a card with the name of a guest being placed by the side of each. A touch of colour was added by strings of lanterns and flags bobbing about in the breeze which blew through the hall and cooled the air deliciously.

After we had taken our places the mayor, in a formal speech, again welcomed us. The pretty waitresses, assisted by *Geisha* girls, then trooped in, bearing small low tables on which the food was tastefully arranged, one table being placed opposite each guest. No one began to eat until all were served, and the waitresses knelt down ready to give any assistance, from pouring out the *saké* to lighting cigarettes. Speeches were made at intervals. One very interesting part of the entertainment was the explosion of a lot of crackers, which was intended to be a special compliment to the war correspondents. As Viscount Inouye remarked:

> They are always worrying to see fighting and smell powder, and we thought we would let them smell the powder now.

This little joke caused much merriment, and the feast ended with the health of the Emperor of Japan being drunk with the greatest enthusiasm.

The tinkling of a *samisan* announced the beginning of the *Geishas'* songs and dances. Against a background of blue sky, a group of girls, dressed in diaphanous robes, posed and pirouetted gracefully, the bright sunlight shadowing their lithesome figures amid flying clouds of softest silk. The announcement that the train started for Seoul at 3.45 broke up, somewhat abruptly, a most delightful entertainment.

There is a very nice club at Chemulpo at which I called, and I met there a friend who saw the fight between the *Variag* and the Japanese cruisers. He said it was all over in forty minutes. The concussion of the guns broke several panes of glass in the buildings in the town, and the Coreans got very excited and dreamt of great things, amongst them the probability of becoming a naval power.

Corean railways are almost as rapid as our own Welsh lines, and although Chemulpo is only 30 miles from Seoul, the journey occupied nearly three hours. On arrival I drove straight to the Palace

Hotel, where I put up. Our arrival meant much to the sedan chair and *rickshaw* men, and most of them were retained by members of the party for the whole day. I started sight-seeing on my own account early the next morning, not being due at the palace audience until 12 o'clock. Seoul is little more than a collection of hovels. The men are tall and swagger along with much dignity, wearing the hat peculiar to the Corean tilted slightly at various angles. This hat is not put on the head but on a "shape," the "shape," like the hat, being beautifully made of very fine horsehair, and fitting so tightly that the skull appears to bulge over it.

The long, white silk coat is not unlike a dress of the Josephine period, and the skirts float out as the wearer stalks along with his pipe and fan. The women wear voluminous petticoats and trousers, like their Chinese sisters, and turned-up slippers encase their small feet. When abroad in the street they veil their beauty and, at the same time, keep off the dust and flies, by throwing a large cloak over the head and face. The children wear most brilliant colours, which, seen down long vistas of the Seoul suburbs, give one the idea of a flock of gorgeous macaws or parrots.

Through the streets pass strings of ponies laden with all sorts of produce, and the everlasting Corean bull with a load that one would deem only an elephant capable of rising under. Dogs have a good time in Seoul. Many of them are decorated with broad bands of various colours, and they roam everywhere, seemingly allowed to do as they like. They are supposed by the Coreans to have souls, which accounts for the singular freedom which they enjoy. The houses are low pitched, with no attempt at ornamentation, except in some cases where a particularly fierce menagerie tiger is painted in staring colours. In an attempt to paper one house, they had used newspapers of various ages and dates, a combination which seemed to gratify the pride of the owner, a tall, venerable-looking man, almost apostolic in appearance. The smells of Seoul are awful, sewage pits, wells and a dried fish store rivalling one another with noisome odours, and among the garbage and offal the younger generation plays happily.

Over the gates of the city stands a three-tiered pagoda, used in ancient times as a guard house and watch tower. The fine old iron gates are now rusting on their hinges, time and neglect have crumbled away the circular wall which defended the portal from frontal attacks, and all the coping stones are broken. The whirr of the electric tram as it rushes through contrasts strangely with this picture of age and desola-

A STREET SCENE IN SEOUL, KOREA

tion. I boarded the tram and was whisked down to the hotel, passing the market which is held in the open street, and where Corean husbands were chaffering over onions and lettuces, the principal items of the family dinner. The all-pervading filth veneers the butchers' shops, and meat is hewn off anyhow in chunks, whilst the feet and head portions are whittled down and sold for soup or glue, there being no material difference in the flavour of either. The white-coated crowd moved leisurely out of the way of the tram-car, while the general traffic picked its way through piles of fish, vegetables, wood and other merchandise which fills an eastern market.

Twelve o'clock was the hour appointed to be at the palace, but the emperor did not receive us personally on this occasion. The chamberlain and principal officers of the palace did the honours. The emperor has two palaces; the one in the city is called the "Palace of Heaven" and the other the "Palace of Prosperity and Virtue." The latter is situated in a most charming spot outside the city, surrounded by a strong wall.

We were invited to the Palace of Prosperity and Virtue, and were received by a guard at the entrance, who inspected our passes and allowed us to go through. The scene inside resembled a beautiful English landscape, the green undergrowth shaded by fine old trees such as might be seen in an English park. A broad, well-kept road winding through a glade of fir-trees brought us to an inner gate, where the palace officials took charge of us. We were first received at the main entrance of the palace, a fine piece of Chinese architecture, brilliant with vermilion, green and purple, which all seemed to harmonise. Here a second official took our cards, which were handed to the prime minister, who shook hands with us before passing us on to some other officers who conducted us into the garden.

There we were left to ourselves, and had some leisure to admire the lovely landscape gardening. Lotus ponds and quaint pavilions of various sizes and shapes dotted the grounds, and the whole garden was almost a counterpart of the familiar old willow-pattern plate. Lunch was served in the chief pavilion, a two-storied building, gorgeously painted and celebrated for the beauty of the red lacquer columns which support the main hall. A flight of stairs led to the upper apartment, where a cold lunch was laid out which would have done credit to *delmonico* or princess. The Corean steward told me, with great pride, that it was cooked and laid out in European style, and that the Japanese were their instructors. There was champagne and other wines.

The guests being numerous, space was limited, and everyone was not lucky enough to stand at the table. I managed to make friends with some Corean gentlemen, who, like myself, had come in late, and we wandered about, with our chopsticks in one hand and a big plate in the other, collecting tit-bits. We then retired with them to the broad, low rail of the balcony, which fortunately was in the shade, and thoroughly enjoyed our picnic lunch together. In praise of the lunch I remarked;

"You owe a good deal to the Japanese."

"We owe everything," they said, "and under their beneficent rule and guidance Corea will become a great and prosperous province of the glorious Empire of Japan."

After lunch we wandered through the beautiful grounds, where cigars, coffee, and cool drinks seemed to appear like magic in every pavilion we entered. Our long ramble ended at a big rock, beneath which gushed forth a clear crystal spring that supplies the palace grounds. A strange Chinese poem is inscribed in bold characters on the face of this rock, and the translation is as follows:

PALACE OF PROSPERITY AND VIRTUE.
Three hundred feet high how far from heaven the waters descended!
Look yonder white rainbow rose and the current makes
The thundrous wind in ten thousand hills.

Our cameras were busy, and probably they were the first ever seen in this ancient glade. We returned to our *palanquins* and *rickshaws* and were driven off in a cloud of dust, our departure being witnessed by a crowd of Coreans, who actually removed their pipes in their staring wonder. The day closed with a brilliant reception at the Japanese Club.

The following day we received our cards of invitation for the emperor's audience. This was to be held in the Palace of Heaven at 3.30 the same afternoon. Our kind hosts told us to be at the Hotel de Palais early, and they would guide us. Most of our party started in *jinrickshaws*, but *palanquins* of ancient construction and painted a dead black seemed to be the favourite conveyance of the elite of Seoul. We started through the narrow dusty street, *palanquin* bearers and *rickshaw* men jostling each other in their endeavours to be first at the palace. We alighted at the gateway to perform the remaining short distance on foot. Sometime previously the palace had been burnt down, but a temporary building had been erected for the purpose of receiving foreign dignitaries.

We were first shown into the large hall, where doors opened into a number of reception rooms. Into one of these the official directed us, shaking each of us by the hand as we passed in. Cigars, sweetmeats and tea were served, but, considering the temperature, the latter might have been dispensed with. The furniture and decorations were in the Tottenham Court Road style, but two magnificent globe vases of *cloisonné* enamel contrasted strangely with the shoddy appearance of the rest of the room. The master of the ceremonies arranged the order in which the presentation was to take place, and the ushers beckoned us towards a doorway with a portiere curtain, which was swept aside as we entered the presence of the Son of Heaven. On a raised dais at the further end of the room, between the two windows, stood the emperor and the crown prince before a magnificently embroidered silk screen. The court consisted of the chief eunuch, a tall, misshapen piece of humanity who lolled against one of the gorgeous pillars, and two military *attachés* who kept well in the background.

The emperor is a stout, rather jovial-looking man, with some dignity, but the merry twinkle in his small eye betokens the *bon vivant*. The crown prince looked rather vacant, and did not seem to interest himself in the proceedings in the least. He has a weakness for garlic, and to counteract the pungent odour he always chews a piece of ginger, which he rolls in his mouth like a sailor does his quid of tobacco. The dress of both father and son was similar—white Corean robes and the peculiar head "shape." As we passed we gave two bows to the emperor and one to the crown prince. Some of our number bowed with considerable deference to the eunuch!

At the conclusion of the ceremony we drove to the official residence of the Japanese minister, where we had supper. This was served *al fresco* and eaten with chopsticks. The band from the palace played operatic selections, and a telegram was read from Admiral Togo announcing a second defeat of the Russian Navy, which news was a splendid ending to our day. The following day we returned to Chemulpo and the ship, and early the morning after we started under easy steam for a secret destination.

This proved to be a wild-looking bay called Haiju, which was the secret base of Admiral Togo during the early part of the war. (It may be remembered that Russian reports accused England of lending Admiral Togo Wei-hai-wei.) The beauty of this place is its secrecy. Admiral Togo used it as a telegraph station, and although it is seventeen hundred miles from Tokyo, messages got through in ten minutes. Takarabe kindly allowed us to land, but warned us not to go into the grass on account of the vipers which are very numerous. The officer in charge of the station showed us round, and we came back to the ship loaded with wild flowers.

We continued our journey the next day, but were stopped by fog—a real Corean fog. We remained hung up by this for about three days. Everyone who has experienced a fog at sea knows the deadly dullness it occasions, but two Japanese artists named Toji and Murasi helped to while away the time by showing us some delightful specimens of their handiwork, turning out trees and flowers like magic. One especially good example was a spray of white chrysanthemums on white paper. Some of us set to work in imitation of them. But I am afraid our first efforts were rather clumsy.

One night lights were seen and heavy firing heard across the water. There was at once a rush from all parts of the ship, and boats' crews stood by the falls prepared to lower in an instant. The excitement, however, soon subsided, when Takarabe decided that, fog or no fog, he would start, and seventeen knots an hour soon placed us out of danger of being captured. I had turned in early, and about nine o'clock my boy rushed into the cabin and hurriedly began screwing in the dead light, explaining something about a flash light and a man-of-war. Here was more excitement, and I groped my way on deck, where I found that all lights were out. In breathless silence, groups of figures were looking eagerly and anxiously ahead.

We heard the guns again and saw the searchlights. Had the Russian fleet come out? Or were they the Vladivostock cruisers searching for us? We continued steaming at full speed, and, although our distance from the firing was not great, the fog concealed us. Further alarms continued from time to time during the night, most of the guests remaining on the deck or in the saloon till after midnight. In the morning an array of bottles in the saloon proclaimed the earnestness of the discussion that had taken place as to what course the Russians would pursue in case they captured us.

On Saturday we anchored in the friendly waters of Haiju Bay once more. The correspondents were, of course, anxious to send off the news of the fighting, but Takarabe would not permit them to do so.

"This is intelligence," he said, "and we don't wish the Russians to have any idea where we are or what we are up to."

When any important news came on board the fire bell was always rung to let everyone know. A furious ringing proclaimed one day that

LANDING AT PINYANG.

VIEW FROM PIPARI ISLAND, CHINAMBO, KOREA.

a go get was to be read out. Captain Takarabe was in the saloon, and with the help of a blackboard he charted and explained the positions of the fleets in the recent battle. He also gave us the unwelcome intelligence that the Russian cruisers from Vladivostock had been sighted in the neighbourhood, and had been attacked by our torpedo destroyers, but with what result was at present unknown. This was evidently the engagement we had seen and, being only a transport, had fled from. The younger members of our party were getting restless and chafed at our inaction, but there was no help for it, for the Russians were particularly anxious to recapture our ship, especially now that it had so many prominent men on board, and we could not afford to run any risks.

Towards the afternoon great excitement was caused by the appearance of five steamers making for the bay, but they turned out to be Japanese transports, one of them carrying relief crews for the Port Arthur fleet. These ships, like ourselves, had come in to wait for news, and soon afterwards we heard that the Vladivostock squadron was homeward bound. We now made a fresh start, steaming up the river. Before noon the following day we brought up at Chinnambo. This place, under the Japanese, is already becoming a large and influential city, but our object in going there was to push on to Pinyang, the ancient capital of Corea. The first shot of the war was fired at Chinnambo, the Japanese driving out the few *Cossacks* who were stationed there. The principal residents and officers entertained us with the regal prodigality to which we were becoming accustomed.

The first stage of our trip to Pinyang was aboard the comfortable roomy steamer *Kiodo Maru*. The River Tai-do-ko (which means "big similar river") waters the plains of Pinyang, the latter name meaning "crop ground." Stretches of mud flats backed by mountains is the general character of the scene from the river, on which many fishing boats, mostly fishing for prawns, were busy as we steamed up stream. Higher up the country changed, wide, fertile plains taking the place of the mud flats. This was the beginning of the Valley of Pinyang—probably the finest rice country in the East. The banks looked very much like those of the upper reaches of the Thames, with the quiet backwaters and shady nooks.

The *Kiodo Maru* was unable to get nearer to the city than three or four miles, owing to the sudden shallowing of the river. The small paddle consort came alongside, and we transhipped. At four o'clock we anchored opposite the gates of Pinyang, which is a typical Chinese walled town. The battlements were crowded with apathetic white-robed spectators, as were the few houses outside. This changeless apathy of the Coreans contrasts very strongly with the untiring, bustling energy of our hosts. Japanese police were lined in front of the crowded walls and songs of welcome were sung by neatly-dressed school girls. The progress that has been made at Pinyang and elsewhere in Corea since the Japanese came is marvellous. Corea is in transition, and rapidly becoming civilised under the touch of these magicians—these Britons of the East.

Over a bridge of boats between the steamer and the shore we trooped, squeezing our way through the ill-favoured crowd to the gateway, where the crowd was even thicker on account of the rain. The reception was held in a windswept chamber of the watch-tower. Afterwards we made a progress through the principal street (which was little better than an irregular trail trodden deep in the mire), the ribs of our umbrellas hooking in the eaves of the houses, many of which were worse than dog kennels. I saw donkeys and pigs in the family apartments, and the people live in indescribable filth. The town hall served as headquarters of the army, and there we were received by the commander-in-chief and shown various specimens of the country's produce and manufactures.

Our next objective was the battlefield of the 1894-5 war, on the summit of which stands a monument to the fallen heroes of Japan. The little enclosure, shaded by fruit trees, is well looked after, and, when we had inspected it, we wandered among the ancient groves of pine trees. We saw, also, the tomb of Prince Ki-Tzi, which is said to be thirty-two centuries old. The highest point of the battlefield is 700 feet, and there the walls of the city join in an acute angle. The view is charming, a Turner tree stands up boldly against the sky and the landscape includes mountain, wood, water, plain, and the ruins of old cities.

By the time we had seen all that was to be seen, hunger began to make itself felt, and we adjourned to an old house where an ample meal awaited us. It is said that many years ago a celebrated Chinese scholar, one Kin-too-gen, came to this house to read some of the old poems which decorate the walls and are contained in a printed book kept there. Feeling that none of the poems adequately described the beauty of the scene he became inspired. Going out on to the verandah he wrote these two lines:

Facing the castle there runs a mighty stream with heavenly eternity.

Viscount Inouye at the tomb of the Chinese Prince Ki-Tzi, Pinyang.

Toward the east of a vast plain mountains are dotted here and there.

The beauty of the place, and probably the reaction after the inspiration had left him, affected him so that he wept bitterly and ran away.

Pinyang is celebrated for the beauty of its women, and it is there that the emperor selects his *concubines* from the school for the training of this class of women. Since the Japanese have been in power the institution is in a very poor condition, and, under their rule, is likely to be abolished.

On returning from this trip we found that a telegram had been received which ran as follows:

The Russian fleet left Port Arthur at 6.30; Admiral Togo's combined fleet have gone to meet them.

Captain Takarabe left, ostensibly for the mouth of the river, in our armed transport, but, as the transport was really a scout, it was thought probable that he had gone to the front. As may be imagined, the news upset our programme, but such happenings are the fortune of war. In the absence of Takarabe, Captain Yamaguchi took charge of the arrangements for our comfort and pleasure. We were not allowed to mope, and Marquis Kuroda—one of Japan's oldest *Daimios*—organised a picnic in one of the lovely spots up the river. A large *junk*, matted and shaded with awnings, was provided, and the tug boat took us in tow. We had a most delightful time, and the trip was particularly interesting as it afforded an opportunity for seeing the Corean farmer at home.

The farmhouses closely resemble those in China. The one we visited was not very prosperous, but the owner told us that as generations of his ancestors had lived and died there he felt bound to remain and look after their tombs. Under the eaves of most of the houses there is a poem eulogising the ancestors of the household. Before we left we brought a camera to bear upon a young bull surrounded by a group of children. The bull resented the familiarity, and, lowering his head, bore down upon the photographer in full charge. The photographer escaped, and the farmer apologised courteously, explaining that our black coats had frightened the bull, as he had never before seen any but white.

We made the acquaintance of the squire of the district, a boy thirteen years of age. He asked us to take him to see the ship, and I, not knowing the habits of the country, referred to him as a boy, which the youth evidently greatly resented, and which was, of course, interpreted to him. A Japanese friend of mine said:

You will offend him very much if you call him a boy. He is a young Corean gentleman, and has a wife fourteen years old, and owns a great deal of property.

When at Pinyang the history of the emperor's favourite was told to me. It is a romantic story, and so essentially Eastern that it reminds one of the Arabian Nights' Entertainments.

This favourite is of very humble origin, her parents being so poor that they found it difficult to support their children, and at the age of thirteen she entered the service of a lady of the court as a drudge, her principal duties consisting of cleaning out the sewers and boiling rice. But she did not long remain in this menial employment, for, one day, being commanded to dress her mistress's hair, she displayed such skill in the execution of the task that her mistress was very pleased and never permitted her hair to be dressed by anyone else.

The other ladies of the court—for women are much alike all the world over—were not slow to notice the elegant appearance of the lady's *coiffure*, and it was not long ere the poor girl had a clientele that embraced nearly all the chief ladies of the land. Perhaps it was her imperial dignity that prevented the late empress from expressing her feminine curiosity and envy until her *coiffure* was the only one in the palace that showed no trace of the magic touch of the hairdresser girl. Then, however, she lost no time in ordering the girl to be brought to her, and from that day forth her *coiffure* was worthy of the imperial head which it adorned.

The hairdresser girl now lived in the palace in constant attendance upon the empress, and it was not long ere the emperor noticed her and fell under the influence, not of her hairdressing, but of her personal charms. A secret intimacy grew up between them and continued uninterrupted, until it was discovered by the empress. The empress was a very jealous woman, and with the knowledge of the intrigue between the emperor and her hairdresser her anger arose, and she turned the girl out of the palace with contumely.

The sudden loss of the services of one who made them appear beautiful in the eyes of the Corean gentlemen caused great consternation among the ladies of the court, and they put their heads together—heads that now, alas! were indifferently dressed—and each agreed to do all in her power to induce the empress to forgive the girl and admit her to the palace again. My informant said that the persuasions of the court ladies had the desired effect, for the empress yielded reluctantly, and agreed that the girl should return, but I have no hesitation in saying that, in this particular, he was incorrect, for it is obvious to the simplest mind that her poorly-dressed hair had broken the spirit of the empress, and that she sighed for the elegant *coiffures* that had added to her imperial dignity.

So the hairdresser girl entered the palace again and resumed her services to the ladies of the court. Now the royal palaces of Asia are seldom free from intrigue, and the Court of Seoul has always been excessively Asiatic. Soon after the girl's return to the palace the enemies of the empress made things so uncomfortable for Her Majesty that she left the court hurriedly and lived in a remote place in as unostentatious a manner as possible. With her departure the little hairdresser rose in the favour and the affections of the emperor, so that she occupied in the palace a position but a little lower than that which the empress had filled. But her day of glory was short-lived, for the empress' faction again got the upper hand, Her Majesty returned—evidently with a determination to pay off old scores—and the girl fled for her life.

She was about twenty-seven years of age at the time of her flight from the palace. In her short life she had ascended the social ladder beyond the dreams of ambition, and now she fell from her high position to the lowest rung. She took refuge with an old friend, a laundry woman, and supported herself by making "cake"—a composition of inferior green peas and rice—and selling it to the common people. It was not a remunerative business, and soon she was reduced to wearing old rags. Her friend the laundry woman could not help her, for she, too, had fallen on bad times, and only earned enough to keep herself from starvation. Providence came to the rescue of the girl in the person of Kaw, a poor clothes dealer of Seoul, who wished to wed her. In her sore distress she agreed; they were secretly married, and in course of time she became the mother of a boy and a girl.

After many months a lady of the court learnt the whereabouts of the hairdresser girl, and at once visited the house of Kaw, where she was made happy by once more having her hair dressed in the inimitable manner. She visited the house often, and began to take an interest not only in Kaw's wife's hairdressing, but in the worthy Kaw himself, and by way of atonement to the injured wife took steps to bring about her return to the court. The death of the empress, on October 8th, 1895, enabled her to gain her end, and once more the girl entered the palace.

She was now supreme in the emperor's favour, for she had no rival, but it is sad to relate that as she occupied the exalted position of the late empress so she developed the jealousy that had characterised her predecessor. Soon after her son, Prince Yin, was born (October 20th, 1899), one of her spies reported that the emperor and a lady, whose name, in English, is Moonlight, had appeared to get too much enjoyment from their friendly conversation at one of the State banquets. She promptly had Moonlight arrested and tortured, although after this somewhat forcible intimation of disapproval she set her free.

Another unpleasant incident occurred when the ladies of Pinyang (famous for their beauty, bravery and musical accomplishments) were invited to the palace. The emperor unfortunately drank more wine than was his wont, and in the enthusiastic expression of his pleasure at entertaining the Pinyang ladies, he seized the hand of one of them. The spies at once reported this regrettable occurrence to the hairdresser girl, and the Pinyang ladies advised their friend to go home to Pinyang. With characteristic bravery the lady refused.

"There is no greater honour," she declared, "than to be permitted to clasp the emperor's hand, and having done so I do not fear to die."

The other Pinyang ladies (who appear to have possessed common sense as well as their more attractive accomplishments) endeavoured to persuade her, and at last she consented to flee from the palace. It was said, however, that she was "lost on the way," which is the cautious Corean way of stating that one of the hairdresser girl's emissaries had waylaid and murdered her.

The hairdresser girl is now fifty years of age. She is paramount in the palace, and is looking forward to the day when she will be officially recognised as empress, and her son, Prince Yin, acknowledged heir to the throne.

CHAPTER 3

We Sail for Togo's Base

When we got back on board the *Manchu Maru* we received the cheering intelligence, by telegram, that:

The Russian Squadron passed the Corean Straits bound for Vladivostock July 1st.

This was the date of our scare when we ran back to Haiju.

Our ship had coaled and watered and we started for the Yalu. The military authorities invited us to Antung, the head-quarters of that district, and after that we should practically look after ourselves, hiring our own *junks* to do the remainder of the journey to Ku-heu-chung, the scene of the first and most important battle. It was at Ku-heu-chung that the Japanese showed the world that their soldiers were equal to their sailors—that they had learnt lessons from Germany as well as from England. The anchorage at the mouth of the Yalu is protected by shoals and rocks, and the intricate channel is always changing.

The hospital ship *Yokohama Maru* and several transports and other steamers were lying there. Unfortunately, the Marquis Kuroda and Dr. Yabi, who were laid up by typhoid fever, which it was supposed they had contracted at Seoul, left us to be nursed aboard the hospital ship. To Dr. Yabi I owe a debt of gratitude. For nine months I had been troubled by a growth on the lower lid of my left eye which three or four doctors had decided was a polypus, to remove which it would be necessary to cut down to the cheek bone. I did, as a matter of fact, go to a hospital to have the operation performed, but, the surgeon being away, the operation was postponed. In the meantime, I started on this trip, and Dr. Yabi, noticing the eye, asked if I were treating it. I told him I intended having it operated on when I returned.

"What for?" said he.

"For polypus," I replied.

"Pardon me," he returned, "but I don't think it is polypus. Will you allow me to see it?"

After a short examination he said:

"I will give you a wash which will, I think, cure it."

He gave me the stuff, and after ten days' application the growth came out whole.

To our great disappointment the military authorities were unable to carry out their kind plans for us, for we received orders to start for Admiral Togo's base, there to await instructions. While we were passing the spot where the big Chinese battle took place in 1894, we carried two of the survivors in triumph round the decks, Captain Yamaguchi being one, and the other a petty officer.

The same day we passed several groups of islands and right ahead lay a long, high island. Behind this island lay the mystery known to the world only as "a certain place"—the rendezvous of Admiral Togo's fleet. Rounding a high, gloomy point, the "certain place" lay revealed to foreign eyes for the first and only time. Long lines of warships, with steam up ready for instant action, lay there, the redoubtable *Mikassa*, flying the flag of Admiral Togo, heading the line. The scene, for a moment, took our breath away. Dream-like the ships looked, shrouding the bay with smoke, yet they conveyed an awful impression of power and strength that appalled the mind.

I have seen many naval reviews, but never have I gazed on a sight so impressive as these steel-clad ships which, like some fabled monsters, breathed forth fire and smoke. The placid haven wherein they lay was secured from attack by booms and mines which closed the ways of approach, and all the time wireless telegraphy was bringing news of every move made by the Russians who were shadowed by the admiral's swift cruisers. High over the fleet frowned a huge segment of rock, strongly resembling Gibraltar.

Glasses and telescopes were busy aboard our ship. The hitherto dissatisfied and impatient members of our company were content. At last we were really within the area of active operations. At any moment we might be actors in a battle that would settle the fate of nations. About twenty miles from these islands, Manchuria with all its bloodstained mysteries showed peaceful and quiet, the white cliffs gleaming like the English coast. In a sheltered bay a big army camp was established, towards which we steered, our hopes running high at the prospect of landing. But when within signalling distance we received a message ordering us to return and anchor, so that after a memorable, though in the end rather disappointing day, we took up our moorings in the outer anchorage, under the protecting guns of Admiral Togo's fleet.

That same evening Takarabe came on board again. He had been up to see General Nogi, the commander-in-chief of the investing army at Port Arthur, and he promised to let us know the result of his mission on the following day. We then learnt that he had been to the front and seen the opposing armies within eight miles of each other, and that on account of the difficulties in capturing some of the forts Port Arthur was likely to hold out for some time longer. In consequence, our proposed visit to Dalny and Talienwan had to be abandoned, for a time at any rate. He told us, further, that as there was a possibility of a Russian raid we were to shift our anchorage, and this was at once carried out, the *Manchu Maru* steaming back to a sheltered and retired bay at the rear of Admiral Togo's position.

A number of fishing *junks* came alongside, and it was very amusing to watch the deals in fish. Not a moment's credit was allowed, the Chinamen hanging on to the fish with one hand until the coin was safely in the palm of the other.

There was great consternation when the following notice appeared on the notice board:

> This ship is immediately to return to Nagasaki.

This was a crushing blow. We had come so near the front and yet were to return without actually getting there. I heard privately that the reason of our return was that the Russians were about to make some important movement and that our position might become critical at any moment. Our hopes were soon raised again, for about 10 p.m. we received a signal to the effect that Admiral Togo would receive us on board his flagship some time on the morrow, but first we were to be allowed to steam within 10 miles of Port Arthur, to view the general scene of operations. After this, we were to join Togo at another rendez-vous—in the Blonde Islands, escorted by the cruiser *Tsukai*, Japan's first ship of the new navy.

We proceeded towards Talienwan Bay, where we saw flotillas of destroyers and torpedo boats going to or returning from their positions on the blockade. We steamed back towards our meeting place and by noon we observed the *Mikassa* and Ashanii right ahead waiting for us. We were cordially welcomed by the officers in the ward room of the

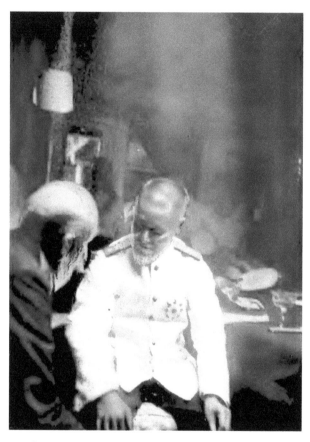

A SNAPSHOT IN THE DARK. ADMIRAL TOGO AND
MYSELF HAVING A YARN ON THE *MIKASSA*.

Mikassa, which was very plainly furnished. A grim relic stood upon the sideboard in the shape of a fragment of the 12-inch shell that cut a piece out of Lieut. Matsumura's leg.

Admiral Togo came in to see us. He is a short, well-built man with rather a slight stoop, and just on the shady side of fifty. We all turned to look at the man whose name was on the lips of everyone in the world. His is a kindly face, but it was marked by lines of care, the result of the anxious watching and thought of the last six months. Although it might be the face of an ordinary, studious man, it indubitably impresses one. The eyes are brilliant and black, like those of all Japanese, and a slight pucker at the corners suggests humour. A small drooping nose shades a pursed-up mouth with the under lip slightly protruding.

He has a large head, which is a good shape and shows strongly defined bumps, and the hair is thin and worn very short. A slight beard fringes the face and it is whitening on the chin, and the moustache is thin and black. Like most great men, he can keep his own counsel. It is said that he can sit for weeks by himself without any desire for companionship except his pipe, for, like Bismarck, he is an inveterate smoker. He did not speak very much to any of us, although he said courteously that he looked upon our visit as a great honour. Champagne and glasses were brought in, and he drank to our health, wishing us a safe journey back to Japan.

The *Mikassa* looked so clean and smart that she might almost have been ready for inspection off Spithead instead of within the sound of the Russian guns, which boomed sullenly at intervals throughout the day. The band played a typically English programme as we sat in groups with the Japanese officers about the deck. The only visible sign of the *Mikassa* having been in action was a shell wound in the mainmast. Before leaving, we were shown round the ship, and the whole crew seemed to show the traces of the anxious, vigilant six months that I had noticed in Admiral Togo. Very few of them ever got more than four hours' sleep in one night.

On our return to the *Manchu Maru* the anchor was speedily weighed, and our head pointed to Japan. Without adventure we got to Nagasaki, where our plans underwent another alteration, owing to the Vladivostock Squadron coming out again on the war-path. We had to change our course, returning by the Inland Sea and leaving the Pacific route in the hands of the enemy. The report from headquarters ran:

Vladivostock Squadron have been reported by fishermen as

coming through the Hokdido Strait.

So we proceeded to Kobe, there to await further orders. At Kobe we could obtain no news of the Vladivostock fleet, and most of our party dispersed—the greater number being bound for Tokyo. I tried to get to Yokohama by the P. and O., but they could not guarantee me a safe passage, and finally they unloaded their cargo at Kobe, and received a wire ordering the ship to return home to England. I therefore went on to Tokyo by train, where I spent my time passing between the Embassy and the Admiralty.

It is interesting to a European to watch the life in Tokyo streets. There is none of the roar and bustle of the west, nearly all the transport being done by porters who carry their heavy loads with noiseless tread. The *jinrickshaw*, which corresponds to our hansom cab, is scarcely audible, and the only noises are the street hawkers crying their wares, and the dismal whistle of the automatic steam pipe cleaner. Now and again troops of merry children going to and from school make a joyous morning concert, and the busy chant of the *coolies* at their work may be heard sometimes. But the silence in the city does not betoken laziness; work, work, hard toil, is evident everywhere.

Every one of the two and a half millions of inhabitants of Tokyo takes a bath once during the day. This is an excellent institution, and might be followed with advantage in many other cities I have visited. Japan is clean from the sea-shore to the mountain-top, and so it is with her people; they look and are clean, and they are always cheerful. They work hard, but there is not that mad rush for riches which is the curse of modern commercialism. Their pleasures are simple; a family excursion to view the cherry blossom or maple, or maybe a *junk* load of happiness drifting leisurely on the river, either of which affords the pleasure of contemplating the wonders of nature which they all enjoy. The Japanese life is an object lesson in the simple life, the want of which is evidently beginning to be felt in England.

Chapter 4

I am Ordered to Sasebo

The days spent in Tokyo were pleasant enough, but I had not come out to the East to remain idly in Japan, and I began to wonder if I ever should see any of the fighting. I was, therefore, not a little elated when I received orders from the Admiralty to go to Sasebo, where I should be appointed to one of the cruisers. On my arrival there I called on Admiral Samijima, who said he had orders for me to go at once. When could I get away?

"I am ready," I said.

"Well," he replied, "there is a ship starting at six tomorrow morning; you had better go straight on board."

I went back to my hotel, packed up, and stepped aboard the ship at seven o'clock the same evening, and found myself once more beneath the pennant of the Rising Sun.

Everything seemed in confusion. The ship was coaling, and the decks were littered with boxes and bales and all sorts of stores. Women as well as men take part in coaling, and they are paid thirty-five *sen* per day, and well they earn it, working in the barges and at the steadying gear, passing the baskets, and, in fact, doing exactly the same as the men, encouraging the work with songs, or what our sailors would call "shanties." They all wear *kimonos* and a Japanese towel bound round the head, which gives them a somewhat coquettish appearance. Their legs are wrapped up in pieces of cloth—a sort of dark-blue putty— and a native *obji* completes the costume. The coal dust covers them, and they are dingy, dirty daughters of Eve, but their bright eyes gleam and their white teeth flash as they laugh and chatter over the rough work. I remarked to the captain that I should be very sorry to see our women doing such work.

"Well," he replied, "if the work is hard, it is honest, and they might

PETTY OFFICERS ON THE TRANSPORT GOING TO FILL UP VACANCIES
CAUSED BY CASUALTIES ON TOGO'S FLEET.

be doing worse."

This untiring industry is, in my opinion, one of the chief causes of the high standard of virtue that characterises the women of Japan, and several of the missionaries whom I met in Tokyo are of the same opinion.

Our departure was postponed until four o'clock the next afternoon, and, as the officers were all busy, I dined by myself. Nakai, my servant, was wrapt in admiration at the way I used my chopsticks. "*A red sky at night is a sailor's delight,*" in the words of the old song, and this evening the sunset was fiery red, and the moon rose in splendour over the hills. It was the festival of *Bom* (the moon festival), which is signalised by dancing and feasting, and corresponds to our harvest moon.

My new messmates were Captain Yamamuchi (whose father was a retainer of the late Shogun), Surgeon-Lieut. Nakamura, of the Japanese Imperial Navy, and eight other officers, to all of whom I was formally introduced. As the sun set the wind arose, and the barometer falling rapidly told us that a typhoon was imminent. The captain, remarking that he had experienced several typhoons and did not want another, decided to run for shelter in Shisiki harbour. After a run of forty miles we arrived there, and found a Red Cross ship and some other vessels which had also come in for shelter. Fortunately, we were visited by only the tail end of the typhoon.

The live-stock on board aroused my curiosity, and I paid the animals a visit. The fowls, indeed, were allowed to run about, which kept them in better health than when penned up. There were also three lanky pigs, livid-looking and miserable from the repeated washings of the sea water.

The weather cleared about midnight, and at 4 a.m. the watch was called and we weighed anchor at 5 a.m. and proceeded on our journey, the Red Cross ship leading.

On board the wearing of the *kimono* is only allowed before eight o'clock in the morning and after eight o'clock at night. My servant, Nakai, asked me if I would take my bath in the morning or in the evening. In this respect we differ from the Japanese, as they bathe at night, and there is a great deal to be said in favour of the evening bath, for when all the work of the day is done the hot bath is most refreshing and encourages sleep. All the officers don the *kimono* after the bath and come up to the ward-room to finish the evening, but, like most Englishmen, I preferred to have my bath in the morning. Some of the ships are fitted with European baths, but many have only the Japanese bath, which is a large square tank deep enough to sit in up to the chin. They soap themselves before getting in, with a little Japanese oblong towel, decorated with pictures, the bath itself being used merely as a plunge. The same towel is used for drying the body, and it is washed and wrung several times during the process, the bather's servant rubbing down his master's back. Whatever the disadvantages of the Japanese bath, it undoubtedly renders the skin supple and fresh.

Meal hours in the Japanese Navy differ from ours. Breakfast is to be had from 7.30 to 9.30. Dinner at noon (the officers who go on duty have theirs half-an-hour earlier). Supper at 5.30, and from 8 p.m. and throughout the evening tea and cigarettes are served, and sometimes *saké*, which is taken hot. It is a notable fact, however, that *saké* is never served when on active service except on very great occasions, and then very little is drunk. The tea, unlike ours, is green and made with water that is not allowed to boil. It is an acquired taste, but, once acquired, one never cares for any other kind of tea. The same may be said of Japanese food, and it has an additional charm for me in that it cured me of indigestion. Indigestion is unknown in Japan.

A table laid for a meal in Japanese fashion presents, to a European, a somewhat curious appearance, although dinner is frequently laid in European style. Knives and forks are unknown at the Japanese table, and small cases containing a pair of chopsticks (which may be

Nakai, my servant.

DINNER ON THE TRANSPORT

The rice tub.   Nakai,
my servant

HOW I LIVED ON A TRANSPORT

ivory, lacquer, or wood) are laid before one, long-ways, after one is seated, and a small china or lacquer bowl is brought containing bean soup, sometimes made with fish and beans, at others with chicken and beans, and it frequently contains a few slices of vegetables, generally *daikon*, a species of large radish. It has a very disagreeable smell, but by no means a bad flavour. This bean soup is a standing dish throughout Japan. The bean is so nutritious that it sustains a man for a whole day.

The next bowl contains rice, which takes the place of bread, and is eaten with the dried or fresh fish that follows the soup, and with the two fried eggs that are generally served in a small saucer. Pickles and sugared beans usually form a part of the repast. Soup without a spoon is a problem to the European at first, but he soon learns that it is quite correct to raise the bowl to the mouth, using the chopsticks to keep the meat and vegetables from interrupting the flow. On the sideboard there is a wooden tub full of rice, and it is served out into the rice bowls with a large wooden spoon. Holding the rice bowl in one hand, one selects such tit-bits as one fancies from the saucers and eats them with alternate mouthfuls of rice.

The usual drink is *Nippon Cha* (tea), which is poured into a tiny cup rather larger than the *saké* cup, but of the same design. During breakfast one generally eats three or four bowls of rice, and the last bowl is often mixed with tea. This mixture has the consistency of Devonshire cream, and has a most delicate flavour. At the conclusion of the meal the boys pour some tea into the rice bowl, with which one washes the chopsticks before placing them in their little wooden case.

The routine on a Japanese cruiser also differs from that followed in the British Navy, and the following is a time-table of the men's daily task:

7. 0. Turn out.
7.40. Breakfast.
8. 0. Medical inspection.
8.15. Wash decks (if there is no ice or frost) and clean guns and arms.
9.45. Stand easy. Smoke for fifteen minutes.
10. 0. Watch on deck. Fall in. Told off for various duties.
11.30. Sweep and clear up decks. Stand easy when finished.
11.45. Cooks of messes fetch dinner. Noon. Dinner.
1. 15. Fall in. Watch on deck told off for various duties.

2.15. Stand easy.

2.30. Carry on work.

3.30. Sweepers.

3.45. Prepare for supper.

4. 0. Supper.

4.45 Quarters.

5. 0. Stand easy.

5.15. Drill for seamen. Exercises for engineers.

5.40. Sweepers, clear up decks.

Sunset. All lights masked. Prepare to resist torpedo boats; that is, guns ready, with ammunition boxes by each, night sights adjusted, and guns' crews told off, one man to keep watch at each gun, the remainder standing between the guns and keeping a sharp look-out for torpedo attack. (This, of course, is a most important piece of organisation, and one which Admiral Togo impresses on all his captains.)

7. 0. Rounds.

7.30. Pipe down hammocks. Look-outs told off for various parts of the ship.

The remainder of the evening the men drink a little tea, and smoke cigarettes and the *Cheesi* pipe ("little pipe"), which holds just enough for one or two whiffs. Sometimes these small pipes are of silver and sometimes of brass. They squat round the tobacco *bon* (a tub with a piece of rope lighted at one end, something like the ancient linstock); some play cards, others chess, and many of them the old game of go-bang. But most of them spend an hour or so each day studying languages or some detail of their profession. They stand about knitting, if nothing else is to be done. They are never idle, and are always merry and good-tempered. There is never any punishment, for none is ever merited. Each man feels that his particular job is as necessary to Japan as Admiral Togo himself, and they are all inspired by one sentiment— "*Bushido*," the literal meaning of which is "duty and patriotism."

In the large ships two cooks are carried, one foreign and one Japanese. All food undergoes the strictest inspection, not only before, but *after* it is cooked. Every day the quartermaster brings in a dish of the men's food—taken haphazard from the coppers—which the paymaster and the doctor taste and inspect, and the same system is applied to the food destined for the ward-room, so that all on board have only the most wholesome food set before them. This excellent system is also enforced in the army.

As with the food, so with the health of each man, for the doctor makes a searching examination in even the most trifling cases of indisposition. Every man in both navy and army is weighed at least once a year, and if he is above or below the weight which at his age he ought to scale, a medical board is appointed to find out the cause. Everything is governed by science and reason even to the most minute detail.

CHAPTER 5

The Chase and Destruction of the "Novik"

Steaming through the Corean Straits, we left Tsuhima Island far astern, being on our port side, and Masampho, on the Corean coast, showing in the distance in a blue haze. We passed over the spot which has since been made famous by Admiral Togo's great victory, and for two days we steamed to the north.

On the morning of the 15th July we heard guns and observed smoke right ahead, which we afterwards learnt was the fight between Admiral Kamura's fleet (mostly built by the great firm at Elswick) and the Russian Vladivostock cruisers. Sometime afterwards I had an interview with one of the officers of the fleet, who told me the true story of the fight, which I will repeat in his own words.

At 5.3 we spied the Russian cruisers, three in number, steering S.W. three-quarter south. At that time the Russians had no idea that we were near, but at 5.11 they suddenly discovered us and immediately altered their course to the east. We opened fire about 5.20, using the 8-inch bow guns, with some effect. The rangefinder gave the distance as 10,000 metres. The Russians soon replied, and a heavy cannonade from both sides ensued. Forty minutes after the action began the *Rurik* seemed to be in distress. The enemy's ships then separated, the *Gromoboi* and the *Roossia* slowing down, to allow the *Rurik* to come up. But she was too badly injured. The battle still raged fiercely, and two of the Russian ships were on fire for a few minutes. We concentrated our fire on the *Rurik*, which was lagging very far behind, and our cannonade was so effective that the ship was set on fire

Elswick's cruisers.

Boats picking up the Russian sailors.

THE GRAVE OF THE *RURIK*

and the rudder damaged.

Although helpless, she continued firing her guns, and the *Roossia* and the *Gromoboi* returned to assist her. Some signals passed between them which, of course, we could not understand, but it seemed probable that the *Rurik* was asking for assistance. We fully sympathised with the Russians, who had to leave their poor helpless consort to our mercy and steer northward for Vladivostock. Our cruisers followed, and after chasing them some time we noticed that the *Roossia* was on fire, and about fifteen minutes elapsed before it was extinguished. The effect was very striking as the long fiery tongues darted out from the ports. The ship seemed to me like a demon flying on wings of flame. We kept up the pursuit for another twenty minutes, and then returned to where we had left the *Rurik*. This was at 11 in the forenoon. We could see nothing of her save a few boxes and wreckage dotting the sea, over which the smoke still lay like a shroud.

The ill-fated crew were rescued by the ships of our squadron which had not joined in the pursuit, and the prisoners were distributed among the various ships. Eighty were sent aboard us. Their wet clothes were removed, and they donned dry uniforms—the uniform of their enemy. Among our prisoners there were three officers and one petty officer and the chaplain. As they were picked up the officers were put in the stern sheets of our boats, and the sailors mixed with the crew. They seemed very weak, and one of the officers (the navigator) had a slight wound on his left arm. Our doctor immediately proferred his services, which were gratefully received. Our sentry at the gangway saluted, which the Russian officer returned.

The Russian sailors were assisted up the gangway by the Japanese, and it was amusing to see the little Japanese bluejackets assisting the wounded Russian sailors, who seemed giants by comparison. There were about ten injured men, and one of the Russian wounded kissed the Japanese sailor who was assisting him, which made the Jap look a little abashed and silly. We supplied them with everything they asked for, and whiskey and soda was served out to them from the medical stores. We also gave them cigarettes and fans. With the exception of the wounded they fell in on the quarter-deck, and were afterwards sent to the mess-deck, the officers going to the sick-room.

We anchored for the night at Tsuhima Island, and the next morn-

THE NOVIK

ing we started for Sasebo, which we reached at 4 in the afternoon. I tried to speak to the Russian engineer.

"How are you?" I said; "I am very sorry to see you here, for you are brave men, and we all admire your courage."

"Thank you, I am quite well," he replied.

They were very gentle and quiet, but held themselves very proudly.

We did not remain at Tsuhima long, as we received orders to proceed to Manchuria. As we passed Port Hamilton I took some snapshots of the crew while they were eating their dinner. The rations were neatly served in a saucer: two small fish, pickles, and some vegetable. The vegetable was *okra*, and is considered very healthy and strengthening. Rice was served out *ad libitum*. My dinner consisted of the following dishes: Tai fish soup, pork chops and onions, rice, a couple of herrings, and, as a salad, two roots of young ginger washed down with *Nippon Cha*. I hit it off very well with my Japanese friends, with whom I talked through an interpreter, and I paid my footing in the mess in champagne and cigars.

I made a tour of the ship, and found that the men's messes on the lower deck were much the same as on a British man-of-war. The petty officers' quarters were adorned with pictures, in staring colours, and plants which are tended most carefully. Many of the men had insect pets, crickets being the favourites. These insects are kept in tiny cages of bamboo, and maintain a lively scissor-grinding noise. They seem to thrive very well on a piece of vegetable, either pumpkin or watermelon, and the fresh water which the men take in their mouths and blow over them occasionally.

At midnight we anchored in a Corean archipelago called the Myangcoan group. This group of islands lie in latitude 34° 12' N. and longitude 125° 56½' E. That magic messenger, the wireless telegraph, brought us some mysterious news. A Russian gunboat was somewhere in the China Sea, and, bearing in mind our valuable cargo, our captain brought up in one of the Tom Cringlest (if I may use the expression) places, devoid of trees, but protected by sandbanks, rocks and islands. The moon, high in the heavens, reflected her image like a broken patch of phosphorus, and the distant islands showed dimly through the passing mist wreaths.

It was such a night, and such a place, as the buccaneers might have chosen to bury their ill-gotten treasures, and, indeed, who could say what hoards might not be lying in yonder sandlet, for in those seas the pirate still flourishes. At six a.m. the clanking of the cable announced

J. Satō.

PORTRAIT OF A PETTY OFFICER—CHIEF GUNNER'S MATE—WITH HIS
JAPANESE AND ENGLISH SIGNATURE.

that the anchor was being raised, and we proceeded, but only for a short distance, for we ran into a fog which enveloped us and rendered navigation in such a place dangerous. There is no sleep on board after six o'clock with the cocks crowing and the crickets chirruping lustily. As the sun gained power, the fog gradually lifted, until only streaks of mist belted the high lands. Three transports which had been fog-bound like ourselves were now steaming in company with us. By ten o'clock the day was quite clear, and the sun shone brightly. We made good progress, and it was thought that Dalny would be reached in forty-eight hours.

Walking round the ship I noticed that two very useful boats of the *sampan* type were carried. Needle-nosed and flat-bottomed, they are propelled by sculling at the side, and are perfect for landing troops. They are capable of holding a fair number of men, who squat on the bottom out of the way of the scullers, and drawing very little water they can go close to the shore, thus enabling the men to effect a dry landing. This is one of the secrets of the Japanese success in putting a large army on shore, as all the ships carry these boats.

In addition to carrying stores we had on board a number of sailors and petty officers for Admiral Togo's ships. The Japanese petty officer is a well-educated, intelligent man, and can be thoroughly relied upon. Of those I met, most could speak, and all could write, English. Many of them belonged to the ancient Samurai families, and these all carried their family swords, many of which were of great age. They gave a sword display for my benefit. These swords are handled with the greatest reverence, for most of them have been handed down through many generations and are highly prized by their possessors. They are carefully wrapped up in a bag of yellow silk and are periodically taken out and examined critically.

So keen is the edge that it requires the most careful handling. The proper way is to hold the scabbard in one hand and lay the flat of the sword crossways, using the case for a sort of rest. By manipulating it gently in a good light all the markings of the temper of the blade can be seen. It is usually connected to the hilt by a peg of whalebone, which is easily taken out, and the maker's name is written, sometimes in gold, on the haft. In the old days the Japanese youth became a man at the age of fifteen, when he was presented with a sword with great ceremony. The hilt is worked with the finest materials, but these decorations are nothing compared with the beauty of the blade. The bluish steel has a silken texture, and it has an edge that can sever a piece of

立神丸甲板上戲写

中島小市

K. nakashima
on deck tategami maru

ENGINE-ROOM ARTIFICER, ALSO CHIEF PETTY OFFICER, TAKING IT
EASY. NOTE THE ZORI (SANDALS).

gauze and a curve that produces an automatic draw in the cut, which make it the most formidable cold-steel weapon even of the present day.

It appeared that we were bound for Togo's "certain place," and I welcomed the news in the hope that it meant that we should see some fighting. It seemed but the day before that, on the old *Manchu Maru*, I visited the Blonde Islands. There was Togo's fleet still on guard, and, indeed, it was all so clearly photographed in my memory that I had not forgotten a detail of the scene, and it will always remain one of the most vivid impressions of the many that I have gathered in my wandering life. We entered the anchorage on this occasion by a passage from the south, which is protected by booms and mines.

As soon as the anchor was down the purser and the doctor went to the harbour master's ship *Taichu Maru* to report arrival and to receive instructions. This is an important piece of organization in the Japanese Navy. All ships on the way to the front report themselves at various signal stations on the journey, and when they pass near a base they call in for further orders. The front is, it is true, approached more slowly, but the value of the system is apparent, for the commander-in-chief and Admiralty are in touch with the ships throughout their journey. And it also prevents strange steamers from entering the military area.

The day after our arrival Port Arthur was attacked from the sea and the land by heavy guns, and we could plainly hear the dull booming of the cannonade.

The *Idzumi*, a cruiser originally built for the Chilean Government by the Elswick company and bought by the Japanese, came in and, anchoring, at once lowered all her boats, and the crew set to work to clean the bottom. This is another important piece of organisation, the Japanese never allowing their ships to become foul.

Most of the petty officers whom we carried had now gone to the harbour-master's ship, to be drafted to their various stations, and the purser returned with the gratifying information that we were to start for Dalny on the following day at noon.

A transport carrying mails came into the roadstead, and passed through the fleet. As she approached a ship for which she had mail bags, four notes were blown on a bugle, and the ship at once sent a boat to her to fetch the letters. The next morning, I arose at four o' clock and saw the sun rise over the huge rock I have spoken of. In the morning light it resembled one of those gigantic pre-historic lizards, and it seemed to be gazing out over the sea to Port Arthur. The harbour had cleared somewhat during the night, for the hospital ship and two or three transports had gone away. The wind had chopped round and was blowing hard from the south, and the captain told me that we should have some "not good" weather.

Admiral Togo's choice of a base was a good thing for the fishermen, for, to ensure a fresh supply of fish for his ships, hundreds of *junks* were regularly employed. These fishermen are half pirates, and up to the time of Togo's arrival had given a great deal of trouble. The Chinese sent some Chusan soldiers, who are themselves little better than bandits, to keep order, and these soldiers made a working arrangement with the piratical fishermen with the result that, until Togo appeared on the scene, the inhabitants of the villages had a very bad time.

On our voyage to Dalny a tragic event happened. When we got outside the roadstead we found there was a heavy sea from the west, which set our ship rolling heavily. The crew were employed in throwing some old shakes overboard, which had served temporarily as cattle-boxes, and the sea kept washing over the waist of the ship, wetting the men to the skin. They were laughing and chaffing each other as the waves broke over them, when suddenly the ice chest with its contents, weighing three or four tons, slipped from its place and glided towards the main mast, and the boatswain was pinned by the leg between this and the iron bits. The limb was crushed to a shapeless mass, and the sailors carried the poor fellow to the ward room, laying him on the floor.

The doctor looked very grave, but proceeded to bind up the fractured leg, although the case was hopeless. The injured man lay with his head supported by two comrades, another was fanning him, a fourth held a glass of water, and on either side four of his ship-mates knelt to secure him from being knocked about by the rolling of the ship. Although the atmosphere was stifling, he kept complaining of feeling cold, and more blankets were heaped upon him. He murmured occasionally, and I wondered if his thoughts had flown back to far away Japan and his little wife and child, or whether his last act of duty still filled his mind. Who could tell? Once only he spoke intelligibly, words which brought despair to the hearts of the watchers.

"It's so cold."

Though heaped with blankets the sailors added more to satisfy their messmate. The doctors had long since given up hope. The heart beat was tested for the last time. His feet and hands were cold, though the brain still lived. It was an easy death, this sinking quietly into Eternity. A bright ray of light shot through the dark pall of cloud as the gallant boatswain's spirit fled. Who dare say that the Great God of all mankind shall not find a place for that Pagan soul.

The body was laid out next to my sleeping cabin, and a small altar was erected with two lighted candles, between which a snow-white cloth bearing rice-cake was placed. Before the altar incense was burning, and at nightfall the body was placed in a coffin with the head towards the altar. The dead sailor's messmates watched by the bier all night, keeping the incense burning, and the ship was filled with the fragrant odour.

I found it difficult to sleep that night, for the deadlights being closed no air could enter, and the pungent scent of the incense was almost overpowering. Sleep came at last in spite of the choking that oppressed me, but it was broken by troubled dreams of the poor boatswain. I was awakened by a big rat scampering across my chest, and I found the cabin swathed in a mist of incense. In the morning the burial took place, the remains being hoisted into a *sampan*, and with his messmates and the priest the boatswain made his last voyage. Some small ceremony took place on shore, the dead man's shipmates passing by his body, one by one, giving a last salute. They left him in his shell on a cliff by a lonely bay, awaiting, within sound of the murmuring ocean, the torch of the cremator. One of the officers remarked to me that the boatswain had died as every man ought to hope to die—"At his duty."

Kwangtung Shan bore due west seven miles. This together with the smaller island of San-Sham and the shoals, covered with mine fields, protected the entrance to Talien-wan Bay. Kwangtung Shan, if fortified with heavy guns, would secure both Port Arthur and Dalny. We heard that the fight at Port Arthur the day before had been very fierce, but that the Japanese had captured two important positions. About three o'clock we passed the picquet boat and exchanged signals with the Red Cross ship *Kote Maru*, which was bound for a secret destination. The water shoaled rapidly as we neared the signal hill (Tai-o-sho).

From this point the land sweeps down in successive slopes, breaking off in low cliffs, and the coast here and there is indented with sandy coves. The country is roughly farmed by the Chinese, and the little bay shelters numerous trading *junks*. As we turned into the bay we obtained a fine view of the sweeping curve of the shore, which is dominated by the lofty mountain Dai-o-noshan, which, being interpreted, means "large monk" or "bishop." This mountain is 2,200 feet high, but it looks considerably higher on account of its isolated position. Bold, stony ridges succeed one another up to the serrated summit, which is somewhat Alpine in appearance.

In the little harbour of Odincove (Taiko-ko) a guardship is stationed, whose crew undertakes the arduous duties of Signal Hill. The bay sweeps round to Dalny, which lies almost immediately opposite. The navigable channel is well marked, but it was, of course, mined in places, and could only be run with special charts and bearings. The natural defences of the place were very strong, and had been still further strengthened by the Chinese, who had built some forts. These alone would prove formidable to approaching ships, but with the addition of mines and booms the place was practically impregnable. We anchored about three miles from the town, where lay a number of ships of the Third Division, under Admiral Hosoya.

The steam launch from the admiral's ship came alongside, and when she returned I jumped in to go to the flagship and present my letters of introduction to the admiral. This, I am afraid, was a breach of naval etiquette, for the admiral sent his secretary to tell me that I must be presented officially by the Port admiral. I returned to my ship and the captain informed me that I must go ashore to the harbour master's office with the doctor (who is also a lieutenant). The purser, and several other Japanese gentlemen who were officially connected with the army, went at the same time.

It was dark when we landed, and we had to scramble over some rough-hewn stones, which formed part of the walls of the dockyard. Threading our way through we at last reached the harbour master's office. I was introduced to Admiral Muira, who was Port admiral, and he asked if I had any letter for him. Having none I showed him my credentials from Tokyo, and explained the object of my visit. He is a young, energetic and good-looking man, and held the position of Port admiral at Port Arthur during the short Japanese occupation in 1894. I heard that it was the intention of the government to reinstate him in his old position at the fall of the place. After a very pleasant chat we returned to the pier with an orderly whom the admiral had sent to guide us. On arriving at the pier we had to send the orderly for our *sampan*, and waited an hour before it appeared. We all bundled in and at last returned to the ship.

I was anxious to present my letter to Admiral Hosoya, but the following morning the harbour master signalled:

All passengers to remain on board."

This, of course, was disappointing, but I made the best of a bad job by studying Dalny and its surroundings through my field glasses. Away to the north-west stood the long flat mountain Nan-San, where the Japanese soldiers won their spurs, but the fair cultivated plateau looked peaceful enough in the bright sunshine of this Manchurian morning. The harbour was full of ships—gunboats, cruisers, auxiliary cruisers, transports, and hospital ships, and yet there was room for many more. The town of Dalny may be divided into two parts. The commercial district is easily distinguishable from the harbour by the tall chimneys and the smoke and dust which hang over it night and day, while the residential part looks almost like an ordinary London suburb with its long rows of houses, broken, here and there, by a church or some other public building.

The Chinese quarter lies at the back and is not visible from the harbour. The public park stretches away towards the mountains, and in its neighbourhood are several large detached houses. Red brick is used in the construction of the houses, and in many cases it is decorated with white *stucco*. A railway runs past the back of the town to the pier and harbour, which at present are under military authority. The breakwater, which is a mile in length, shelters this part of the harbour from the north-west storms, and I noticed that the sentry boxes on the breakwater were painted with the regulation black and white oblique bars of official Russia. The mountains make a picturesque background to the town. The most prominent is called Little Fugi, on account of its resemblance on certain bearings to the huge mountain of that name in Japan.

The next day the bombardment of Port Arthur began again, three days' rest having been taken to refresh the troops after their last effort. The Japanese had been steadily closing in upon the city, and there seemed little doubt that ere long they would capture the town and thus achieve the greatest feat of arms of modern times. The sullen boom of the guns was heard throughout the day.

A torpedo-boat came alongside and took in twenty-five tons of water in less than an hour, and we also coaled some of the small craft. Coaling and watering their ships is a simple matter in the Japanese Navy, and differs slightly from our method. When they come alongside, the hatches are opened, the coal is passed down in bags and the water is taken in at the same time.

THE *AKAGI* COMING ALONGSIDE.

TORPEDO DESTROYER. NOTE THE *MANTELETTES* FOR
PROTECTING THE BRIDGE FROM SHELL SPLINTERS.

Reinforcements of soldiers arrived daily, and at once went off to the front, which showed us that the capturing of Port Arthur was proving no easy task. Raw troops stepped ashore at Dalny and in less than five hours were becoming veterans in the trenches of Port Arthur.

A gunboat came alongside for coal and water. She had been laying mines off Port Arthur and showed signs of pretty hard service. The trim, smart look of the man-of-war was hidden beneath a covering of old rope hanging in coils around the vital parts of the ship. The bridge especially was covered by this curious "armour," converting it into a protected conning-tower. These rope fenders are technically known as *mantelettes*, and they are very effective in stopping shell splinters.

I had received no word from Admiral Togo in reply to my letter, and I found the waiting for instructions monotonous. To pass the time I amused myself by trying to catch some big fish that were constantly cruising around the ship. It was tantalising sport, for although the fish frequently smelt and mouthed the bait, they never once even nibbled.

The *Akagi* was lying in the harbour during our stay at Dalny. She is the gunboat which, in the Chinese war, had a shell burst in the chart house, killing Captain Sakamoto. She was undergoing the repair of some trifling damage she had received in an action with a Russian gunboat. The duel was fought at long range for two hours, when the *Akagi* plumped a shell well into the Russian, who at once steamed off. There is another very interesting vessel lying in the harbour, a paddle-wheel saloon boat, which would make an excellent admiral's yacht. She was at Dalny when the Japanese captured the place, for the Russians, fondly imagining the occupation of Dalny was only temporary, sunk her in the harbour after heavily coating her with paint inside and out.

I was fortunate in being allowed to visit the dockyards at Dalny. The machine sheds were in a state of dilapidation, as they had been burnt by the Russians, but the electric light works had not been touched. Work was proceeding briskly everywhere. Gangs of *coolies* were clearing away debris ready for new buildings, permanent and temporary, to be erected, and in the dry dock three torpedo-boats were undergoing repairs. While I was ashore I noticed a crowd of Chinamen talking together excitedly, and the cause of their excitement was revealed to me when a firing party of bluejackets marched by with a Chinaman in custody. He had been tampering with the water supply, and in a little while I heard the rattle of a volley, and soon afterwards met the firing party returning.

When I returned on board, I found that news from the front had been received. The great battle of Liaoyang had been fought, and it was rumoured that Kuropatkin had been severely wounded, and only 12,000 of the Russian host had escaped death or capture. The news seemed too good to be true, and we anxiously awaited the official report. The battle of Liaoyang was the critical phase of the campaign, for had Kuropatkin defeated the Japanese army Port Arthur might conceivably have been relieved, although even in such an eventuality Kuropatkin would have been unable to have taken the aggressive until he had been heavily reinforced.

Captain Mimura of the destroyer *Ikadzuchi* (Thunder) came on board and dined with me on the evening of my visit to the dockyards. He had just come in from the blockade, and he told me the Russians would certainly come out and fight again. The Japanese had laid a number of contact mines outside the Russian mine fields, and it was a case of mine and counter mine. These contact mines were floated about six feet below the surface, and could also be exploded by electric wires connected with the torpedo boats. This alternative was to prevent the possibility of the Russians sending small steamers and clearing them away. Two or three days before, Captain Mimura told me, the *Sevastopol* had come out from Port Arthur and shelled the army positions, but Togo attacked her and soon drove her in again. She touched a mine on her way back, which blew a hole in her port side and nearly sunk her.

While I was talking to Captain Mimura the *Chitose* cruiser entered the harbour and signalled that the *Novik*, a Russian ship that had escaped from Shanghai, had been sunk off Saghalien. The story of the last voyage of the *Novik* was told to me afterwards by one of the officers of the ship that sank her:

In the afternoon of the 10th August, after the big battle off Port Arthur, the *Czarevitch* ran to Kaiochaio Bay, seeking to take advantage of German neutrality, and the *Novik* took shelter at Shanghai. Having chased the destroyers to Cheefoo, the *Chitose* received orders from Admiral Togo on the 11th to chase, and, if possible, capture the *Novik*. Thinking the Russian gunboat was bound for Vladivostock, and knowing that in such case she would have to go by the Pacific route, the *Chitose* ran through the Corean Strait to head her off. A wireless message was received from Kagoshima informing them that the *Novik* had passed that place steering north. Receiving no further message when they reached Tsugalu Strait, they went on to Hakodate. There they were joined by the third-class cruiser *Tsuma*, and both coaled. They received another wireless message from Admiral Togo to proceed to Soya Kaikyo, and after steaming some distance a second wire came from the admiral: '*Novik* has passed Etologh Island.' After receiving this message, they felt confident of getting her.

Cruising about the strait, on the afternoon of the 21st, expecting to meet her, they received at five o'clock another wireless message: '*Novik* coaling at Colsacot Bay.' This bay is in Saghalien Island, and, hearing firing, they went off at full speed, and found the *Tsuma* and the *Novik* engaged. Before they came up night fell and the fighting ceased. Both vessels received some damage, but the *Tsuma*, being a small ship, was not so much damaged as the *Novik*. It appeared that the *Novik* had tried to get out of the bay, but the *Tsuma* had headed her back, cruising off the mouth of the bay and blockading her, and, at the same time, making good some defects.

The *Chitose* ran into the bay. The *Novik* was there, but the night was so dark they could see nothing of her. They cruised to and fro all through the night. At dawn she was sighted and reported to be on shore, and the Japanese ships ran in to within three thousand metres of her and opened fire. It was like shooting at a target, and the shots soon took effect, for the Russian seemed to settle by the bow, and by the volumes of smoke that came from her it was evident that she was on fire. The crew got away in the boats, and, seeing that the *Novik* was done for, at seven o'clock the Japanese steamed off to Sasebo. The *Chitose* remained at Sasebo and the *Tsuma* went on to Yokosuka, where she was docked.

On a cruiser off Port Arthur during the blockade.

Inspecting the ammunition on a cruiser

CHAPTER 6.

Togo Appoints Me to the "Tainan Maru"

On September 1st Paymaster Aihara came on board and informed me that Admiral Togo had appointed me to his ship the *Tainan Maru*, and that he had come to fetch me. It did not take me long to pack up, and, taking leave of the captain and my messmates, I stepped into the steam launch with Aihara, and proceeded to take up my new appointment. I was given the rank of ward-room officer, but my duties were light. I had my station at fire-quarters and boats, and fell in by the chief engineer at divisions. As I stepped on board the sentry saluted and the officer of the watch came forward to receive me. I was an object of some interest to the sailors, who were grouped forward and gave me a smiling greeting.

The officer of the watch introduced me to Captain Takahashi, the commander, who, like all the Japanese I have met, is a thorough gentleman. After a few remarks, he preceded me to the ward-room, where I was heartily welcomed by my messmates. Tea and cigarettes were served, and I soon began to feel at home in my new surroundings. The *Tainan Maru* was an auxiliary cruiser, and the ward-room was the ordinary roomy saloon, well-lighted and airy. Two long tables stood on either side, capable of accommodating about forty people. Our ward-room complement, however, was only twenty-five, so that we were by no means crowded.

In the centre of the room, beneath the dome, a Japanese garden was arranged on a square of oilcloth. There were dwarf trees, shrubs, a rice plant, and some wild bushes and plants taken from the mountains of Nansan. There was also a small pond containing a Chinese eel, who kept himself very much to himself by burrowing under the pebbles at the bottom of the little pond, and sometimes we had to stir him up with a piece of coal to see if he was alive. A lively young green cricket chirruped merrily as he browsed on the tender shoots of a tiny fir-tree, and a pair of quails nestled among the picturesque pots, darting out at intervals to pick up stray grains of rice or crumbs.

Although I had already dined my kind hosts insisted that I must be hungry, and a good meal of fruit and fish was placed before me with bread, the first I had tasted for ten days. I had become so accustomed to chopsticks that the knife and fork which I used felt heavy and awkward. After dinner the captain and senior officers invited me on to the bridge, where we sat enjoying the glorious, golden sunset through which we could see the beams of Port Arthur's searchlights shining faintly.

Every day the captain gave me such items of news as he could, consistent with his duty. On that first evening he told me that the Japanese soldiers were hard at work entrenching and digging parallels nearer and nearer to Port Arthur, keeping the Russians ever on the alert. The lurid flash of the heavy guns was reflected momentarily on the clouds as we sat on the bridge, and some seconds after each flash the dull report fell on our ears. I also heard that the mine ship which had been coaling alongside my late ship had been blown up whilst "creeping" for mines. One of the men was frightfully mangled and several were drowned. Navigating these seas is a dangerous and nerve-shattering task, for at any moment the ship may touch a mine and go down with all hands.

A torpedo-boat came in with a *junk* in tow bearing one hundred horses, pigs, and poultry, destined for Port Arthur. It was a valuable prize, and one likely to prove a useful addition to the transport service of our army. There was something humorous in the attitude and looks of the captain and crew of the captured *junk*. The tow-rope attached to the *junk* was so short that the muzzle of the 4.6 almost rubbed the nose of the Chinese skipper as he steered. Probably the old craft never before went at such a pace.

Every man Jack of the crew felt that he was under sentence of death, and looked as he felt—a sadder-looking set of men I never saw. The captain stood bolt upright at the tiller, and the grinning muzzle of the gun had a strange fascination for him. He had, probably, never relaxed a muscle of his body for many hours. Scared to death, his lips glued together with terror, he returned no answer to the chaffing Japs. The blazing sun scorched his eyes, which did not blink, and his face

226

JAPANESE TORPEDO DESTROYER WITH CAPTURED *JUNK*, PORT ARTHUR BAY.

was blanched to an ashy grey.

I turned in at 10 p.m. My cabin was lofty and roomy, but the ventilation not very good, the dead-lights being tightly closed to prevent any light from showing outside. The orders from Admiral Togo insisted upon this rule being strictly observed. I fell asleep with the boom of the heavy guns sounding in my ears.

I was awakened in the morning by Arai, my new boy, opening my scuttles. He greeted me with a pleasant "*ohayo*" ("good morning"). I turned out and went on deck to inspect the ship, and some description of a Japanese auxiliary cruiser may be of interest to my readers. On the forecastle and aft we mounted two 4.7 guns (Elswick) on turn-tables. In the well between the forecastle and saloon-decks were a number of coils of wire hawser for the laying of mines, those terrible engines of destruction which have formed one of the chief features of the present war.

On account of the hot weather the awning and screens had been rigged up to shade this part of the deck, where the men sleep and take their baths. A windsail directed what little air was stirring down the forehatch to the quarters of the crew. On the boat-deck were the usual number of life-boats, and on the shelter-deck below a 12-pound 2.7 gun projected over each quarter. Two 3-pounders also were mounted on the shelter-deck, and a number of contact mines completed the armament. Over the after hatchway were the booms on which four boats of the large *sampan* type were stowed. Beneath these boats the sailors do their washing, and the space was taken up with clothes-lines from which the little Japanese towels were fluttering. The watch below were smoking their tiny pipes, laughing and chatting merrily, and several of them, their curiosity aroused, got up to look at me.

The second-class cabin space was given up to the warrant and petty officers. Two long tables ran down the centre of the saloon; the men's chests were arranged in a row close to the bulk-head, and at one end of the cabin was a small set of lockers, one for each member of the mess. Two 60,000 candle-power searchlights were fitted to the ship, one on the shelter-deck, and the other abaft the funnel, with both of which we practised every night. The bridge was much the same as in any other steamer, with the exception that it was fitted with a range-finder. The lower deck, where in ordinary circumstances the third-class passengers would be accommodated, was used by the crew. Swing shelves held the mess traps (an iron plate and cup, knife, fork and spoon), and ditty boxes wherein Jack keeps his photographs and little treasures.

Soon after my appointment to this ship the staff engineer was ordered to Sasebo, and I was much struck by the "send off" we gave him. The ship's company was drawn up to wish him a pleasant and prosperous voyage, and, in reply, he made a neat speech to the men, complimenting them on the way in which they had performed their duties when under his orders, and expressing the hope that they would continue to do so under his successor. He then shook hands with each officer in turn and left amid hearty *"Banzais"* and waving of handkerchiefs and caps. This ceremony, I was told, was always observed when an officer left his ship, and it is a very good custom, for it tends to keep officers and men in sympathetic touch.

At breakfast the next morning the conversation was of mines, their advantages and dangers. Several of the officers were strongly of the opinion that mines should be carried in parts and put together when required. Such a system would involve additional drill to enable the parts to be riveted together and the mine laid in the shortest possible time, but the proposal undoubtedly is worth consideration. It occurred to me at the time that this destructive weapon might be used with advantage against submarine attack, and I have no doubt that as the submarine becomes more general in the world's navies the mine will be the weapon that will be used against it with most success.

The cook made me a special dish for breakfast, which pleased me so much that I felt I should like to give him some tangible evidence of my satisfaction. I proposed to give him a glass of *sake*, but I was told it was quite contrary to regulations. No one is allowed to give drinks without permission, and this permission is as difficult to obtain as it is for a captain to get his promotion.

The sound of the bombardment continued day after day. The Russians generally opened fire after lunch, continuing firing until 4 p.m., when there was usually a lull until 9 p.m., when the booming began again and continued until after midnight. This methodical action of the Russian gunners amused the Japanese greatly.

The harbour work was carried on with great regularity. Steam tugs, towing strings of *junks* laden with *coolies*, crossed over to Kyu-ju-ton, the small town ten miles off, where store sheds, roads, and a landing-place are being constructed for a new military base. Sometimes a transport or hospital ship passed on her way to Japan, filled with sick and wounded soldiers.

One evening after dark the captain invited me to go fishing from

MYSELF SKETCHING ON THE DECK OF THE MOTHER SHIP.

TORPEDO FLOTILLA ALONGSIDE "MOTHER" IN A CERTAIN HARBOUR

the boats astern. Our outfit was simple, consisting merely of a fairly large hook on a short line and some small fish for bait. These small fry swarmed round the ship in their efforts to evade the ceaseless attacks of the swordfish, and they were easily caught for bait with a dip-net. We had very fair sport, catching about twenty fish, many of them with their tails bitten off by their ravenous brothers. They are not nice to eat, although the Chinese are very fond of them. But, as one of my Japanese friends said, the Chinaman is half pig and half monkey, and will eat anything.

We sent ashore a landing party of bluejackets one day, and I noticed that their rig differed slightly from that of the British Navy. The blanket is carried over the left shoulder, and, instead of in a haversack, the rations are carried in a sort of long bag, worn over the right shoulder, bandolierwise. This is of blue canvas, and is technically known as the *Bentu fukuro* (lunch cloth). The water-bottle is worn in the British manner, and so are the belt and cartridge cases. They left in very high spirits, for they were going to meet the enemy, but I could not help wondering how many of them would return.

When next I went ashore I was determined to see Dalny thoroughly. After landing, we walked through the dockyard and across the railway until we reached the Chinese town, in which most of the streets were very narrow and crammed with people. The streets of Chinese towns are always narrow and always crowded. In the main street, in front of the low shops, were long rows of booths made of bamboo and canvas. Vegetables, fruit and provisions, most of them of revolting appearance, were for sale at these booths, and the proprietors appeared to be doing a flourishing trade. I had intended to visit the Chinese theatre, but it looked so dirty that I changed my mind and set off for a ramble in the suburbs. The road was crowded with two-wheel carts, each drawn by a horse or mule, and with a donkey or cow tied to the side of the cart. There were long strings of them carrying stores to the front.

The Russians laid out good roads and splendid boulevards in Dalny. The *boulevard* which runs due west is planted with trees, and ends in a fine *jardins des plantes*, the greater part of which is enclosed by a low wall. We entered through the gap where the gate had stood. The turnstiles and offices were in ruins, the broad pathway grass-grown, and the ornamental shrubs and trees choked with weeds. It was now the fruit season, and on many of the trees the pears still hung, notwithstanding the Chinese boys. The first building we came to was the bear den, with two fine animals from the Himalayas. A magnificent specimen of the Bengal tiger, fat and sleek, tenanted another den, and this was the animal which, it was said, was given a Japanese woman to eat for a treat. But this, of course, is a yarn.

The gardens are delightful. A stream runs through which in the rainy weather becomes a raging torrent, but its waters are always clear, and are fed by the springs in the mountains behind the town. Flowers blossom everywhere—zinias, marigolds, and the everlasting flowers grow to perfection, and among other plants I discovered was the Cape gooseberry. Trees of almost every variety seem to flourish in the gardens. We called on the curator, a most intelligent gentleman, who was comfortably installed in the house of his predecessor, who was, of course, a Russian. The glass of the doors and windows is coloured red and green, for the purpose, I believe, of preventing snow blindness. I had a long talk with the curator, and he invited me to see the animals fed.

"Although," he said, "after your beautiful zoo this is not worth speaking of."

We went with him and saw a live woodcock thrown to the tiger, and the great beast caught it like a tame cat catches a sparrow. Our host showed us also the remains of the aviaries and other houses.

"We shall soon have all this repaired and tenanted," he explained, "and if you return next year the gardens will be in perfect order."

He hopes eventually to be able to compare his gardens favourably with any similar gardens in the world. We returned through the town, where the houses again reminded me of those of the London suburbs—the familiar semi-detached villas standing each in a small garden. The houses were occupied by the troops, or turned into storehouses, and the gardens served very well for picketing horses. The town hall and government offices overlook the square, which has a large garden in the centre, beautifully laid out with flowering plants, but of course the weeds had choked everything, and the place had become a wilderness. Nevertheless, we succeeded in gathering a lovely posy, and then returned through the dockyard.

At the pier we saw some diving boats—big *sampans* decked with moveable planks, beneath which the various stores are placed. The divers live on the boats, sleeping and eating on board, the mat awnings protecting them from the weather. They were employed in bringing up the mines, and there were about fifty boats engaged in the work.

"They handle these mines like new-born babes," Captain Taka-

CLEANING THE BOTTOMS OF THE BATTLESHIPS AT THE RENDEZVOUS, PORT ARTHUR BAY.

hashi told me, and I answered that I was not surprised.

When we got back on board we were treated to a bit of old Japan, for a number of the men had donned the ancient, picturesque costume and were giving a display of fencing. The weapons used were made of bamboo, the length of the two-handed sword, and with their armour of bamboo, cloth and silk, the men presented a striking contrast to the bluejackets who stood around them, watching the fencing with critical eyes.

The following day the crew was busily cleaning and painting the ship's bottom. This operation is constantly performed in the Japanese Navy, so that the ship may always be in a condition to steam her fastest. It was very inconvenient for everyone on board, for the ship was heeled over to an angle of fifteen degrees. To heel over the ship, the water ballast was pumped out from one side of the ship, the other remaining full, and to increase the angle the boats were lowered to the surface of the water and the big iron lifeboat was suspended from the derrick. The boats were then all filled with water, which, of course, careened the ship to the required angle.

Our captain treated his men like children, and they all seemed to look up to him as to a father. When off duty the officers fraternise with the men almost as if they were equals, and I believe there is no instance on record of a man taking advantage of this affability on the part of his superiors.

News reached us that two of the Russian searchlights at Port Arthur had been destroyed by the Japanese guns. The first was hit by a lucky shot, but in the second case the guns were carefully laid in the daytime, and when the first flash came from the searchlight a 100lb. shell smashed the whole apparatus to pieces. This was a serious loss for the Russians, as they had only a few small searchlights left.

Everything was got ready aboard the fleet for an attack on Vladivostock as soon as Port Arthur should fall.

I breakfasted one morning on the root of a tiger-lily. Its flavour was something between a baked apple and roast chestnuts, and it was of the consistency of mashed potatoes.

I found the mosquitoes very troublesome, so I got the purser to serve me out a green mosquito canopy, such as the sailors use to cover their hammocks.

An interesting chat which I had with one of the officers revealed to me some of the causes of the destructive effect of Japanese gunnery. The Japanese shell charged with Shemoshi powder damages armour

A MINE EXPLODING
IN PORT ARTHUR BAY
SEPPINGS. WRIGHT
04

ITSHIKUSHIMA, ADMIRAL YAMADA'S SHIP.   MINE SWEEPER.

far more than the projectiles used by the Russians. The Japanese, too, are better marksmen than the Russians, and the reason is that they always practise at long range—from 10,000 to 12,000 yards. At this range they make excellent practise, large rocks which they make their target being blown to pieces. They generally open fire on the Russian ships at 10,000 yards, and it is noteworthy that their practise is never at a shorter range.

The Japanese sailors wash the decks differently from any other sailors. They squat behind each other in long lines, and the front rows scrub and those behind mop. They hop along like frogs, and the washing of decks is a decidedly interesting sight.

A contact mine blew up in the harbour one day, in the midst of all the shipping, and the report continued to reverberate around the harbour, fragments hurtling and screaming through the air like shells, but nobody seemed to mind. A few pieces came aboard us. There is a sporting uncertainty about navigating mine-sown waters.

One of my strangest experiences aboard the ship was when I was shaved by the ship's barber. The Japanese barber is as thorough as the rest of his countrymen. He had a wonderful assortment of tools, which included a circular brush and a case of razor blades, the smallest of which were more like flattened bodkins. I asked him to explain the use of these small blades, and he told me they were for shaving *the inside of the nose*, and at once proceeded to give me a demonstration. He first took a piece of wet lint with a tiny pair of tweezers, and dexterously manipulated it until the hair inside was sufficiently softened. He then used one of the small razors with marvellous delicacy and precision, and removed all the hairs without a scratch. It was a ticklish operation, and I did not find it a very pleasant one, for it made my eyes water for some time afterwards.

CHAPTER 7

Togo Sends for Me

I had begun to tire of the life at Dalny and long for something more exciting when I was suddenly ordered to join the *Nikko-Maru*, another torpedo ship, lying in a secret harbour almost within gunshot of Port Arthur. This was welcome news, for it seemed that I was about to witness all the torpedo and mining operations. I was to travel to my new ship by torpedo boat No. 67, which was to report first to Admiral Togo and then go on to the secret harbour. Before leaving I called on Admiral Hosoya in the flag-ship and also boarded the *Kobe-Maru,* the hospital-ship, to see a doctor whom I knew. He told me that Togi and Murati, two artist friends of mine, had been enquiring after me, and hoped to meet me on my return.

I dined on the *Kobe-Maru* and afterwards was shown round. Everything was beautifully neat and clean, the operating rooms being fitted with appliances for keeping a regular temperature under any atmospheric conditions. The cabins had large square windows, instead of the usual round scuttle, and the promenade deck was given up to the convalescents. Every patient wore the same style of dress—a white *kimono* and white cap—which was very cool and comfortable. While I was on board two patients arrived from the front, and they were hoisted on board in a case of bamboo splints. This contrivance is an excellent invention, as the spring of the wood saves the patient from being jolted. At one time the *Kobe-Maru* ran between Glasgow and America.

I returned on board the *Tainau-Maru*. Searchlights were at work, and I passed my last evening sitting on deck talking to the captain and paymaster and enjoying the lovely moonlight. Torpedo boat No. 67, commanded by Lieutenant Taira, came alongside for me at 8.0 the following morning, and I stepped aboard with Arai, my boy, whom

COMING ALONGSIDE THE MIKASSA AT THE RENDEZVOUS OFF PORT ARTHUR.

LAYING A QUICK-FIRER. THE OBJECT IS A RUSSIAN DESTROYER THAT KEPT HOVERING ROUND.

WE CAPTURE A *JUNK* FULL OF DONKEYS.

MAKING FAST THE PRIZE.

the captain had kindly allowed me to take with me. No. 67 bore the marks of war. There were a number of dents in her sides, and a patched hole through the companion, the work of a Russian shell which wounded a man who was going downstairs at the time. Another circular patch on the deck marked the spot where a 4.7 shell entered, exploding among the machinery but, strange to say, doing little damage beyond cutting the steam pipe in half. All this happened during the third blocking operation of Port Arthur. The little vessel looked pretty, though weather-worn, and she had been all through the blockade without a breakdown. She was built entirely by the Japanese.

Amongst the assorted cargo the deck was lumbered with mails, a number of bags of fresh bread for Togo's ships, and my portmanteau. We sped along at the rate of seventeen knots, although our course was rather erratic owing to the presence of vagrant mines, which we sunk by rifle fire. There were many *junks* out, and the long sea line was broken by the battleships belonging to the Fourth Squadron, whose head-quarters lay at the harbour for which I was bound. That harbour was one of Togo's quiet little places for repairing, refreshing, and general refitting. In two hours we hoped to reach the fleet.

There was another passenger on board besides myself—Commander Yoshitaro-Mori, a headquarter-staff man on special duty. His station was at Chefoo, and he told me that a small steamer plied between Dalny and Chefoo to bring *coolies* over to work on the railways as transport, camp cleaners and so forth. He did not tell me his particular work there and I did not enquire, as I knew that the Admiralty's orders were that officers must not mention their business or even refer to their duties when travelling together. He had been up to see General Nogi, a friend of his, and was very keen on seeing the final assault on Port Arthur. He told me his friend the general was going to send him a telegram when the time was ripe.

Togo's squadron was farther south than its usual beat, which lay between a certain island and a point opposite Wei-hai-wei. At about one o'clock we came up with the fleet, which looked grim and powerful in its war paint. The ships were lying with their heads towards Port Arthur in double column, and provision steamers and colliers were alongside some of them. A collier was lying by Togo's ship, and I noticed the bridges and tops were protected by rope *mantelettes* and hammocks. The moment we came alongside Admiral Togo sent for me. He was waiting for me in his cabin, and in his left hand he held a fan which he used throughout the interview. He asked me if I had

Bunch of artificial flowers.

Shell that nearly killed the Admiral.

Dwarf trees presented to Togo by Count Okuma.

The Admiral's chair.

SMOKE AND CHAT WITH TOGO IN HIS CABIN ON THE *MIKASSA*, OFF PORT ARTHUR

lunched, to which I replied in the affirmative, whereupon tea and cigarettes were ordered.

His cabin was furnished plainly. On the mantelpiece there stood a basket of artificial flowers made of feathers, a present from some of his admirers at Kobe, and in the fireplace, over which there was a curtain, stood two little dwarf trees in the familiar china dishes; one was a cedar 500 years old, the other a fir, probably the same age. These were presented to the admiral by Count Okura. There were two sofas, one on the starboard and one on the port side, and on the left-hand sofa lay two drawings of the last battle off Port Arthur.

"They were done by my steward," the admiral said, "and they are a very good representation of what occurred."

One showed the position of the ships and the blowing up of the *Petropaulski*, but the second drawing was more a plan of the battle. Over this sofa was an oil painting of the training squadron in a typhoon on its voyage to Australia, when Admiral Togo was in command. A few photographs adorned the walls and yellow curtains shaded the scuttles. On the right-hand sofa there was a blue pillow and a rug; this was evidently the couch on which Togo took his afternoon nap. A small knee table, above which was a rack stuffed with charts, a table and two or three chairs completed the furniture. There were in the cabin three grim reminders of the war, one being the Russian shell that nearly killed Admiral Togo and a splinter from which cut deep into Lieutenant Matsamura's leg, another a shot with the point knocked off, and the third a whisker of a torpedo that had stuck in the net. The fragments of the shell had been carefully collected and pieced together with cement.

The admiral talked to me of Dalny, of Tokyo, and of painting. His secretary joined us, who knew England well, and our conversation then turned on England and Togo's impressions.

"I liked England well," he said.

He admired our cities and spoke very highly of the many friends he made whilst serving his apprenticeship on an English training ship. Through the doorway, opening out on to the stern gallery, shining white like the rising moon (so white that it cut deep into the blue of the sea and sky), stood the solitary island that marked Togo's rendezvous. Admiral Togo speaks English imperfectly, but he understands it thoroughly. During our conversation the coaling was proceeding, and consequently the doors and windows of the cabin were closed to keep out the dust. He got up to open one or the other occasionally, com-

Sketch of
the battle of
Port Arthur,
done by the
steward.

ADMIRAL TOGO PLANNING THE BLOCKING OF PORT ARTHUR IN HIS CABIN
ON THE MIKASSA. ROUND ISLAND IS SEEN THROUGH THE OPEN DOOR.

plaining of the heat. He pointed out to me the island, saying:

"Do you know the name of that rock?" I said that I did, and he continued, "I shall remember it all my life, I have looked at it so long now."

I looked at it again, studying the details more closely. It is almost circular, although there is one strongly indented bay from which a broken, indistinct track leads to the summit. On the summit was a flag-staff, and from the pole floated, in large folds, the Rising Sun of Japan. Two or three rock islets nestled against the side of the main rock, around which the perpetual movement of the sea encircled a lace of foam. We sat there for some time gazing upon the island, and occasionally our conversation wandered back again to England. He wished to know where I lived, and on my telling him his face beamed with interest.

"Why, I know that place," he said. "I have passed it on my way from London to Portsmouth."

But his face soon became reflective again, and the serious lines tightened on his lofty brow as some thought of the magnitude of his responsibilities entered his mind. Twice I asked if I were interrupting any business, but he said:

"No; go on."

I was sketching him at the time, and he said:

"I am afraid I have given you much trouble in coming out here."

"It is a great honour," I replied, "and a great pleasure, and I hope you will let me come again."

"As often as you like," he said, "the torpedo boat will always bring you."

I felt very gratified by the manner in which the great admiral received me, but I was anxious not to encroach upon his valuable time, and made an effort to leave. He put his hand on my arm to stop me, and rang the bell. The secretary reappeared, accompanied by the steward, who brought three glasses of champagne on a lacquered tray, and we drank to one another. The admiral fanned himself throughout the interview, and, as I was leaving, he asked me to paint him a fan. He looked about the cabin for one, but without success, so he produced his album and asked me to paint the rock as it appeared framed in the doorway of his cabin. I set to work, and in a few washes produced a picture which seemed to please him greatly, and, with hearty good wishes and assurances from the admiral that we should meet again, I turned to leave. As I passed through the cabin door he said:

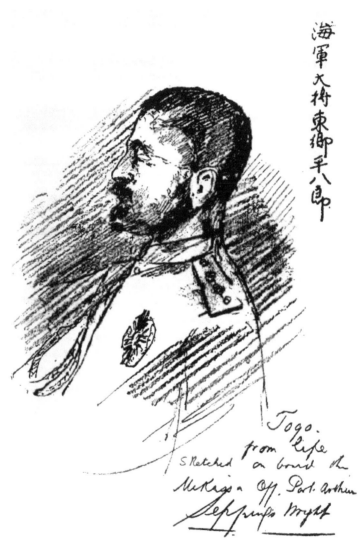

海軍大將東郷平八郎

Togo.
from Life
Sketched on board the
McKisson Off. Port Arthur
Seppings Wright

SKETCH OF TOGO BY MYSELF

"Don't forget. Whenever you want to see me, you come."

On our way back to the harbour, about halfway between the rendezvous and Dalny, we saw an innocent-looking *junk* hugging the land, its crew rowing for all they were worth. Now the strongest point in a Chinaman's character is his marked objection to exertion of any sort, so that this display of hard work was suspicious. Commander Mori called the attention of our Captain, Taira, to the extraordinary energy displayed by the usually apathetic and happy-go-lucky Chinaman. After a brief conversation the captain ordered a shot to be fired in the direction of the *junk*. The shot struck the water half a mile ahead of the Chinamen, but they instantly complied with the delicate hint to heave-to. Moreover, they appeared so anxious to come to an explanation that they began rowing with renewed energy in our direction.

As soon as they came within hailing distance the honourable captain of the *junk* was told that he must condescend to bring his exalted person on to our miserable little torpedo boat. The Chinaman made a great show of his anxiety to come alongside, displaying a wholesome awe for our 12-pounder, which was trained round on the *junk*, and he frequently waved a deprecating hand at the silent, menacing gun. As she steered alongside, two of our sailors, with fixed bayonets, jumped on board, taking charge in the name of Japan. The captain, who had been apparently eager to come on board, now showed a strange reluctance to leave the helm, which seemed to require a good deal of adjustment, and he deputed his first mate to come on board to settle the matter. An amused smile played around Mori's face as he said:

"I would like to see the captain if it is not too much trouble for him to explain whence and whither he is taking those fine young donkeys."

There were about fifty donkeys on board, and the captain of the *junk*, nervously watching his chief officer out of the corner of his eye, became busier than ever at the tiller, pretending not to see the mate and also seeming to be afflicted with deafness, as the latter explained that the invitation to board the torpedo boat applied to the captain personally. At last, with an impatient gesture, he left his self-imposed task, and came on board the torpedo boat quickly, with an engaging smile. In offering explanations he mentioned, casually, that as he was rather in a hurry and wanted to get on, he would be glad if we would let him go quickly.

"Certainly," said Captain Mori, "when you have answered my

THE *JUNK* WE CAPTURED FULL OF DONKEYS.

. John Chinaman when
He lost his junk

SKETCH OF THE CHINAMAN WHO LOST HIS *JUNK*

questions."

John Chinaman then assumed a jaunty and confident air, that seemed to say: "I'll settle this little business," and, saying something about "chits," he went on board his *junk* and returned with a bundle of letters, which he handed to the officer, and then squatted down on deck with an air of rollicking confidence as to the result of the enquiry. Nevertheless, he narrowly watched the inscrutable face of our commander for some sign of his fate.

Captain Mori came to a decision in about two minutes. He gave a brief command, and the *junk* was made fast to the stern of the torpedo boat, and we started off once more. As the *junk* felt the strain of the tow rope, the Chinaman cried out:

"If you go so fast my *junk* will be broken to pieces."

His little pig's eyes quivered and sparkled with rage, but meeting the eye of Mori he immediately became submissive, and wept slowly and softly with his head always fixed in one position. I made a sketch of him as he sat there.

"This is a very old dodge," Captain Mori said to me, "and a very transparent one. The donkeys are supposed to be for a friend of his at Kiaokiao, but the letter that I hold in my hand gives him away, for Kiaokiao lies to the south, and he should have been a hundred miles from here in that direction. He told me a ridiculous story about some wonderful and mysterious current that brought him off Port Arthur. But what convinces me that the *junk* is a lawful prize is the statement in the letter that these donkeys are worth £45 apiece. Now the price of donkeys throughout China is never more than two or three pounds, and the only people who would pay such a price as £45 are the Russians in Port Arthur. These donkeys will be very useful for our army."

The remainder of the journey passed in silence on the part of the Chinaman, but there was a good deal of laughter on our side at the dignified air which our prisoner had assumed, refusing to speak when he was addressed.

We anchored for the night at Dalny, and the prize and its contents were sent to join the fleet of prize *junks*. As the sun had set and the channel was mined, we were compelled to remain at Dalny for the night, and I took advantage of this circumstance to visit my old ship, the *Tainan Maru*, where I received a most hearty welcome. On my arrival the side was piped with due formality, and the sentry presented arms. My servant and orderly accompanied me everywhere on ac-

"RESTING" JAPANESE DESTROYERS IN A CERTAIN HARBOUR.

CAPTAIN MYAKI AND CREW OF NO. 67.

count of my rank in the service. After a pleasant evening I returned to the torpedo boat, and early the following morning we started for the secret harbour, taking the western passage. This is a very difficult passage on account of mines and booms, and a few weeks ago it was well-nigh impassable, as the Russians had mined nearly every square yard of it.

Torpedo boat No. 67 belonged to the First Division, and she could steam twenty-five miles an hour. She took part in the battle of August 10th, attacking the *Askold* and discharging torpedoes at the range of 1,000 metres. None of them exploded, however, probably on account of the rough weather. The coast scenery we passed on our way to the harbour was bold and striking, and one great rock reminded me of the "Parson in the Pulpit," the well-known rock standing out of the sea between Dawlish and Teignmouth.

We sighted two ships of the Fifth Squadron, and soon afterwards I was startled by a report and concussion that made our boat shiver from end to end. I learnt afterwards that it was caused by one of the searching vessels exploding a contact mine that had been found. The mines were an ever-present danger, and I always felt an apprehensive curiosity as to what might be concealed in each wave into which our bows plunged. The officers told me that they all had experienced this nervousness at first, but use had become second nature and their nervousness was a thing of the past. A pair of destroyers suddenly popped out from a concealed cove and steamed off to Port Arthur, which was right ahead of us, though hidden by the point of Niko-Shai. At last we cleared the point, opening out the Bay of Port Arthur. The town lay to the west, deep in the haze created by the smoke and dust of battle. The batteries perched high on Liao-tau-shan and the crest of the mountains along the curved front of ten or twelve miles were wreathed in smoke and flames, and might have been mistaken for a huge range of active volcanoes. When we arrived the Fifth Squadron was engaging a new battery which the Russians had unmasked.

The Japanese system of intelligence is complete, and we were able to get news from the signal station of the position of affairs at the front. The army, we learnt, had nearly finished the bed for the 11-inch gun, and as soon as it began firing the position of the battleships in Port Arthur harbour would be critical. Thousands of reserves were still arriving at the front, and within two days a general assault would be made. This, it was hoped, would drive the Russians into Togo's arms.

We ran alongside the admiral's ship with orders from the commander-in-chief, and when we had delivered them we steamed between the rocky islets that protect the harbour's mouth and took up our station in the First Division. The harbour was Togo's advanced base, and it was there that the Fourth Squadron had its headquarters. Torpedo flotillas, mine ships, mine searchers, and tugs all sheltered there. It is one of the prettiest places in the world, and, topographically, is unique. A natural breakwater of high mountainous islands runs parallel with the mainland, forming one of the safest anchorages that can be found, and about midway along this chain of islands a flat neck of sand connects them with the mainland. The value of this position could not have been fully realised by the Russians, but the Japanese recognised its importance and captured it early in the war, and it was from this base that all the subsequent operations connected with blocking, torpedo and mine work were carried out.

Over the sandy neck of land stands the Chinese town which gives its name to the harbour. The huge mountain beyond, from which the spiral puffs of smoke darted upwards, was Liao-tau-shan. This mountain rears its head 1,500 feet above the sea level, and the indefatigable Russians had fortified it and armed the forts with heavy guns of large calibre, which opened on any of our ships that approached within range. A nearer shoulder of land, cutting the slope of Liao-tau-shan, was Golden Hill, and other hills shut off from view the remainder of the Port Arthur defence works.

At the foot of Golden Hill is the entrance into Port Arthur, and on the opposite side is Tiger's Tail. On the latter the Russians had fixed a searchlight, which at night was constantly sweeping with its brilliant beam the waters of the bay. Its light used to enter through my cabin scuttle, illuminating the walls for a brief space ere it passed on, leaving the cabin in greater gloom than before. The general character of the scenery is very similar to Bantry Bay, with its rude, roughly-tilled farms and low thatched farmhouses. Nearly all the islands are occupied by poor Chinese farmers—the entire live stock on one island, exclusive of chickens, consisted of one donkey and one black cow. The smaller islands would afford good grazing for sheep, but the rough grass and undergrowth is reaped by the farmers for winter fodder.

There is a storm-swept look about these islands, and on the weather side the cliffs are smooth and look as though they have been black-leaded. There is no sign of trees. On the outermost island there is a fine colony of pigeons, and I and the chief engineer paid them some visits later on, with the result that we had some very good dinners of

LIEUT.-COMMANDER MYAKI,
MY TORPEDO CAPTAIN.

pigeons and rice. Beyond the islands Admiral Yamada kept guard, from dawn till dark, returning every night to the friendly protection of the haven. It was the first link of the blockade. Closer in—right between the jaws of the bay—the five flotillas of chasers crossed and recrossed, keeping an unwearied watch.

The tide eddies and sweeps around Port Arthur Bay, and it bore with it vagrant mines which had broken adrift from their moorings in the mine fields at the entrance of Port Arthur. Each morning the mine sweeper, with its huge net, swept the channel, and mine creepers, in pairs, towed their grapnels on the bottom to discover and destroy any mines that the Russians might have laid in the fairway during the dark, foggy, or moonless nights. Terrific reports throughout the day testified to the industry of these useful craft and to the necessity for their labours.

On several occasions during my stay I watched a mine-ship steaming out on its dangerous errand, and more than once it was only a boat's crew of terribly mutilated sailors that returned. The mining and counter-mining went on unceasingly. Each night our small picquet-boats sneaked along the coast, slipping from headland to headland until they approached the enemy's harbour. There they made a bold dash, and a hail of Russian shot and shell would surround them, as they daringly laid their mines and scuttled back out of the bright beam of the searchlights. But sometimes they never returned.

No. 67 was a second-class torpedo-boat, but by means of bamboo and canvas her appearance had been changed so that in the distance she might easily be mistaken for a first-class destroyer. She was the third boat in the 4th flotilla, and her position in the line of blockade was immediately opposite the entrance to Port Arthur harbour. She was commanded by Lieutenant-Commander Myaki. With three other torpedo-boats we one day left the anchorage and put to sea by way of the inner entrance. A strong south-west gale was blowing at the time and it severely tested the sea-going qualities of our small craft. We made straight for rendezvous B, within the long-range radius, and a shell from the top of Liao-tau-shan mountain welcomed us by splashing into the water with a loud roar and bursting harmlessly some distance from us.

The commodore of the flotilla ignored the Russians' gentle hint, and we continued to cruise to and fro on this rendezvous, keeping in touch with the 3rd and 5th flotillas at either turn. The 3rd flotilla was composed of big destroyers, and the 5th flotilla of torpedo-boats.

To thoroughly enjoy a trip like this one needs a strong stomach and no nerves, for both are tested to the uttermost, the one by the active and restless jumping of the vessel, the other by the knowledge that at any moment the boat may run against a Russian contact mine. Only a short time before a chaser of the 2nd flotilla had thirty feet of her stern blown away, although, strangely enough, no one was injured. Two of the officers were in the ward-room at the time, and their escape was little short of miraculous. Being built in water-tight compartments the little vessel did not sink, and she was at once towed back by her consort. It was thought that in dipping in the heavy sea which was running her screw had touched the mine.

About five o'clock Myaki and myself tumbled down to the tiny ward-room for supper. Everything in the ward-room, including ourselves, was kept in a state of perpetual motion, but our boy succeeded in getting us a big pot full of tea and a tin of biscuits, with which, together with some ham and eggs nicely cooked by Myaki himself over a big brazier in the cabin, we made a good meal. Myaki had been in several engagements. He had never been wounded, but he told me that some of the actions had been so fierce that he was soaked to the skin by the water which the shells splashed over the vessel.

"I never thought I should come out of it alive," he added.

We spoke of our homes and families, and he showed me a photograph of a beautiful, clever girl who was waiting for him in Tokyo. She was dressed in the semi-European costume of the Japanese school-girl, and was pictured playing her violin.

The life of a Japanese naval officer, Myaki said, was very hard.

We are always on duty and seldom get leave, but we are not discontented, for we love our emperor and his navy so much that we do not complain, however much is asked of us. Our wives are, of course, left very much to themselves, but to pass the time what is there pleasanter for them than study and work? My girl has taken to music, and is a thoroughly earnest student.

He went on deck to relieve the second officer, a sub-lieutenant, who came below and cooked his own supper while I smoked my pipe. We both went on deck when he had finished, he to the forebridge, and I hanging on to the guard-rail. The wind, in the meantime, had dropped, though there was a considerable sea still running, but the motion of the boat was much easier and had lost that obstinate jerking motion which is so unpleasant when steaming against a head sea. The

Panorama of a certain harbour—from my mountain.
One of the prettiest harbours I've ever seen.

A Russian compliment. The usual shell practice at us.

night drew on, and one searchlight after another shot its beam over the waters of the bay. The big searchlight at the harbour's mouth fixed its eye steadily on us for a minute or two.

"Now look out for a shell," Myaki said; but nothing happened.

"I suppose they don't think us worth wasting a shot on," he added.

There was no moon, so we made a deviation in our course which brought us closer in. We expected the Russian torpedo-boats to come out and meet us, and in preparation for this we had a private signal which could only be seen at a distance of five or six hundred yards, and would enable us to distinguish our own boats. It seemed, however, that the whole energies of the garrison and the sailors were devoted to beating off a land attack. The roar of the guns and the sharper cough of the bursting shells was continuous, and the bright star rockets made a fine display. The firing was maintained until after midnight, when it suddenly ceased. We learnt afterwards that the North Fort had been captured several times, but the Russians were too well entrenched in commanding positions with machine guns for the Japanese to hold it. I remained on deck until past midnight, fascinated by the thrilling drama that was being played before me.

We were experiencing much the same weather as prevailed when the destroyer was blown up, and I confess to feeling "creepy" at times. However, I turned in and slept well until early dawn, when the sea calmed down and lay a rich, deep, violet-blue beneath a dome of indigo. The stars faded and the beams of the rising sun flashed upon the strongholds of Port Arthur. The bay looked peaceful enough, and were it not for the meteor-like spark of the bursting shells, we might have imagined ourselves on a pleasure cruise. Any such vain imaginings were rudely dispelled by the sudden explosion of a contact mine a few yards ahead. As it burst it threw up to an enormous height a vertical column of spray mingled with a transparent brown smoke. For a minute I thought one of our flotilla must have gone, and I counted them several times before I could convince myself that all four were safe. As the day became lighter I noticed two *junks*, one painted red and the second white, like mark boats at an ordinary regatta, and I learnt that they were moored in their positions to define the limits of rendezvous B.

From the deck of our boat we could plainly see the windows of the houses in Port Arthur, count the guns on Golden Hill, and detect the trenches, shelters and traverses knit together by a network of tracks. We could even see some of the Russian battleships, whilst the masts and fighting-tops of all towered high over the Tiger's Tail. Two triangular white spots high up the hillside facing the entrance were the beacons to guide ships through the channel by certain cross bearings.

The battle raged continuously throughout the day, but we saw little of it, for our army was struggling for the possession of a fort that was out of our range of vision. Presently a violent explosion on land shook our little vessel and it was followed by a dense cloud of white smoke, rising slowly and majestically out of the earth and gradually expanding into a shape like a gigantic mushroom and larger than the biggest thunder cloud I have ever seen. Three times we saw the huge smoke cloud, and three times there was a deafening roar of gigantic explosions. We clapped our hands and shouted "*Banzai!*" hoping that the Russians were blowing up the magazine before giving up the fort. But on our return to the harbour the captain of the *Nikko-Maru* told us that the terrific explosions were caused by a new and terrible weapon of destruction known as a land mine.

I was studying with great interest the coast line and general character of the cliffs at the entrance of Port Arthur, where the Russians had sown thousands of mines and placed booms which effectually prevented any vessel without the key of the channel from getting in, when a three-funnel battleship glided out and anchored in the outer roads (of dramatic memory). We could not distinguish her name, but our leader signalled orders and we all turned seaward, gliding through the waters like a flock of divers. The Russian fired several times, but the shells fell wide of us. Our 11-in. shells soon found her out, and drove her to cover off Tiger Island. She was the *Retsivan*, one of the finest battleships afloat. Nothing was talked of now but the possibility of our being sent to attack her at night, but she put an end to our conjectures by returning to harbour before sundown.

The Russian mine sweepers had not come out that day, and as the reports from our army stated that several small steamers had been sunk in the harbour, it was probable that they were among the number.

At breakfast our commander again undertook the duties of cook, and turned out a very tasty omelette. Our beat of twenty-four hours was up at midday, and we were relieved and returned to harbour for the usual twenty-four hours' rest. As we had used up most of our coal and water and other provisions, the commodore signalled to us to go alongside the mothership. Four of us went alongside, increasing the number to seven, three being there already, which made quite a raft of torpedoes,

Japanese shells.   11 in. shell with shimose powder.

THE SEBASTOPOL.
    OUTSIDE THE
    HARBOUR.
STOPPING A WEAPON. -'!'

Russian mine sweepers.

The *Bezstras...*
Russian destroyer.

New Russian battery
    on the Point.

all busy coaling. A torpedo boat on active service presents a very different appearance from the spick and span review-order neatness to which we are accustomed in time of peace. The sides are scratched and scarred with hard service, and the deck has the appearance of that of a tramp steamer with a deck cargo. The rope *mantelettes* around the bridges and exposed parts make her look heavy and clumsy.

The masts in a torpedo catcher are fitted with a canvas crow's-nest (reached by a Jacob's ladder), where the look-out is stationed. The rigging is heavier than that of a torpedo boat, and a small yard is fitted with blocks for signalling. There is also a long slender bamboo topmast which seems to pierce the sky, from which floats the Commodore's flag, and a small yard for the wireless telegraphy. A canvas bath occupies the gangway of the port side, and around the funnels the men wrap their small Japanese towels to dry them. Between the funnels there is a clothes-line, and packing-cases, boxes, bales and crates of poultry lumber up the deck. Right aft a pair of falcons or, perhaps, pigeons are perched on the side rope, the pets or mascots of the vessel. One torpedo boat's pet was a duck, which used to fly all over the harbour, returning now and then to see that his ship was still in position. Bright patches of colour were introduced into the grey monotony of the torpedo boats by the staring red of the blankets which were often hanging out to air.

The weather becoming thick and wet caused some excitement amongst us, for it was ideal weather for the Russian fleet if they intended to slip out. Everybody was on the *qui vive*, we expected to receive at any moment the warning signal, and I looked forward to an opportunity of witnessing a fleet action—one of the ambitions of my life. The private or warning signal is very short and to the point, and consists simply of five red lights—dot—three dashes—dot. When it is seen every ship in the harbour must get under weigh and steam for its appointed rendezvous at full speed; it is, in fact, the signal for a concentration or mobilisation of the whole fleet. The torpedo boats' station, in the event of the signal being given, would be at the rear of the fleet, for in a general action we take the position of reserves and are a sort of "Marine Cavalry."

The day passed without any alarm, and the following day I obtained permission from Admiral Togo, by wireless telegraphy, to inspect the signal station—"Togo's eye," as I had christened it. The picquet boat took us to the small town where it is situated, and after some difficulty on account of the shallowness of the water we managed to

Land mine exploding, as seen from torpedo boat, off Port Arthur.   Rendezvous B.

LAND MINE EXPLODING, AS SEEN FROM TORPEDO BOAT, OFF PORT ARTHUR, RENDEZVOUS B.

land by going alongside a big Chinese *junk* and from thence walking ashore along her gang plank. The signal station is perched up on the highest point of the peninsula, and is reached by a rough pathway cut in the mountain side, up which we scrambled. The captain had come ashore with me to give me a personal introduction to the officer in charge, a young lieutenant.

Chinese towns are always dirty, and this was no exception. The houses backed against the beach, conveniently for the depositing of the family refuse and filth, which remains until a tidal wave or some other rare convulsion of nature clears away the rotting mass of garbage. As the streets of the town were no better we walked by the beach, keeping close to the edge of the sea, and struck the track at the foot of the hill. After a sharp climb we came to the signal camp, which consisted of one tent and a long marquee supported by iron wire guys and protected from the fury of the storms by a strong wall of stones. We called first at the tent to see the officer. After tea, cigarettes and compliments he led us to the summit to see the simple, yet important, signalling arrangements.

On the very top the rock had been flattened over an area of about 12 or 14 square feet, and a bamboo flagstaff firmly embedded. The look-out was stationed on a knife-like neck connecting the outer cliff to the mainland, and a telescope of great magnifying power was fixed on a tripod, with a packing-case for a seat. One of the three sailors always had an eye glued to the telescope, watching every change and movement at the entrance of the harbour of Port Arthur. Signals were sent to Admiral Togo hourly if all was quiet, but any movement on the part of the Russians was, of course, signalled immediately. I looked through the telescope and could plainly distinguish the Russian soldiers. The enemy's signal station was in full view, and the Russians constantly indulged in a little target practice at our flagstaff, which they never succeeded in hitting.

We remained at the signal station for an hour admiring the view, which as a cliff subject is, from an artist's point of view, incomparable. The point of the peninsula runs straight off in perspective into the ocean, and the crags rise up sheer from the blue sea, the wild waters of which have undermined the cliffs with caves and quarried wonderful arches as proportionate as if they had been designed by an architect. The sheer drop of the cliff on either side of the telescope platform made me feel dizzy, and a short time after I heard that one of the sailors had fallen over and, of course, was killed instantly.

CHAPTER 8

Another Interview with Togo

The *Nikko-Maru* was the "mother" of No. 67, and the deck officer, Lieutenant Matsumura, kindly showed me over her one day. She was built at Nagasaki by the Mishi-bishi Company, is of steel, and is one of the best and latest additions to Togo's fleet of auxiliary cruisers. She carried eight guns, and her quarter-deck was packed with war material, chiefly the long packing-cases containing the deadly 18-inch torpedo. Amongst her other "maternal" duties she provided the torpedo flotillas with coal, water and provisions, and she ran a canteen on board where officers and men could purchase many useful trifles, and some luxuries. I occupied the pilot's room when not aboard No. 67, and there I wrote, painted, and developed my photographs. My friends from the torpedo boats used the room as a sort of club, where we all met and discussed Port Arthur Bay and the events in which we were participators.

It was in the "club" one night that I heard that an English captain had had a very narrow escape. The story was told to me by one of the officers who had just returned from the rendezvous. A small English ship of only 650 tons, bound from Hankow, was proceeding to Wei-hai-wei when, getting out of her reckoning, she struck a mine near Port Arthur. She was a wooden ship and was blown to splinters, and the crew of Chinamen and two English mates were drowned. The captain, however, managed to hang on to a life-buoy, though badly wounded in the wrist, and he was rescued and taken to the *Mikassa*, from whence he was sent to Sasebo to be handed over to the British Consul. If it had been the Russians who captured this Englishman, instead of the Japanese, I am afraid it would have gone hard with him, for, as my Japanese friends said, they would probably have shot him first and tried him afterwards.

My cabin on the *Nikko-Maru* was interesting from the fact that

A TORPEDO "MOTHER" IN A CERTAIN HARBOUR

IN A CERTAIN HARBOUR.

a mysterious Mr. Thomas had occupied it at one time. He was very highly spoken of and popular with the officers of the ship, who said that he and I were the only Englishmen who spoke with enthusiasm of the wonderful state of efficiency of their navy.

The bathroom being next door to my room, many of the officers attended these club meetings in their *kimonos*, either going to or returning from their bath. Two little Chinese chow dogs, recently captured from a blockade-running *junk*, also made it their headquarters when I was at home. The mother was a handsome chestnut-brown dog with eyes soft like a woman's. Cheesi, the son, was a brilliant black puppy, with tan marks, the peculiar and interesting point about him being the lower jaw, which was so small and undeveloped that it gave him quite a weird expression. Cheesi found a great difficulty in opening his mouth to eat, and this drawback made him very irritable. He was very sensitive about his deformity, too, and if I pointed my finger at it he strongly resented it and went for me. But he was a nice little fellow, and we were great friends.

The alternate beat out into the bay and return to the harbour was becoming as monotonous to me as his beat is to a London policeman, except sometimes when we afforded the Russians a little target practice. A change came, however, whenever I took a run out to the *Mikassa* to see Admiral Togo, who was always at his post. I asked permission to land, as I was desirous of making a picture of the Port Arthur fighting from as near a point of view as possible. He enquired as to what arrangements I proposed to make, and I told him I had my tent and camp outfit with me and only wanted his permission to land. He told me to make my mind quite easy, and he would arrange everything and let me know by signal. I returned to the *Nikko-Maru* in high spirits, and at once looked up the camp gear and saw that the tent was all ready and the guy ropes, pegs, and other paraphernalia in good working order.

Whilst waiting for Togo's signal to me I made several interesting trips, one of the most exciting of which was in the mine sweeper. Mine sweepers are destined to play a prominent part in future naval operations, but in the present instance an ordinary merchant steamer was used. A derrick was stepped in the forecastle, and there were four long spars fitted with gear for holding the net at the corners. At the foot of the net were two blocks, and a pulley is rove from the ends of the upper spars to these blocks, to ensure keeping the net at least thirty feet away from the ship. This big net is lowered about twenty feet in the water, and the ship steams ahead fishing up the mines, the method being not unlike prawn fishing on a large scale.

Our fishing did not result in a catch, but I was glad of the opportunity of seeing the method in operation. It is, of course, highly dangerous work, for if the net fails to catch the mine the latter inevitably strikes the vessel. Several vessels were lost in this manner by the Japanese, therefore vessels of any great value were not used for the work. The captain and officers took great pains to explain everything to me most thoroughly, and after their valuable information I shall be able to construct a vessel which will do this work with more certainty and less risk to her crew. The persistent work had very nearly cleared the fixed mines in the vicinity, and those that had broken loose and were carried by the tide were what we principally sought.

The following day I went ashore to select a place for my camp. I took my sketching materials and a day's rations. The pinnace ran me ashore in less than half-an-hour, and Lieutenant Matsumura, a petty officer, and two bluejackets accompanied me as a sort of guard, as it was thought that my foreign appearance might lead to my being mistaken for a Russian. On landing, we went to the Chinese merchant's store, which, like all the buildings, was in a state of dilapidation and dirt, which seemed to indicate stagnant trade and extreme poverty.

The whole family, with the exception of the women, seemed to be behind the counter, as is usual in Chinese shops, where it always appears to me that there are more sellers than buyers. The wares consisted of all sorts of rough agricultural implements of native manufacture, and some European goods, including bottled beer, and in one corner stood a large jar about the size and shape that one pictures those that play an important part in the story of Ali Baba and the Forty Thieves. At first I thought this jar must be a large fly-trap, for the outside was deeply incrusted with dead insects. In a rack by its side stood several loathsome-looking, greasy vessels, fashioned out of gourds and with long bamboo handles. I was wondering what these filthy utensils were used for when the oldest Chinaman present transferred to one of them some of the contents of the great jar, and as he ladled it out I saw that it was oily, rancid stuff of the consistency of golden syrup. It was the liquid butter which is used by the Chinese in cooking.

We had considerable difficulty in making my wants known to the Chinaman, and Matsumura described Chinese characters in the air and on the counter to intimate that he wished to write. After a while the Chinaman understood, and produced his brush and ink and paper, whereon Matsumura inscribed my wants. It is a curious fact that although many Japanese visit China for business and pleasure, they find as much difficulty in speaking the language as Europeans do, in spite of the fact that the Japanese language is written, to a great extent, in Chinese characters. Therefore, although they cannot talk with each other, they can communicate by writing, as I have often witnessed in out-of-the-way islands which I have visited whilst with the Japanese navy. If there happened to be no writing materials at hand, a clean space on the road, or a field, or the sand of the shore, served the purpose, and quite a long conversation was often maintained in this way.

In the compound at the back of a Chinese house we passed was stationed one of General Nogi's pickets, and the officer in charge told me that he had received instructions concerning me; that I was to tell him where I wished to pitch my tent, and he would advise me as to its suitability, for the big guns of the Russians occasionally searched the hills in the neighbourhood. Hiring a donkey for the day, and loading him with water-bottles, rations, and painting materials, we set off as merrily as a lot of schoolboys. Our way lay through the town, the first portion being a rough esplanade, which seemed to have been appropriated by a rope-making business, the temporary gear being put up without the least consideration for the traffic, and the work carried on amid all the bustle of the street.

It was further blocked by various tradesmen—smiths, shoemakers, and others—and every other available part of the street was occupied by hawkers. It appeared that the shopkeepers' premises extended to the centre of the road, and they charged the hawkers a small rent, or "squeeze "as they call it in China. The traffic threaded its way as best it could through this improvised bazaar, the Chinese policeman ignoring the obstruction, for the shopkeepers all gave him a little "squeeze," which relieved his mind of any further responsibility in the matter.

On leaving the town our path skirted a large brackish piece of water in shape like an irregular triangle, and on one side is the city of the living, and on the other the city of the dead. The refuse of the town and the drainage of the burial ground are probably filling the place with *bacilli*, but the ducks seemed to enjoy it, swallowing the loathsome stuff, including cubic yards of germs, greedily. The family washing was also done there, and should any unnatural Chinaman think of taking a bath I have no doubt that he would go to that spot and add to its unwholesomeness.

There is a wild beauty about the barren-looking mountains, and they are further interesting from the fact that a battle was fought there early in the war, when the Russians made a very strong effort to retain the position. The Russians had set up both telegraph and telephone between this place and Port Arthur, which, as my Japanese friends remarked, "was very kind and thoughtful of Alexieff, as it saved the Japanese a lot of trouble." The wires had, of course, been diverted to Nogi's headquarters, thus placing him in direct communication with Admiral Togo. At the foot of the mountains the path crosses the rocky and boulder-strewn bed of a mountain stream, but, the season being dry, water was only to be obtained in the deeper holes. Native Chinese paths are not remarkable for smoothness, and the one we ascended was no exception to the general rule. The first part of the climb made me feel that I was very much out of condition.

The sun shone brightly, and on the way up we met but little traffic, only a fish hawker and a Chinese pedlar, carrying their goods in the usual milkmaid style, and a small string of donkeys with their burdens and some Japanese cavalrymen leading their horses. The mountains were somewhat barren, being clothed chiefly with coarse grass, hardy, stunted bushes, and a few small Canterbury bells, ox-eye daisies of a salmon tint and thistles. Here and there a vine clung to the rocks, and a species of dwarf oak with large leaves peeped out from between the stones. There was strong evidence of mineral possibilities, for a large number of quartz reefs showed in well-defined lines amongst the slate. It is good sheep country, and I noticed flocks of Angora goats and also some good, hardy horses. We toiled up and up until we came to the pass on the top of the first ridge, where a cool breeze tempered the heat, and we found it very refreshing after our stiff climb.

From this point we saw a sight that thrilled us—a battle in progress. It was distant, but near enough for us to distinguish the rattle of the small arms from the roar of the big guns and the sharp cough of the exploding shells. But we had yet another mountain to scale, and much as we would have liked to watch the fight, time would not permit. We followed the devious course of the shoulder of the mountain until we got to a small track, which led us to a gently inclined plateau, sheltered from the north winds by a natural rampart of rocks. This seemed to me a suitable place to pitch my tent. The mountains descended to the sea in a succession of huge steps, some of which were thirty feet high, and beneath me, like a map, lay the whole of Port Arthur Bay, each rock and island and every ship being clearly visible. The waters of the bay spread out to the high horizon, the farthest distinguishable point being Togo's rendezvous and the great circular rock a dark blemish in the polished silver track of the morning sun. The smoke of Togo's battleships traced dark lines in the heavy atmosphere, and I could see the flotillas going out to relieve guard in the bay, and also, with the aid of my glasses, the islands which marked the limits of the blockade.

The top of the mountain (So-Cho-San), some 400 feet above us, was yet to be climbed, and we trailed our feet up the zig-zag goat track, slipping on the short smooth grass, and through another broken cliff reached the summit. The panorama was one of the most remarkable that was ever spread before my eyes. A triangular plateau with a beacon was the actual top of the mountain, and my view was uninterrupted save in one direction where the peak of Sho-cho (Double-headed) masked a very small portion of the fighting area. Westward, in the din, dust and smoke of battle, lay Port Arthur, the hills in and around the city seamed and scarred with a network of trenches, and their tops scraped brown and bare of every particle of vegetation by the terrific raking fire of the Japanese guns.

The sky was blue above and around us, but the city was enshrouded with clouds. Every variety of cloud seemed to be there, from the light cirrus to the black thundercloud and the heavy rolling *cumulus*. But from these clouds death and destruction fell, for they were, literally, clouds of war. The lighter ones issued from the parachute-like burst of the shrapnel shell, the heavy *cumuli* were caused by the black powder smoke of the heavy Russian guns, and the Shimosi powder gave the thunderclouds with circular lightning darts as the powerful explosive rent the shells. The roar and rattle of these death-dealing missiles jarred horribly on our ears as we gazed upon the fair view before us.

Six mine boats were working at the mouth of Port Arthur harbour, and several torpedo-boats and fishers crossed and recrossed the small area of water which was all in the wide expanse that mighty Russia could call her own. Beyond Port Arthur rose the tragic 203 Metre Hill, and away to the left rose the peninsula of Liao-tau-shan, from the highest peak of which spouts of smoke marked the position of the heavy guns on its crest. On that eminence the Port Arthur generals said they would make their final stand.

I turned and faced the east. The peaceful Bay of Dalny gleamed like an emerald, and the smoke of the tall chimneys suggested industry. The mountains between us and the beautiful bay already bore names bestowed on them by the conquerors. One small, peaked hill had been named (after the sacred mountain of Japan) Little Fujiyama. Around

My expedition up the mountain.

My escort on the mountain.

its base swept the military road made by the Russians to connect the harbour below with Dalny. It passed through the rich plain, with the ripening corn standing on either side—a beautiful picture of peace. The panorama was completed by the continuous range of the mountains to the north.

We remained watching the progress of the fight until the declining sun warned us that we were due at the beach before dusk. We hurriedly scrambled down, reaching the shore at 6.30, but we were compelled to wait until 7.00, on account of the lowness of the tide, and even then had to take a sampan to get to the launch.

I was very glad to see in command of the launch one of my friends, who had gone away the night before on a mine-laying expedition off Port Arthur, and not returning when expected had caused us much anxiety as to his fate. He told me that the reason of his delay was that he had been unable to get away until the moon rose, and then he had to lie low behind a promontory until he got a chance of running the gauntlet of the Russian guns successfully. He seemed to treat the matter as a joke, although the captain told me he had not expected to see him again, as he had ventured too far.

On our way out a mechanical mine exploded at the other end of the harbour, and a pillar of black smoke shot up quite two hundred feet into the air. I reached the ship at 7.30, and sat watching the various coloured lights of the different shells and star rockets before turning in.

In the morning I breakfasted early and went ashore with the usual escort and First-Lieutenant-Commander Yonehara, who wanted to see the fighting. I had some difficulty with the donkeys, having to hire two fresh ones, as the poor creature who carried my pack the day before had gone lame. The news of my presence must have been noised abroad, as all the town, apparently, had turned out to see the first Englishman who had ever landed there. I found the road hard, and my feet were tender from the previous day's climb. On reaching the summit of the first mountain we saw that the fighting was still going on, but in more desultory fashion, for the Japanese, having captured a position the day before, were taking things more easily. I noticed, however, that the Russians had mounted a new battery of four guns.

The most interesting sight was seaward, where the mine creepers were busy at work assisted by some torpedo catchers, while over against Liao-tau-shan one of our gunboats carried on a quick-firing duel with a Russian ship, which finally retired to Port Arthur. This, together with the fact that they had been clearing a passage through their own mines at the entrance, seemed to indicate that they were thinking of making a dash for Vladivostock.

Just below us we saw a torpedo catcher discover a floating mine, and from our position we were able to see the whole procedure. After shooting at the mine without result it was set on fire, and the torpedo catcher raced away for dear life at 25 knots an hour, her consort steaming towards her in case of accident. But this mine behaved very mildly, expending its energy in smoke and flame. The *Nishen* and *Kasuga*, the two Italian cruisers sold to the Japanese by the Elswick company, lay about ten miles to seaward, while further off, and too far to distinguish clearly, a cruiser was coaling from a collier.

The sun having scorched me rather badly, I did not accompany Lieutenant Yonehara and one of my escort in their climb up the higher mountain (Sho-cho), where they hoped to obtain a more extensive view. They went off like school boys but came back tired, hot and dusty, with their tongues hanging out for want of water. A bottle of cool beer, however, soon restored their exhausted energies. I had been sketching during their absence and I found that my Chinese donkey-man was quite an art critic, for, in the intervals of hunting insects in the neighbourhood of his pigtail, he criticized my drawing freely.

We started back earlier this time and by a shorter track, but, before we left, Yonehara took some photographs of us with his plate camera, which turned out very well. It was very amusing to watch the Chinese women in the fields scuttle away at our approach, but we did not regret their shyness, for their appearance was too revolting to make us wish for a closer view of them. We halted at the mountain stream for the donkeys to drink, and I noticed then, as I had noticed before, that the Chinaman is generally kind to his animals.

I got back to the ship at 6.00, winding up the day with a good Japanese supper of chicken soup. My tea-pot would not pour out properly, so Fuki-Shima, my new boy, seized it, blew down the spout till it gurgled and then triumphantly filled my cup. I said nothing, and meekly drank it.

The Japanese shells had been exploding well inside Port Arthur, and it became a question of how long the Russians could stand the racket, but the next morning the forts and batteries were silent; the Japanese were digging, and the Russians were evidently determined not to waste their ammunition.

I had no companions on my next trip ashore, as all hands were busy coaling ship. Down in the bay the Russian mine boats were busy, and one torpedo boat was watching at the entrance. Togo's fleet was more to the westward, right opposite the entrance to Port Arthur. The same evening, I was pleased to hear from Admiral Togo that I had his permission to pitch my tent in the vicinity of the military lines, where I could paint my Port Arthur picture. I again got out my tent for inspection and made a list of things that I might require for repairing it.

A torpedo boat came in towing a big *junk* with the usual unhappy crowd of Chinamen aboard, and later in the day it was rumoured that the remainder of the Vladivostock Squadron had put to sea again with the intention of trying to form a junction with the Port Arthur ships.

My tent was a Cabul and an object of interest to the sailors. I pitched it on the shelter-deck and inspected all the fittings, so that, when I landed, everything would be in order. My camp kit consisted of the tent, bed, sheepskin blanket, canteen, tea-set, saddle and saddle-bags, bamboos for various purposes, flour, rice, jam, biscuits, sardines, butter, candles and matches, besides my personal baggage. I estimated that six donkeys would be necessary, for two donkeys would be wanted for the tent alone. My companions were to be two bluejackets, to act as guard, and my servant. My sheepskin sleeping bag was well-shaken and aired, for some fleas from the dogs had found the soft fleeces very cosy. A little insect powder and the sun drove them from their snug home. The arrangements for my comfort were very complete. Water was to be sent from the ship, and it was arranged that the doctor should pay me a visit at least once a week. Two sailors were to live with me as a guard, and if the ship should have to go to Sado Point for a day or two and they had to join her the *Kioto Maru* was to take over the duties of supplying me with a guard.

"You see," the captain said, "we are responsible to Admiral Togo for your safety."

I rose early the next morning and packed. The tent and a month's supplies had been already placed in the large *sampan*, and everything was ready by eight o'clock. As I went over the side the doctor threw the Cheesi dog into the launch. The novelty of his surroundings seemed to terrify the little animal, and he shivered miserably throughout the passage. With the officers and bluejackets, who had been sent with me to pitch my tent and see that I was made comfortable in my camp, I landed on the wet beach, for although the place has been in existence since the time of Confucius there is no pretence of a landing-place. The crowd of Chinese loafers and idlers greeted me with the usual apathetic curiosity. I paid a visit to the store to arrange for supplies of fuel (wood and charcoal), and my boy picked out some old oil jars which he said he intended to convert into a furnace. Soldiers were there, the sentry being comfortably seated in an armchair at the doorway. I called on the officer, and he introduced me to another gentleman in uniform, who turned out to be a Chinese interpreter. This was a piece of luck, as I was able to make all my wants understood, and, through his influence, I procured six stout donkeys and some donkeymen of about the same order of intelligence as the animals in their charge.

I had engaged a number of *coolies* with spades and hoes to clear the camping ground, as I had decided to pitch my tent with the opening facing Port Arthur. After a great deal of trouble, owing to the rough and rocky character of the ground, we managed to pitch the tent. The usual artillery duel was in progress, and I noticed that some of the guns from the new battery were trying the range of Admiral Yamada's flagship, and that several of the shells burst on the shoulder of the mountain only about 500 yards away from us. I was beginning to doubt the wisdom of my choice of camping ground, when two officers and a cavalry picket appeared and confirmed my doubts.

The Russian gunnery had improved very much since the beginning of the fighting and, the senior officer said, smiling, the gunners were very clever at hitting tents. This officer was in command of the district and he told me courteously, but decisively, that I must move out of the danger zone, which I was willing enough to do. Accordingly, the whole camp had to be struck and repacked on the donkeys, and a new site selected. I finally decided on the small plateau which I had first chosen. It was late in the afternoon ere I was comfortably settled, but I found my new situation an improvement on the first, as it was sheltered from the keen wind. The officers insisted on my giving them a list of everything that I might require, and what they could not get from the ship they promised to order from the Chinese store. I walked part of the way with them on their way down, leaving them at a small gorge which I called the gate of my estate.

There was one almost insuperable difficulty in organizing my new mode of life, for of my establishment the two Japanese sailors could not easily make themselves understood to the half-dozen Chinamen, the Chinamen could not easily understand me, and I could not speak the language of either. But we managed to get along. My livestock consisted of fowls, donkeys and the little Cheesi dog, who seemed to grow large with the dignity of his self-assumed office of watch-dog. He barked fiercely at the Chinamen, the fowls and even the donkeys, and when my bed was made he jumped into the middle of it, coiled himself up and went to sleep, feeling, no doubt, that he had begun his duties well and fairly earned a nap. In the meantime, I had begun to think about supper. My Japanese servant had been unable to make the furnace out of the earthenware jars for the simple reason that he had no tools, so my only load of wood was quickly burnt out in boiling the kettle. My supper consisted of tea, biscuits and *bouille*. My two sailors brought their mats and blankets into my tent, and the Chinamen roosted among the rocks some distance away—a precaution which, owing to their filthy habits, was absolutely necessary.

CHAPTER 9

The Night Attack

I awoke in the morning feeling very fit—the effect of sleeping in the beautiful, fresh mountain air. My first thought was a bath, and this I was able to enjoy after waiting a while, one of my donkeys coming in after a journey of six miles to the mountain torrent to fetch it. My water buckets were old paraffin tins, well scoured with hot water and soda. For breakfast I fancied a broiled chicken and gave orders accordingly to the Chinese cook when he came ducking at the tent door. I tried to make him understand what I wanted by scratching Chinese characters on a bare piece of ground in front of the tent, and after arguing and shouting in various languages he at last became aware of the fact that he was to kill a fowl.

I had a small Japanese dictionary of terms, but the only words I could find bearing on the subject were "Fowl" and "Corpse," so I ordered him to "corpse a fowl." The fowl was duly "corpse" and the body brought to me for further instructions. From the Chinaman's signs I gathered that he intended to cook the bird with its feathers on, and he did not think it necessary to clean it! I set to work and gave him a lesson, which he learnt readily enough, but when I told him to cook the bird he said that there was no fire. This was annoying, to say the least, and after all my trouble I had to fall back on the *bouille* beef tin and biscuits and water.

With my field-glasses I was able to scan the whole country, and I was glad to see the party from the ship crossing the sandy spit with my supplies. It would take a couple of hours for the supplies to reach my camp, so I went to the mountain top to watch the progress of the fighting.

The Japanese had succeeded in establishing themselves in a very strong position, which the Russians were endeavouring to retake. It

a pickel—

A small party of blue jacket: Keep look out on the Russian: Mining boats. —

was a most important position, for it commanded a portion of the harbour and town. The fighting was very severe, and I heard afterwards that the casualty list on each side was terribly heavy.

About noon the donkeys, packed with my supplies, arrived, coming up to the camp at a run. One donkey was loaded with the much-needed wood, a bag of charcoal, and two earthenware pots. The Japanese sailor, like his British prototype, is essentially a handy man, and, with an iron tent-peg and the mallet, he proceeded to manufacture a furnace. A square hole was knocked in the front of one of the pots and two or three holes at the back to ensure a draught, making an excellent stove, which he immediately put to use, boiling the rice and grilling the chicken. I set the *coolies* to work to dig a trench round the camp, in case it should come on to rain, and in the afternoon I went up to select a spot on which to plant my easel.

It was difficult at first to get the Chinamen to understand what I wanted, but I made one carry the easel and water, and the second the paint boxes and my camp stool, and in a few days this became a regular routine and my paraphernalia was daily taken up and fixed while I breakfasted. Nearly every day one or other of the officers came to see me, and my two sailors were relieved as regularly as when on ordinary duty. It was easy work for them. Each pair spent twenty-four hours in my camp looking after me, and, in fact, never losing sight of me, their relief from the ship coming at 8.0 the following morning and so on for the four or five weeks of my stay, so that, during my residence on the mountain, I had altogether nearly half the ship's company to guard me. In fact, I was treated almost like a royal personage. The doctor paid me a visit twice a week, and any officer who might be passing to the hill top invariably called to see me.

I ran my tent on the lines of a Japanese house. On the floor I spread grass mats, and I and my friends always took off our boots before entering. This ensured absolute cleanliness. I wore the *kimono* and did a good deal of my work on the floor in Japanese fashion. At first I was troubled with flies, but I moved the kitchen further away and kept the donkeys on another hill, and the few flies that remained were killed by my Japanese guard, who fashioned an ingenious flapper of a pliant splint of bamboo, with which they stalked the wily fly and never failed to kill, clearing the tent completely of the pests.

I soon settled down in my new surroundings. I spent the greater part of each day on the mountain top with my field-glasses and water-colours, generally remaining there until the sun sank in splendour

280
206
1620
5600
57620
Round Rock
Cap rock
Oct. 9. 1904. – On my mountain.
Manchuria

behind the mountains on which the fighting raged, the figures of the combatants standing out in sharp silhouette against the red disc. Throughout the nights the big guns boomed, but the mine-laying boats were unable to work effectively on account of the bright moonlight.

On my second morning I bathed in the fowls' drinking pan, which had been cleaned out for the occasion, and one of my sailors scrubbed my back and swabbed me down. A little later one of my guards ran in to tell me that my friend the interpreter was coming up the mountain with a present for me—a fine tai-fish. The tai-fish is a sort of sea perch or red snapper and is justly called the salmon of Japan. It is equally good hot or cold, and, by the Japanese, is esteemed a great delicacy when eaten raw. Of course I had to leave everything to meet my friend and express my pleasure at his gift, and I invited him to stay and share it. He was a charming and well-informed man and gave me a great deal of information about the surrounding country—the names of the mountains and valleys, and the spots where the fiercest battles had been fought.

The big mountain Sho-cho, he told me, was the scene of one of the most ghastly battles on record, and, although some weeks had passed, many of the dead Russian soldiers still lay where they fell. It was on this mountain that the enemy first used stones and rocks to hurl down upon the attacking force. He pointed out the new position of one of the Russian searchlights. We could plainly distinguish it on the nearest point of land held by the Russians, and we could also see that it was masked by a projecting cliff from the Japanese guns.

The new Russian battery was getting a "dusting" that morning, and the concentrated fire of a number of batteries and an 11-in. gun was gradually crumbling the ridge that protected it. I could see the Japanese shells dropping in the battery and bursting among the guns, and I marvelled how anything could remain alive in the place. I could see men being carried away and several motionless figures lying prone, which revealed the deadly nature of the Japanese fire; but the Rooski stuck well to his guns and maintained the fight all day.

I found the autumn sun too strong in the afternoon, and, my fingers beginning to sting and nasty-looking red blotches appearing on them, I postponed working until after four o'clock. It was good weather for the haymakers, and every patch of grass and herbage was mown. A rough sort of sickle, something like a large knife-blade inserted into a handle at an angle of forty-five degrees, was used by the

A "PAINTER" ON THE BATTLEFIELD.
PHOTOGRAPHED BY THE BOATSWAIN.

mowers. Whole families turned out, with donkeys, to help with the haymaking.

I was told by some officers who came from the ship that a big battle was imminent, as the Japanese intended to capture the Double Dragon, or North Fort. That formidable work had been nearly taken more than once, but the rapid fire of machine guns from different protected positions effectually prevented our soldiers from holding it. The shell storm began as we settled ourselves among the rocks on the mountain top and looked over towards Port Arthur. The general plan of the ring of the forts could be distinguished and we could see the military road connecting them at the back, and also discern the movements of the Russian troops. So far as I could see the road was perfectly safe for traffic, the Japanese shells passing over it.

From where I sat my position was as good as that of an umpire at military manoeuvres, for I could see both sides—the attacking force, and the defenders. The ball opened with one of the most terrific bombardments that it has ever been my lot to witness. The number of guns in action could not have been less than 500. The position was roughly as follows: The Japanese army had already captured the first line of defence and Fort Kuropatkin had also fallen, so that the Russians were hemmed in behind the permanent defences of the city, and the battle I was watching was an attempt on the part of the Japanese to break through on the flanks and capture the remaining defences.

The tide of battle rolled from right to left, white globes of smoke expanded and floated away like folds of lace, and the dirty black of the Shimosi powder seemed to tear up the earth as it burst, with a terrific report, from the shells. Through my glasses I saw a snow-white cloud which appeared to descend to the earth, and, as I watched, it was suddenly riven asunder and drifted like morning mist to the hill tops. It was the smoke of the 11-in. gun.

Suddenly the Japanese guns ceased firing. The infantry were marching to the assault. I watched the broken ranks as they hurried forward, led by a man wearing a noticeable white belt, who, I learnt afterwards, was General Ichenohe. The advance was stopped by the Chinese wall, which seemed an insuperable barrier, and there was a halt. But suddenly a terrific explosion rent the air, and when the smoke cleared away I saw a breach in the wall through which streamed forward again the conquering army. Hundreds of small Banzai flags sprang up in the ranks until they resembled a grove of flowering trees.

The position was won, and this time it was held. With the excep-

28th Sep. 1904

Dear Sir,

We send here some wooden peices & coal you requested and also your cleaned shirts & trousers.

My captain thanks for your kind invitation but at present the enemy's battle-ships in the port are receiving the severe attack by our cannons & perhaps within a few days they will be pushed out into the outside of the port. In that case our ship must cut off the cable & run away. Accordingly now the captain's responsibility

is very heavy and he can not pay it visit to you.

I think you can consentrate your all power of painting day by day and you are very comfortable. May I visit you? I like I spend day in the tent of the hill.

Assistant paymaster
U. Ohnos

Our venerable gentleman
Mr Seppings Wright
On the hill

tion of a few desultory shots, the battle was over. It lasted from morning until just before sundown, and in the night the Japanese made their position secure. The following day there was a lull in the fighting, for both sides paused to rest and bury their dead.

My daily donkey brought me a letter from Mr. Ono, saying that as the Japanese guns were searching the harbour it was thought likely that the Russian ships would come out, and in such case the torpedo boats would fall back behind the fleet.

My fuel went very quickly, for I found the Chinamen used—or said they had—a donkey-load to cook one chicken! Some beef was sent from the ship, which my Japanese sailors cooked with sugar, and I found it excellent. Hitherto I had been busy with my sketches for my big panorama picture, but the day after the assault I spent lazily putting the camp in order and generally "taking it easy." I found my Chinese cook straining the soup through his towel, which also did duty for a dish rag. I remonstrated with him, and at first refused the soup, but he seemed so hurt that finally I gulped it down. But it stuck in my throat and became no more palatable when he removed a drowning fly from it with his tooth pick.

Two magnificent eagles kept flying and circling around me, so low down that I could plainly distinguish their eyes. I found, however, that I was not the attraction; the birds had designs upon Cheesi doggie, who was gnawing a bone quite unaware of his imminent danger. I picked up a stone, and as I prepared to throw it at the great birds I noticed that it glinted in the sunlight. I examined it, and found it was highly mineralized, and I brought it home and had it tested, with good results. My Chinese boy brought me a bunch of wild chrysanthemums. The blossoms were very small, but they were of the richest yellow and made a nice, bright splash of colour in my tent.

Heavy firing began again in the evening, and I ascended the hill to watch it. The star-studded sky, paling at the horizon, silhouetted the mountains, and around Port Arthur the land was a dusky purple. The beams of five searchlights formed a huge, brilliant star which swept the surrounding country and threw the mountain tops into strong relief, resting now and then on points where the Russians thought our guns might be concealed. Sometimes the powerful light rested upon me as I stood upon the summit, and I wondered if a shell would follow. Fortunately, however, the Russians did not make a mark of me. In the defiles of the beleaguered district the watch fires of the enemy flickered—a thousand points of light.

The heavy guns boomed with business-like regularity, and there was a dramatic moment when the beams of the searchlights concentrated on one point, high against the sky, and the graceful lines of a solitary rocket traced its fiery path and burst with a thousand falling stars, which lighted the whole scene. In an instant the hills were sheathed with flame, for, from the darkness of the Japanese position broke forth tongues of fire, and the roar of the unmasked guns was awful as they poured forth a hail of shell into the Russian lines. A night attack was in progress. In places the electric rays seemed blurred by the rush of projectiles.

Shouts and battle cries and the rattle of musketry arose, and by the vivid light of the star rockets I could distinguish the attacking army, pushing forward like black shadows on a white sheet. The thunder of the guns, the glaring flash of the bursting shells, the dark, rolling clouds of smoke, and the small, black imp-like figures darting forward through the awful turmoil, almost persuaded me that it was a vision of hell upon which I gazed. But the fierce attack subsided in less than an hour, though the searchlights continued quivering and flashing, here and there, until they steadied to the normal, regular movement. I was spellbound by this exhibition of the death-defying valour of the Japanese soldier, and the memory of it remains with me—every detail of that bloody half-hour vividly pictured in my mind.

I heard, a few days afterwards, that all this wonderful heroism had been wasted, and that, in future, night attacks would, if possible, be avoided.

As I returned to camp the weird call of the mountain wolf fell upon my ears, and it was well attuned to the desolate thoughts that oppressed me, but in the bright morning the gloom caused by the events of the night left me, and I took up my pencil and set to work diligently. My fourth drawing was nearly finished and there remained but the fifth to complete the work.

My sailors had often pointed out the distant Sho-cho and asked me why I did not visit it, and at last I decided to make the trip. From my camp to the summit of Sho-cho was two hours' walk, and I set out with the two sailors and one donkey and a Chinaman to carry my provisions and sketching materials. We descended into the valley by a somewhat abrupt declivity to save time, for the path was long and circuitous. We reached the main track, which followed the course of a mountain torrent that wound through the valley, and everywhere were traces of the Russian defences, chiefly hastily constructed rifle-

A NIGHT ATTACK ON PORT ARTHUR. VIEWED FROM MY TENT.

pits and breast works.

The mountainous character of this country is well adapted for defence, and, in consequence, difficult for attack. We half slid, half rolled down the four or five hundred yards to the road which followed and, at times, even ran along the dry bed of the stream. Chinese farms and tumble-down shacks nestled snugly between the ribs of the mountains. By the side of each muck heap stood the family tomb—a rough shrine, generally built with loose stones and having two little window spaces and a tiny doorway to let the spirit pass in and out. One tomb I noticed was rather more pretentious and had sides of a single slab of slate. Firs, fruit, and other trees flourished in these sheltered vales, and corn, millet, vegetables and cotton were roughly cultivated.

Many of the farmers were gathering in their crops, and the scene was biblical in its simplicity and primitiveness. The ox was treading the corn on the threshing floor, women were separating the chaff from the grain, and there were many Ruths gleaning in the fields. Donkeys came down from the mountains, bearing bundles of coarse hay, which is composed of everything that grows, even the dried stalks of the millet being stored for forage for the animals' sustenance during the long and severe Manchurian winter. Half-starved curs guarded the dirty compounds in which the houses stood. Wild flowers bloomed everywhere—chrysanthemums, campanels, lilac and purple marguerites—and wild vines trailed in unrestricted luxuriance.

A species of wild cucumber climbed the low bushes, and the brilliant yellow fruit glowed in the sunshine. Almond, apricot, and walnut trees shaded the narrow track, and among their boughs the familiar magpie chattered, seeming, indeed, to be the only specimen of bird life in the valley. At the further end the Russian engineers had made a military road, which zig-zagged up the hill with an easy gradient, but we followed the donkey-path in order to avoid the dust. At the top of the pass were deep rifle-pits, which ran for miles along the mountains on either side, and high up on the slopes of Sho-cho were gun-pits and emplacements which commanded the valley. The rifle-trenches were not part of a hurried defence, but were carefully planned and well made by the finest military engineers in the world.

Several hastily-made graves marked where the Russian soldiers were buried where they fell, but the Japanese graveyard is carefully planned and neatly laid out, and the small, square, wooden tombs, with the names and records of the fallen, stand in rows on a sunny, flower-spangled slope, shaded by a grove of their beloved fir-trees. The shell splinters and crumbled rocks told of the terrible nature of the artillery fire.

The grand old head of the mountain could only be scaled by an expert climber, for about 200 feet of cliff with scarcely a foothold separates the higher slopes from the narrow top. It was there that I realized the utility of the Japanese *zori* or pliable straw sandal. The knife-like ridge of the summit is only about twelve to fifteen feet in its broadest part, and slopes away at an impossible angle to the southeast. There is a rifle shelter roughly thrown up—what is known in South Africa as a *schaan*, a method of defence which the Boers used frequently on the *kopjes*. A few feet in front a dead Russian was buried; there was no earth in the grave, but big stones and rocks half concealed the gruesome, foetid corpse. The head was gone, but the boots still held the leg bones. A few yards from the grave I picked up the jaw bone, which some animal or bird of prey had carried away, and I restored it with all reverence to its place in the grave.

We spent some time scanning the various positions until the westerning sun warned us to be off. We left the Russian hero in his loneliness and turned to descend. Getting to the summit had been hard enough, but the descent was considerably more difficult. At the foot of the crags I rested, looking across at a deep defile sheltered by high hills. I could see Japanese cavalry picketed, the Army Service Corps, the white tents of the soldiers, and what I took to be the correspondents' camp. We started for home and made good time, reaching the ridge of our mountain range at dusk. The moon was not yet up and Port Arthur, to our right, lay wrapt in gloom. I enjoyed a well-earned supper, which my Chinese servant had, for once, cooked really well.

The next morning, as I was expecting a visit from the captain, I gave orders to have everything cleaned up for inspection and for a better dinner than usual. My first disappointment was the fish, for, instead of tai-fish, the donkeyman brought me a small shark. This pleased my Chinese followers, but it annoyed me very much, knowing Captain Kamamura's weakness for tai-fish. However, I had some good fresh beef and also told the cook to "corpse" a fowl. My guest turned up in good time, and we went up the mountain, where I showed him the new naval battery. He told me that our army had mounted four more 11-in. guns, so that five of these huge weapons were now dropping shells into Port Arthur. He expected the Russian ships to make a bolt for it at any moment, but such a course was by no means easy, for, in the first place.

Port Arthur being a tidal harbour, there was only sufficient water at high tide for battleships to go out, and the evolution of taking the squadrons out would necessarily be slow. Secondly, the mine fields would have to be cautiously threaded by the ships, one by one, and they would have to form up outside. Such a manoeuvre would not be easy under conditions of peace, but with shot and shell around them and mines beneath, it seemed hardly possible that the entire fleet could get out to sea.

After dinner we sat in the tent looking out towards Togo's fleet. Two cruisers and one battleship were slowly cruising to and fro between Signal Hill and Cap Island. At 4 p.m. the captain left, and I went as far as the defile to see him off. On the way I picked up a purse, which turned out to be his, and he explained to me that his servant had brought a warmer coat for him to put on when he reached the pass and, in changing, the purse must have dropped out.

One of my bodyguard having to remain on duty for an extra turn was the cause of some amusement to me, for the two good fellows nearly quarrelled in their desire to be the one to take the extra duty.

The military officer from the town called to wish me goodbye and introduce his relief. He had been promoted to some post at Dalny. I was sorry to lose him, for he spoke a little Chinese, and was very useful in getting me provisions. My interpreter friend, too, turned up with some tins of butter.

I taught my cook to make an Irish stew with beef, potatoes, pumpkin and onions. While the cooking was going on I went for a walk, getting back at eight o'clock. The stew was only half done when I returned, but because it was eight o'clock the Chinaman thought it must be dished up. It took a long time to explain to him that it was more important for it to be cooked.

Over Port Arthur dense clouds of smoke were rising, and I counted six distinct columns which seemed to indicate that the Russian ships were going to move.

CRUISERS AND TORPEDO DESTROYERS OFF PORT ARTHUR.

A beautiful cloudscape grew up over Dalny, and I tried to paint it. Several strong puffs of wind failed to warn me of the approaching change in the weather, and I was caught by the full fury of an icy blast, which sent down the temperature to freezing point. But half-an-hour before it stood at 80°. My tent began to flap about in a very disconcerting manner; presently a guy-rope snapped, and then a tent-peg flew out. The torpedo boats ran for shelter to the western arm of the harbour, and the storm broke with an advance guard of dust and small stones, which swept away my tent, kitchen, and everything over the mountain side. Everyone tried to save something, and for a time there was a panic. Fortunately, the tent dropped, like a spent balloon, among some rocks which were sheltered by an overhanging cliff. There, among the stones and rocks, we propped up what remained of it, and collected our things inside. With much labour and difficulty, we got the uprights fixed, when the ridge pole broke. We overcame this difficulty with a piece of rope, and finally got the tent up.

The Chinamen long since had burrowed among the caves, like rabbits, with the exception of our old cook, who succeeded in making a fire in a sheltered corner and brewed us a kettle of hot tea. We then set to work again, strengthening the tent ropes, until nightfall, when my two sailors and myself turned in. The Chinamen, a fantasy of plunging donkeys, whirling pigtails and dust, had started for the town. All night it blew, and at 2 a.m. away went the fly, and the constant jerking of the ropes loosened all the pegs. At 2.30 all hands were out in the freezing blast holding up the poles and trying to secure the tent. We spent an hour or so thus, and then the gale lulled and we managed to secure the ropes once more. But we had very little sleep, for at six o'clock the tent fell flat on top of us. We put heavy stones on it to keep it where it fell, and crawled into one of the caves and lighted a fire.

No Chinaman or donkeys turned up in the morning, and, after a council of war, I decided to go to the town with one of the sailors, take the ridge pole for the smith to repair, buy rope and mats, and build my home again. The wind was so strong that all the shops in the town were closed except that of my merchant, who fortunately had the Japanese troops billeted on him, as they objected to being boxed up in the store. I discovered a smith, who at first refused to do the work until the next day, but by dint of threatening and cajoling I managed to change his mind, and in half-an-hour he had turned out a neat job. As no steamboat could come from the ship owing to the weather, my excellent henchman could not be relieved, and he willingly returned with me.

While the smith was doing my work I could not help noticing again what dirty beasts Chinamen are. Words cannot describe the dirt and vermin that encrust their bodies. Even on the working, visible parts the colour of the skin is only apparent through the cracks of this loathsome coating. Men, women and children all wallow and sleep in dirt, and the women and girls are, of course, crippled by the way in which their feet are compressed.

I made my purchases and loaded up the donkeys with fresh vegetables, firewood, and some food, and once more ascended to my airy dwelling. We put up the tent, and with the new guy-ropes it seemed fit to stand a typhoon. The sea was smiling, and there was no trace of last night's storm save a larger number of mine sweepers and lookout ships. After such a blow many of the Russian mines would have broken adrift and make the work of the blockading squadrons highly dangerous. The Japanese in the bay were having a little gun practice at some of the floating mines.

I regretted more than ever that I had brought no gun, as I saw a large number of wild duck within easy shot, and I kicked up quail as I walked along. Rock pigeons were quite tame, and large flocks of geese, making their way south, almost touched the ridge of my mountain. The southward flight of these birds told of the near approach of winter.

It seemed to me that Port Arthur could not hold out much longer. The whole of the east side of the Russian position was being raked, and nothing could possibly live in such a cyclone of shells.

I got some fresh eggs the day after the storm, which were a welcome addition to my stores, and the needle and thread arriving from the ship my sailors started to repair the damages.

I was awakened suddenly at dawn the following morning by the loudest crash of thunder I have ever heard, and *pit! pit!* fell the rain in large drops. Then with a roar and a rattle hail showered down, and the lightning seemed to dart among the rocks. I began to think that mountain life was sickening. I could see nothing except the grey screen of hail. Only once before have I seen anything approaching it, and that was in South Africa. The storm at last seemed to roll over the edge of the mountain and sink beneath my feet, and tore its way out over the sea.

Just below me was a miniature harbour which I had often wished to visit. It first attracted me by reason of its resemblance to a little cove in Cornwall, and afterwards by the possibilities it presented for obtaining a constant supply of fish. I took the usual party—the bodyguard, my boy, the Chinaman, the donkey, and the Cheesi dog. Although the cove was directly beneath us we were stopped, after going a few hundred yards, by a huge precipice, which necessitated our making a detour of nearly a couple of miles. The inhabitants in this part struck me as being unusually clean. There were half-a-dozen families in all, with about the same number of boats.

The men were employed in mending their nets, and the women in digging *diakon* (a sort of radish) from the small enclosures. Through my boy I made them understand that I wanted fish, and they immediately launched a boat, and dragged a net, with the disappointing result of half-a-dozen fish no bigger than sprats. They explained that the weather was getting too cold. They lived in this peaceful hamlet all through the war, and followed their usual avocations even when the battle raged above them. One object of interest that they showed us was the case of a six-inch shell, which one day came like a meteor, and exploded with a deafening noise against the cliffs which shut in the houses. This piece of shell is looked upon by them as a sort of god, and it stands on a pedestal in the middle of the beach.

We did not waste much time at the hamlet, but started to the opposite side, skirting the coast to see an old Chinese shrine, which stood in solitude on a promontory some two miles distant, and from which we hoped to get a better view of the entrance to Port Arthur. We spent half-an-hour there, and wended our way back through one of the wild valleys that are a feature of the neighbourhood.

The following morning, hearing that the Russian battleships were coming out into the bay, I hurried up to my observatory on the mountain top and saw one of them, the *Retsivan*, guarded by four destroyers, leaving the protection of the harbour for the outer roads, where she anchored. She was in a rather exposed position, and had already been struck several times. As she moved slowly and majestically out Japanese shells burst around and over her, until she rounded a point of Tiger Island, which gave her some protection. Four mine ships were sweeping ahead of her, evidently to clear a channel. This seemed like the beginning of the end, and I had a fine view of her throughout the day. One of my Japanese guard remarked:

"The Rooski have not much *mesimese*." *Mesimese* is Chinese for food.

The Japanese flotillas swarmed in the bay, so that the fate of the

Retsivan seemed as if it would be settled either by torpedo or shell. She was between the devil and the deep sea. All the ships in Port Arthur harbour were firing up, but Togo's fleet was right opposite and barred their way. Two battleships steamed slowly in as if to challenge the *Retsivan*. If the rest of the Russian ships had come out they would have experienced a similar fate to that of the Spanish ships at Santiago.

Every Japanese battleship, cruiser and torpedo boat was on the move. A shell fell within two hundred yards of my tent and burst, tearing up a pit in the ground three or four yards broad and quite as deep, as was testified by one of my sailors who stood in the hole for me to see. This decided me to prospect for a safer spot. I had noticed, some three or four hundred yards away, some huge boulders, and towards these Cheesi and I strolled. These boulders were about the size of an ordinary two-storied English villa, and two of them lay at right angles to each other, the triangular patch between them being sheltered from every wind but that which blew from the south.

The herbage in this spot was more luxuriant than elsewhere on the mountain, which convinced me of its mildness. There was a cleft in the angle of the rocks about two feet wide through which the north wind might blow, and to prevent this I had it neatly blocked with stones. I then set my Chinamen to work to clear the space of all small rocks and level the ground, and on this pleasant site I pitched my tent. Although the position was so sheltered, I could still enjoy a full view of the bay. My new arrangements were scarcely finished when the Russians gave a grand display of shell fire. They seemed to have got suddenly angry, and every gun in Port Arthur appeared to be doing its utmost to fire away all the ammunition.

The doctor called and spent a long day with me, telling me all the news. General Nogi was reinforcing his army, and a big battle was expected in about a month's time. Some Japanese fishermen had been becalmed before Port Arthur, and a Russian picquet boat came and took all the fish, offering them two yen in payment, but the Japanese refused the money, saying that the Russians were welcome to the fish. The Russians then made enquiries as to the strength of the squadrons stationed in our harbour, to which the fishermen made diplomatic answers. The *Pobieska*, one of the Russian battleships, the doctor told me, had been struck by two shells which did some damage and set her on fire for a few minutes.

I witnessed an exciting scene in the bay that day, some of the Russian destroyers coming out and apparently attempting to make a dash for Chefoo. While I was peacefully writing my journal I was startled by the bursting of a shell a little distance away, followed by two or three more. I wondered what the Russians' object could be, for there were no guns or troops on my mountain, and it seemed a sad waste of ammunition. The firing continued, and I and all my followers ran up to our look-out. During the thickest of the rain the Russian destroyers and a gunboat had left the harbour, and we had a grand view of the action between them and our flotillas.

All the guns of the seaward batteries in Port Arthur that could be brought to bear maintained a ceaseless fire on our ships, but apparently without much effect. The Russians' double column formation was broken and two of the rear ships lagged behind. Then a terrible explosion took place as one of the lagging ships ran against a mine. She sank, and in spite of the Japanese shells that splashed thickly around, her consort stopped and picked up her crew, and then slowly took her place with the six others and proceeded to sea. The driving rain obscured my view for a while, but it cleared, and I was able to see all the subsequent movements.

The Russian destroyers formed into single line and steered straight towards the *Chenyen*, Admiral Yamada's flagship, which was just off the signal point in company with four destroyers. As the Russians made this move two of the Japanese destroyers (apparently a part of the 2nd flotilla) steered in from the bay to meet them, firing as they approached. These two headed, the Russians, going straight for them, and a third destroyer left her position near the flagship to reinforce them. The *Chenyen* was firing her bow guns, which, with the fire of our torpedo-boats, caused the Russians to swerve, and they followed the curve back to the entrance to the harbour, where they remained. The gunboat which had come out with them had stayed there all the time, and she appeared to have received some damage at the beginning of the action.

I had noticed the sound of heavy firing to the south-west, in the direction of Encounter Rock, the scene of one of Togo's battles, but I could see nothing on account of the rain. When it cleared, however, I saw two steamers coming in, partially hidden by a thick squall that was driving up behind them. The two Japanese torpedo-boats had started back to take up their first position, and it seemed to me that they were now making for these two steamers. These were, however, again screened by the squall, and successfully reached their journey's end at Port Arthur. These steamers carried provisions and medical comforts

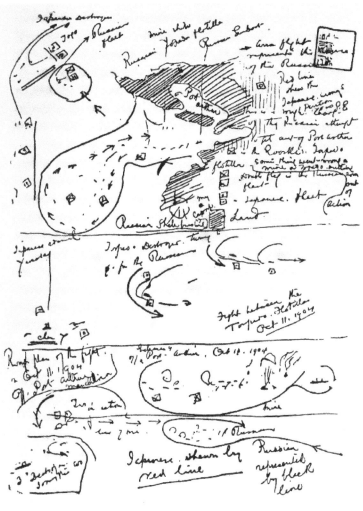

LEAF FROM MY JOURNAL.—SKETCH PLAN OF THE FIGHT.

to the beleaguered garrison, and the Russian torpedo raid was merely a blind to cover the approach of these two blockade runners, so that it was a good day for the Russians.

My last drawing being finished, my stay on the mountain came to an end, and I went to the top of the hill for a last look out over the bay. The donkeys were then brought up and the camp was struck, but the north-west wind blew so hard that the donkeys bearing the tent could scarcely make headway. However, after one or two minor accidents, we reached the beach, and I signalled for the boat. The reply was: "Too rough, will send later"; so I had to remain in the dirty town, doing nothing, until nearly sunset, when the wind dropped and the big *sampan* came in tow of the picquet-boat, and I made the final journey together with all my belongings.

All the sailors who had composed my guard lined the rails to welcome me, and I had a most gratifying reception. The ward-room officers gave me a special dinner, during which I heard all the news. The Russians had received a crushing blow at Mukden, and the rice crop in Japan was the best for twenty years. It was said, too, that if the next attack on Port Arthur were successful the Japanese fleet would be split up, some ships returning to Japan for repairs, and one battleship, a cruiser and the torpedo flotillas being told off to watch Vladiyostock.

The cold weather had set in again and everyone was trying to keep warm. I went into the captain's cabin, as it was the warmest place in the ship, and he gave me a very interesting description of his first cruise as captain. It was up the Yangtse, and he had kept a most complete record and made a chart of the river. It is in this that the Japanese officer excels. He is never content with the government charts, but works out his own, and very often he discovers errors in the official charts. The captain's mail had just come in, and he read to me letters from his wife and child. The one written by his little girl, who was eight years old, ran:

Dear papa, I love you so, but if you stop much longer I shall forget your face. Look at the moon so that your face may be reflected in it, and I can look, too, and see you.

This poetical strain runs through the whole Japanese nation, as, too, does the intense patriotic spirit, or *Bushido*. The British naval *attaché*, talking over the Japanese naval successes with me, attributed them all to *Bushido*. *Bushido* means, literally, "military-knight-ways," and may be freely translated into "duty and patriotism." The word burns deep in the heart of the nation. It was in olden times the guiding word for the knights, or *Samurai*, who were the retainers of the *Damaio* or feudal barons. The code of honour among this military caste was high. Fair play in fighting, protection of the weak, the upholding of justice, and the laying aside of self for the advancement and benefit of the native land, were their leading principles and these principles have existed for thousands of years and coloured the whole life of the people, down to the present day.

Bushido is, indeed, a practical religion, and it is its tremendous moral force that has enabled Japan to stand up before such odds, and were these odds multiplied, *Bushido* would still carry her through. As recent events have shown, the Japanese will never turn their backs on a big bully, and they will never willingly harm an insect. There is nothing the Japanese people hate more than meanness and deceit, underhand practices being so foreign to their own high nature. Many of the older people view with regret the growth of commercialism, on account of the somewhat lax morality which seems inseparable from keen business. But the Japanese realise that they must descend from their lofty station and take their place in the markets of the world. For many reasons this is to be regretted, not the least being that it will destroy the simple life which is characteristic of Japan.

A Japanese father hopes that his son will emulate the *koi* fish, that always swims against the stream, over waterfalls and every obstacle, until at last it reaches the head of the river. In the battle of life, the father does not wish his son's way to be easy; he would rather he nerved himself for the struggle, determined to succeed or die. *Bushido* is kept alive by the Spartan mothers of Japan, and from them the children learn to bear pain and disappointment in silence. The suppression of the emotions is learnt in childhood, and a mother who loses her only son on the battlefield shows no outward sign of her deep grief, but seeks to heal her breaking heart by fancifully imagining her lost boy is a child again, absent from home in his hunt after butterflies, and as, with a bleeding heart, she goes about her household work she sings softly:

How far today in chase I wonder
Has gone my hunter of the dragon fly.

Asist. Pay-
master Ohno.   Supplies   Com.   Capt.
             Wright.   Yonekura.   Kimura.

CREW MEMBERS

CHAPTER 10

Life in Port Arthur

Soon after my return to the ship Commander Yonehara photographed a group, consisting of myself surrounded by my bodyguard—that is, all the men who had been on duty at different times at my camp.

The Russians must have laid an enormous number of mines, for over a thousand had been accounted for by the Japanese, and no doubt there were others still in Dalny harbour. Mine sweepers were very busy after the gale, and I went out with one of the flotillas to peep into Port Arthur again, though on this occasion I was on a destroyer. I went out trawling one day in the favourite fishing ground—the channel which runs between the islands. We hoped to get some tai fish, and we went off in the big sampan, with four sailors to attend to the baiting and work the boat.

We set the trawl (which carried about a hundred hooks) round the base of an island, and the captain suggested that we should land, with our lunch, and leave the fish to catch themselves. Landing amongst the rocks proved no easy matter, on account of the swell, but we succeeded at last, and climbed the cliffs to the rounded summit, where a small flag—a surveyor's mark—was blowing bravely out from a bamboo staff. The herbage was similar to that in some of the sunny nooks on the mountains, and the late autumn flowers were still blooming. The captain and myself filled our arms with flowers and took them back with us to decorate the wardroom table. After lunch we descended the cliff and explored the rock pools. The seaweed was not so brilliant as that found on the English coasts, but there was a very beautiful sea anemone of exactly the bright green colour of the Jersey lizard. The only sign of life on the island was a colony of rock pigeons.

We got into the boat and hauled in the Hue, but no fish were

297

hooked. We had, however, brought with us some dynamite cartridges, and these proved more effective, for we got several bucketsful of fair-sized fish, and among them was one particularly fine fellow of the tunny species.

We returned on board and found the commander making all preparations for sea. We were going to Dalny, and the water shone like glass as we steamed away. Heavy firing was still going on at Port Arthur, but we were travelling in the opposite direction. On account of the mines we had to steer a very long course, and did not head for Dalny until we had sighted Togo's fleet. We passed quite close to Kwang-tan-shan, a double island, consisting of two mountains joined by a silver strand about half-a-mile wide. A small island (Cheesi kwang) nearby looked like a boat at the stern of a ship, and might be compared with the Calf of Man. Right in the centre a black dome marks a huge ocean cave, big enough to swallow a ship, and the entrance to it is guarded by two monster pinnacle rocks. These islands together are about the same area as Jersey, but the only inhabitants are the lighthouse keeper and a few fishermen.

As we entered Dalny Bay the gunboats were busy searching for mines, for there were still many to be cleared out. We anchored in the harbour outside my old ship the *Tainan-Maru*. At four o'clock, however, we weighed again and proceeded to another anchorage, about a thousand yards nearer the dockyard. The captain left to report our arrival to the flagship, where he was informed that the order for leaving the other harbour had been "erased," as he put it, and consequently we were to return the next day. All this lost time would have been saved if we had been fitted with wireless telegraphy, as we could have been communicated with at any time during the passage.

Before leaving the next morning I went to see my old messmates on the *Tainan-Maru*, who greeted me warmly. Everything was the same on the ship except for some changes among the junior officers. I would have liked to remain with my old friends, but it was my duty to keep as close as possible to the scene of active operations.

We anchored again in the "certain place," and I went ashore in order to watch the effect of the land mines which, it was said, were to be used that day. From my point of vantage, I watched the storming, when suddenly the land mine was fired. It seemed to blow a huge section of the hill away, and what was before a symmetrical slope became chaos, and the air was black with falling stone, earth and human bodies. This put a stop to the fighting for a time and a short truce ensued.

We received a telegram from England that day which said:

The Baltic fleet fired on and sunk an English fishing boat in mistake for a Japanese cruiser.

Everyone collapsed with fits of laughter, and there were many who would not believe the story. The next morning our flotilla started out, taking up the usual rendezvous, but nothing of any importance happened except that the Japanese guns set the Russian oil reservoir on fire, and we witnessed a most magnificent sight, the flames leaping high in the sky and the black smoke floating, like funereal plumes, as far as Togo's ships, where it seemed to hang. This fire must have been a serious mishap for the Russians, as they had not much coal or other fuel.

November 3rd is the birthday of His Imperial Majesty the Emperor, and is the most important in the Japanese calendar. On that day both services are entertained at His Imperial Majesty's expense. For the past two or three days I had noticed an air of mystery about the sailors, and on the morning of the 3rd, as I entered the ward-room, the secret was revealed. The room was bright with the bloom of many-hued flowers. There were chrysanthemums of all colours, including blue and green, and the delicate lilac-tinted wisteria hung in graceful clusters and festoons from the beams. They were all made of paper, and in the record time of three days. The panels ornamenting the temporary stage that had been erected were composed of trophies from each part of the ship; the engineer's panel was quaintly designed with spanners, nuts, and other things used in the engine-room; the gunner had his trophy of revolvers, bayonets, and cartridges; the carpenter's was made up of the fire hose, and so on. The back of the stage and its wings and curtains were draped with flags of all nations, the most conspicuous being the Union Jack and White Ensign.

At eight o'clock the ship was dressed rainbow-fashion, as is done in the English Navy, and the forenoon was given up to sports. There were sack races, potato races and the usual items of a sporting programme. There was one very appropriate race. The sailors competing lay in their hammocks, and at the sound of the bugle they turned out, dressed themselves, lashed up their hammocks, and running to another part of the ship, got their rifles and field kit and raced round to the other side, where the deck officer and another ward-room officer inspected them, the prize, of course, going to the first properly-dressed sailor who came in. There were wrestling matches, too, in which the sailors gave an exhibition of their prowess in the art of *ju-jutse*.

At 11.30 all hands (myself included) fell in on the upper deck for inspection, remaining at attention until twelve o'clock, when the salute of twenty-one guns was fired, and we gave three great "*Banzais*" that might have been heard in Port Arthur. As the last puff of smoke floated away the boatswain piped down, where a special lunch with champagne provided by the emperor was served. His health was drunk with wild enthusiasm, and immediately afterwards King Edward's health was proposed, and this toast was received almost, if not quite, as enthusiastically. Being the only Englishman present, I had the great honour of returning thanks. The King of England was the only European monarch who was toasted.

After lunch, chairs and tables were cleared away and the spacious saloon turned into an auditorium. It was crowded to overflowing, for as many of the crews as could be spared from the torpedo flotillas had been, invited. The officers occupied the lockers round the sides of the saloon and the men squatted down in rows on the floor. The acting was really good. The old Japanese drama was presented with all its flowery rhetoric, and also a modern, up-to-date melodrama entitled, *The Russian Spy*. The dressing and acting of the latter play would have done credit to any provincial theatre in England, and, in fact, the chief character looked like an English actor and was a perfect artist.

During the intervals biscuits and sweetmeats were handed round by a humorous tar, who shouted his wares like a hawker, much to our amusement. The evening closed with a sort of variety entertainment, from the organisation of which our London managers might have taken more than one useful hint. Tea and cigarettes closed one of the most enjoyable days of my pleasant sojourn in the Japanese Navy.

The next morning, I went out in torpedo-boat No. 65. I noticed that her mast was stepped abaft the funnel, and I was told that it was to support the derrick in lifting the boat in and out. The winter had come suddenly, and we were all muffled up. The Japanese sailors wore long military great-coats and Wellington boots. The coat has a hood and a cape as well, and a white muffler is worn to protect the throat and mouth, and warm white gloves. I found my furs very comfortable when on board the torpedo-boats.

A mine blowing up in the harbour close to our ship gave us a fright the next day, for we were full of explosives. My prospective trip in another mine boat came to naught, for she got close under a Russian battery during the thick weather, and the fog suddenly lifting and revealing her the Russians promptly put five shells into her and sent her to the bottom, only a few of her crew being saved. As Captain Kamura said, they were getting very clever at shooting from the lower batteries, and had improved their charts and cross bearings so that they knew well where to aim.

A carrier pigeon flew on board, evidently tired out, and a general scramble amongst the crew ensued to secure the bird, but they only succeeded in scaring him to another ship.

We had a quantity of apples and pears on board, which had formed part of the cargo of a would-be blockade runner which had been captured. As we ate them we felt that we had really to be thankful to the Russians for something, although their feelings, had they seen us enjoying the luxuries that were intended for them, would not have been of the pleasantest.

One day, when we were out in the bay, the Russian destroyers and a gunboat suddenly came out of Port Arthur. All the flotillas at once concentrated to meet them, and the cruisers closed in. We indulged in some long-range practice for about half-an-hour and some of our shells told, but the nearest approach to a hit made by the Russians was when a shell fell so close to our boat that it splashed the water all over us. They returned to the harbour, and apparently their coming out had no definite object. It was one of their quite incomprehensible movements, to which we were becoming accustomed.

A queer little Chinese Temple was my excuse for another trip ashore. The compound in which it stood looked like something between a stable and a penny show. Three gods presided over some burning joss-sticks, and they were brilliantly coloured with vermilion, blue and gold. The *frescoes* at the back of the niches in which the gods stood depicted the element over which each of these deities presided. The carving around each shrine was very elaborate, and at the doorway were two pillars of stone on which ancient historical calenders were carved. The yard was knee-deep in stable litter and old coal bags. On leaving the precincts an unusually large contingent of armless, leprous beggars craved our pity and alms, and a few pieces of cash, scattered broadcast, brought an overpowering weight of blessings upon us. Nevertheless, we were very glad to make our escape from the poor stricken creatures.

My Cheesi dog had a tremendous feed of chicken on the chaser that day, which made him look as if he had swallowed a torpedo.

A number of little flags dotted over the islands and cliffs showed

Entrance to Port Arthur.

Liao-tau-shan.

Russian destroyers.

Japanese chasers.

A RUSSIAN RAID.
REPULSED BY JAPANESE
S. W.

RUSSIAN TORPEDO RAID STOPPED BY OUR FLOTILLAS.

that Japan had taken possession of the land and was surveying her new territory. Some of the Russian charts placed the harbour on top of the mountains four miles distant, so that a fresh survey was obviously necessary.

The movements of the Baltic Fleet were duly reported in the ward-room, but it did not in the least disturb the equanimity of the officers. They amused themselves with the gramophone and Go Bang, and predicted a big surprise for the Baltic Fleet if it ever got within reach. General Stoessel, we heard, had sent a message to the *Czar*. Of course, we did not know what the message was, but, taken in conjunction with other signs, we concluded it must refer to the surrender of Port Arthur.

The weather clerk of Manchuria is a lightning-change artist, and the seasons come with astonishing punctuality and suddenness. Winter begins in the middle of November, and on the morning of the 15th we awoke and found the land was duly white with snow. It was quite a pleasant change from the monotonous khaki of the hills and gave the whole country a new aspect, bringing into prominence capes and headlands that were not noticeable before. The shape of the bay, too, seemed changed, for the snow-clad hills brought out the curves of each tiny bay sharply against the blue-green of the water. Liaotan-shan looked like the top of Mont Blanc placed on a jasper table. Everything stood out plainly in the clear atmosphere, and from the deck of the chaser one could discern the Russians as they crouched in the trenches.

The Japanese and Russian trenches had approached so closely, we were told, that in each the footsteps and voices in the other could be heard. The combatants seemed to be very well disposed to each other, the Japanese often throwing cigarettes to the Russians. The black smoke of the Shimosi shells frequently appeared to obliterate them, and we would wait anxiously until it cleared away to see the result. Everyone felt a sense of staleness at certain times, as in most campaigns, and at this time the feeling was very general, for everything seemed to have come to an *impasse*. The enemy would not come out to fight and we could not get in.

One night, however, we had some excitement. At midnight the commodore signalled "chase," and my boy aroused me, saying something about Rooski ships coming out. I rushed on deck, but could see nothing but that we were racing through the water like an express train. Something must be happening, I thought, and enquiring

Mine blowing up.

Russian shell.

MORNING GREETING, RENDEZVOUS B, PORT ARTHUR BAY

of one of the officers, he told me that one of the Russian destroyers had slipped out and was right ahead, steering for a Chinese port. We gradually closed in on him until daylight, when we reached Cheefoo, and saw in the dim light three men-of-war. These turned out to be Chinese cruisers. Some explosions and smoke in another part of the harbour drew our attention, and we found it was caused by the Russians destroying their boat. It was an exciting race, but terribly cold.

The next day, when I returned to the *Nikko*, I heard, a story from some prisoners aboard a *junk* alongside that an English steamer of about 3,000 tons had been blown up by a Russian mine, the survivors being paid to say nothing about it. The *junk* sailed off before I could learn any more, and I was unable to find out how far the story was true.

The arrival of the mail from Sasebo was always a great event with us. *Sampans*, steam launches and boats of all sorts raced from their respective ships to be first alongside.

Christmas was approaching and several of my messmates who had been to England spoke of the English Christmas and how much they enjoyed it. One of them said that when in England at Christmas time he was invited out to dinner, and afterwards they had games and forfeits and kissing. He said that his hosts were very much amused because he did not know how to kiss.

A foreign telegram we received caused much astonishment. It said:

Baltic Fleet one portion coming through the Red Sea shadowed by the English Army.

At last I thought. Army Reform has produced some tangible, and, indeed, striking result.

It was reported that the Russians had only 8,000 fighting men in Port Arthur. Many of the heavy guns were said to be damaged, although they still had plenty of machine guns fit for use. A big German steamer was stopped in the bay by the Japanese cruisers, and, when overhauled, was found to have a cargo of medicine, medical comforts and fur-lined great coats. I saw her start for Sasebo and I decided to make a bid for one of those fur coats, although I doubted if I should be allowed to have one as it seemed likely that they would be served out to the Japanese soldiers.

One of the transports brought presents from the Japanese school children to the officers of the fleet. They were books containing pictures and poems and mottoes, and the drawings were remarkable con-

PATRIOTIC P–Cs. CARDS DONE BY SCHOOLCHILDREN FOR DISTRIBUTION AMONGST THE FLEET.
THE CHILDREN'S AGES RANGE FROM SEVEN TO ELEVEN

sidering the ages of the children (7 to 15) and typical of Japanese art, having the characteristic beauty of line and composition. Fugi, the sacred mountain of Japan, seemed to be the favourite subject, although battle scenes were numerous. There were also several humorous subjects, and each page was signed and stated the age of the artist. It was a beautiful idea, all these children working to show that their fathers and brothers were not forgotten. The books possessed a fascination for me, and I would have liked to possess one.

It may be news to the world, but the Japanese had calculated that this war would last three years, and they have a large reserve of force and material which will carry them on almost indefinitely.

Some very interesting, though unwilling, visitors came alongside one day in one of the torpedo chasers. They were Hindoos from Port Arthur, and they said that they were very tired and afraid to remain in the town. The people, they told us, lived in caves between the houses. It appeared they were servants of the Russian bank at Port Arthur. They were captured by the destroyer twelve miles out. One of our stokers knew a little Hindustani and he drew from them some interesting details of the state of things in Port Arthur. The Russians, it appeared, were short of fuel and no coal could be spared to warm the houses. Food, too, was scarce, and they lived in constant fear of shells. The big shells, the Hindoos said, had sunk one large vessel and about six smaller ones. The garrison hoped that the Baltic Squadron would arrive about February and force the blockade.

The name of the destroyer that captured the Hindoos is *Shinonome*, which means "Eastern Cloud." The names of many of the Japanese destroyers are very poetical. "Morning Mist", "Morning Tide", "Sudden Shower", "Spring Rain", are some of the names, but one of the most curious is *Sirau-Nissa*, which means "Don't Know Light." This is the name of the sea which, so runs the legend, is illuminated by a bright light on dark nights which so puzzled the fishermen that they referred to the light which they could not understand as the "don't know" light, and the sea became known by the same name.

At the request of Admiral Togo, the big guns of the army concentrated their fire on the Russian fleet, and from the signal station it was reported that four or five of the big battleships were moving about the harbour under a full head of steam. It was then confidently hoped that they would come out and we were all standing at the guns in readiness. My station was to help the doctors. I spent the night on No. 67 rolling about opposite Port Arthur.

THE SEARCH LIGHT ON THE
TAINAN MARU.

RUSSIAN MECHANICAL MINE ON
THE DECK OF THE *TAINAN MARU.*

THE DINNER-HOUR ON A
JAPANESE CRUISER. NOTE THE
PETTY OFFICER IN THE
FOREGROUND KNITTING WARM
STOCKINGS FOR THE USE OF THE
ARMY.

CHINESE *SAMPANS* DREDGING UP
COAL BAGS LOST OVERBOARD IN THE
HURRY OF COALING.

I had a talk on religion one day with one of my officer friends. His idea of God was succour or help. His idea of heaven was a place inhabited by the father of priests; but God to the Japanese was nature. They speak of, but do not worship this supreme being.

Often in the evening we had gramophone concerts. We had a lot of Japanese records—songs, and recitations—and among them I recognised the familiar *Geisha* music.

It became absolutely necessary for the Japanese to occupy the mountain known as 203 Metre Hill, for it commanded the forts and the town. There were still some heavy guns to be mounted, and although they were not difficult to mount, the bed, being made of concrete, required about a month to dry firmly, thus occasioning delay.

At last the great attack, the details of which all the world has heard, was made, and the Japanese established themselves on 203 Metre Hill. That proved to be the beginning of the end.

I received a signal the next day as follows:—

Seppings Wright from Commander Yonehara, *Peresbiet* greatly damaged, crew left her; *Retsivan* heeling over on port side, moored by a hawser which is made fast to the land; *Poltava* sunk upper deck awash; one destroyer received one shot.

Port Arthur was in darkness that night, for the first time for nine months. No searchlights were working. The night before Admiral Togo had warned all ships to keep a bright look-out, as the Russian destroyers were expected to come out any time the following night. It was possible that they might try to make a raid, but it was probable they would make a dash for Chefoo and blow the vessels up, the crew either taking refuge on the Chinese ships or on shore.

The end seemed to be near. Japanese troops were waiting opposite Mukden for the rivers to freeze and facilitate crossing, and a signal from the shore stated that the Russian battleships were nearly all destroyed. Port Arthur lay at the mercy of Japan. The Japanese admiral was already appointed as harbour master, although the place was not yet in our hands, but with that thoroughness of organization which distinguishes the Japanese services, the moment the Rising Sun floated over the town the admiral and staff would enter and take over the dockyard and stores.

I sent in my application to go back to Dalny to the *Tainan-Maru*, so that I might see the fall of Port Arthur. Captain Myaki, my late torpedo commander, came to bid me goodbye, for he was off to Japan, the

暁夜左之報知ニ接シ此間至再敵情一報
申上げ度

十二日を
セッピング ライト 殿

日光 東京

昨日敵艦砲撃ノ信果左ノ如シ

戦艦ペレスウォート 大破損 乗員ハ居ラサルカ如シ

全 ヒトウヰザン
非常ニ左舷ニ傾斜シ頭震ヲ防ク為メ陸上ヨリ大索ヲ取ヘ居シリ

全 ボルタワ
沈没シ海水上甲板ニ及ブ

右ノ外一隻二本煙突ノ駆逐艦一隻ニ命中セリ

This is the original signal

blockade being practically at an end. Many of the ships were leaving, and whole fleets of *sampans* were sweeping for bags of coal which had tumbled overboard in the hurry of coaling the flotillas. They gathered a rich harvest, several of the boats sculling ashore loaded to the gunwales. Fukishima, my boy, was at work packing my things. As the regular "correspondent boat" (which, by the way, was one of two torpedo boats that kept up a constant communication between Dalny and the various fleets and harbours) was to leave punctually at 8 the following morning, a friend of mine offered to take me on No. 62, of the 20th flotilla, which would start a little later.

By 9 o'clock my packing was finished and Captain Kimura sent for me to come to the ward room. All the officers were there and the captain bade me *adieu* in the name of the ship, adding some very complimentary remarks. We then drank *saké* together, and I made a little speech thanking them for all the kindness I had experienced while on board.

The *Sevastopol*, the only remaining Russian battleship, came out of the harbour, apparently with the intention of putting to sea and making a desperate dash for freedom; but her captain evidently changed his mind, and she came to anchor in the outer anchorage. It appeared that she had been lying quietly in the dry dock while the Japanese believed her to have been rendered useless by a mine which she struck a few months before. She had, however, been thoroughly repaired and, during the night that we remarked the absence of the searchlights, she was taken out of dock. But between Admiral Togo and the army she had a very poor chance.

At 9.30 I stepped into the steam launch, with farewell "*Banzais*" from my shipmates ringing in my ears. I felt the parting with them very strongly, for they had been good friends to me and had done all in their power to help me, making my stay with them the most pleasant time I have ever spent campaigning. For a long time, the officers and men continued to wave their adieux.

At once No. 62 got outside the harbour, and we darted from wave to wave followed by the remainder of the flotilla. After an hour's tossing we rounded the south point into the calmer waters of Talien-wan Bay. On entering the harbour of Dalny, the *Tainan* was nowhere to be seen, so I had to go alongside the *Fuso*, Admiral Yamada's ship. From the *Fuso* I learnt that the *Tainan-Maru* was mine-sweeping and would not return until the evening, so I went to the *Canton-Maru* and climbed on board. This splendid steamer was formerly a Russian and had been captured off Dalny. The Japanese had made her a machine and repairing ship—a sort of floating dockyard. We ranged up to her alongside the Russian destroyer which had been captured by the Japanese in Chefoo harbour. She was undergoing some slight repairs to enable her to reach Japan, where she was to be put in thorough order before being attached to one or other of the flotillas.

The *Canton-Maru* was commanded by Captain Naicao, a smart looking sailor, who received me very graciously in his own cabin, and ordered lunch for me. His conversation was very interesting, as he was in command of the ill-fated *Hatsuse* at the time she was blown up. He said:

> I was standing on the fore-bridge and at 10 a.m. we struck a mine which did very little damage, but quite enough to prevent her steaming, and we were taken in tow by the *Asahi*. At noon a tremendous explosion shook the ship, and in a minute and a half she sank, carrying down nearly all the crew. The main mast seemed to be projected over the forebridge, and fell, crashing through the deckhouse. I recollect struggling in the water, and being sucked down for about ten feet. On coming to the surface I struck out and was rescued by one of the boats. It was a terrible experience and a great loss, for half the crew perished and the *Hatsuse* was one of our best battleships.

He took me into the ward room, where I amused myself for the rest of the afternoon examining some splendid swords and looking through the pages of a most interesting old book containing drawings of all kinds of swords and showing the different temperings. This book, as well as the finest sword in the collection, belonged to Lieutenant Sata, who told me that he had about seventy swords at home and would be pleased to show them to me whenever I went to Tokyo.

The *Tainan-Maru* was signalled, and by sunset the pinnace of the *Fuso* put me on board. I was warmly welcomed by all hands. Arai (my boy) showed me my old cabin, which looked as if I had only left it an hour before. But the crickets were all dead and the little garden under the window quite woebegone, although the Chinese eel was as lively as ever when stirred up. Captain Takahasi told me he was then employed in minesweeping duty, going out every day at 8.0 and steaming across Port Arthur bay in the search.

Dalny had grown since my last visit, and rows of new barracks had sprung up for the accommodation of the Port Arthur prisoners when

GOING ON LOOK-OUT. MINE SEARCHING
Captain Takaliashi.   Lieut. Kubo.

ON THE BRIDGE OF A MINE SHIP.

they arrived. There was a new harbour master, and his flag was flying on the *Taiko-Maru*, the sister ship of the *Tainan-Maru*. As I have already mentioned, he had been appointed harbour master to Port Arthur, the position he held ten years ago, after the Chinese War. He was confidently looking forward to raising four of the sunken Russian battle ships and adding them to the Japanese Navy.

At 8 o'clock the following morning we started to run the line opposite Port Arthur. The wind blew strongly from the north, which made the work more risky than usual as, in such a wind, the mines were often concealed just under the surface and it seemed likely that we should run on the top of one of them. All the 20th flotilla had taken refuge in Dalny, lying low all day. The extra look-outs were, as usual, at their posts to command a large field of vision, two being in the crow's-nest at the foremast head with a field-glass, three or four stationed on the forecastle, one or two on each side of the boat-deck and one at either end of the bridge.

The wind died down somewhat, and as we returned the look-outs reported a mine in sight. The navigating officer immediately took charge of the ship and manoeuvred her so as to get about 300 yards to windward of the venomous-looking little black spot in the water. The captain and officers were on the bridge, the lieutenant at the range-finder, and, besides the ordinary look-outs, everyone that could be spared came on deck to watch. A sub of the watch mustered on the shelter-deck under the command of the gunnery lieutenant, and at 300 yards the men opened fire. The firing lasted about three minutes, for the motion of the waves made the mine very unsteady. Several hits were recorded, but until the cap was struck no explosion took place. At last the mine blew up with a tremendous report, a thick heavy cloud of smoke arose, and the water was blackened all around by the gun cotton.

We returned to our anchorage at 6, and a collier, the *Westminster*, came alongside, her bows being coated with ice from the frozen spray. Every day we went mine searching, and after the recent gale we expected to find several of these dangerous derelicts. The *Sevastopol* was still outside the harbour, and lay so close to the mine-fields that it would be a dangerous venture to attack her. The weather had become very wintry, and the water in the men's bath-tubs was solid blocks of ice. I noticed, too, that the sea was smoking in parts—a sure sign that it was on the point of freezing.

A fleet of hundreds of *junks*, bound for Chefoo, came in sight, sailing calmly over the waters. Suddenly a mine was found to be floating amongst them, and immediately they fell into the utmost confusion, and it was very amusing to watch them scatter as we rounded to windward to come into position for firing at the mine. It was blown up almost immediately, for the water was smooth.

There was little doubt that many of the *junks* that left Port Arthur laid mines for the Russians. The method adopted is very simple. The caps of the points are removed and the mine is slung beneath the *junk*, the weight of the chain keeping it down. When at the required spot, the anchor is thrown over from the stern, the rope which fastens the mine to the *junk* is cut, and the mine is laid.

The admiral having signalled us to stop in harbour that day, I went ashore in the afternoon. We were expecting orders to proceed to some station in Japan to rest and repair, but we should not leave until the last Russian battleship was destroyed. Dalny was very busy and tugs were panting about the harbour with heavily-laden *junks* in tow. The dock-yard pier was four deep in ships. On landing we made straight for the Chinese town, as I wanted to buy some furs, if any were to be had. The Arctic cold was so penetrating that furs seemed to be the only suitable wear. We passed through a city of commissariat, and mountains of forage and hills of supplies lay alongside the railway to facilitate their transport to the front.

I bought a sheepskin coat, unlined, at a Chinese store, which seemed capable of keeping out the cold, and we then made our way to the square. A Chinese orator was holding forth on some subject which we could not fathom, booths crowded the roadway, shoemakers were sitting at their work, and the tea-stalls doing a thriving trade. The Chinese kettle is a combination of teapot and stove. The fire is made in the kettle itself, the tea being placed in the bowls; scalding water is poured on, and the tea is made. Chinamen must have throats and stomachs of brass, for they drink their tea while it is absolutely boiling.

We went out into the country to see the cavalry drilling. The river was frozen, and on the bridge that spans it we saw a Chinaman with a handsome bird in a beautiful bamboo cage. The bird was singing, and its sweet notes were not unlike those of the lark, but had greater volume and intensity. The Chinaman held the cage at arm's length in the sun, and encouraged the bird by means of a low droning chant. A group of Japanese soldiers stood around, very interested, but at last the Chinaman covered the cage with a blue hood and went off. The soldiers were all muffled in loose greatcoats, with high fur-lined collars.

THE RANGE FINDER. MINE-SEARCHING.

FIRING PARTY SINKING A RUSSIAN MINE, PORT ARTHUR BAY.

In addition, they all wore helmets of soft wool, fitting tightly round the head, a huge woollen comforter and warm gloves. Most of them wore tinted glasses to protect their eyes from the snow glare.

We cut across country to the park and there found a regiment of recruits being taught skirmishing. We also visited the tigers and bears and the temporary mortuary. The mortuary occupied one of the biggest houses in the park. One of the rooms was fitted up as a shrine, and standing on a sort of altar were hundreds of small boxes, each about four inches' square, and containing the ashes of a soldier with his name and regiment inscribed on the front of the box. Two candlesticks and a vase with the lotus flowers stood in front, and a Shinto priest guarded the remains. We made obeisance to the ashes of these heroes, and inscribed our names in the visitors' book.

We returned to Dalny, where we vainly sought for some restaurant, but the only approach to one that we could find was in a dirty store, where a temporary dining-room had been rigged up in the oratory, the altar serving for a sideboard. We had roast fowl, potatoes, rice, tea and four eggs each. Only one of my eggs was eatable, for freshness is not considered essential in China; in fact, a two-year-old egg is esteemed a delicacy.

After our meal we passed through the principal part of the town and crossed a bridge over the railway, all cracked and splintered by a Japanese shell. The troop trains were passing beneath, the soldiers squatting down in coal trucks, but chatting as comfortably as though they were travelling in a Pullman. At one of the shops I bought a cap of sea-otter skin, so that if the winter things I was expecting did not turn up I should nevertheless be well protected from the cold.

On my arrival on board I heard that the torpedo-boats had attacked the *Sevastopol*, and that it was reported that she was sinking. At 8.30 the next morning we started on our usual mine-hunt. A fleet of transports passed us with various stores. The ships belonging to the military authorities have a plain funnel, and their flag is white with a broad zigzag across the centre, and those for the navy bear two narrow bars on the flag. Ships bearing munitions of war fly the government flag with a red ball, the water ship has a blue band round the funnel, and a collier two white bands. We passed a dangerous reef, a long jagged rock nearly a mile long, like a large Eddystone, where the Japanese will certainly put a lighthouse when peace is restored. I felt the benefit of my new furs, being much more comfortable than I had been for some days.

EXPLODING A RUSSIAN MECHANICAL MINE, OFF PORT ARTHUR.

I witnessed a very interesting ceremony in the captain's cabin, namely, the presentation of the long-service medal to the petty officers. The medal is a pointed silver star, and each man was introduced separately, and the captain handed the reward, together with a certificate signed by the emperor himself. Each petty officer received the certificate reverently, it being retained by the recipient for ever, although the medal is returned on promotion to higher rank.

Snow and fog prevented us from seeing the mines and added considerably to the dangerous nature of the work. We sighted another mine sweeper which was running the line which our unfortunate consort was working when she was blown up. All of us, myself included, were anxiously looking out for mines, each hoping to win the good conduct badge which is the reward of the lucky finder.

Two more steamers were sunk in Port Arthur that day, and, with the destruction of the Russian Navy, Port Arthur will be reinforced by 8,000 sailors. Since the capture of one of the north forts the army had advanced some five hundred yards to a second and better position, where they were sheltered from the machine guns. In the evening the news signal stated:

Sevastopol settling down by the head; two torpedoes got home, striking the bows.

The weather became still more severe, our decks being frozen, and the anchor becoming a lump of ice as soon as it was raised from the water. A remarkable piece of organisation is the official weather bureau, and the Japanese are as thorough in this as in all their undertakings. As the army advances weather stations are established, to send information of approaching blizzards, and, in consequence, the troops are never caught by the weather unprepared.

The following day was brilliantly sunny and quite warm—so warm, in fact, that the frozen decks (which were so slippery as to make walking difficult) thawed, and at noon they were streaming with water. The captain promptly seized the opportunity to wash decks.

During the day the captain and officers inspected some Russian rifles that had been captured, and the gunner took one to pieces so that we could examine the mechanism.

Every letter leaving the ships, with the exception of those of the officers, had to pass the censor. This, of course, entailed an enormous amount of work. The men in batches brought their letters to the ward-room, and any officers that were there at the time invariably

First attack on the *Sevastopol*

gave the censor their assistance.

One day a sailor brought me a small English book and asked me to hear him read. I willingly did so, correcting his mistakes and setting him a short exercise. Some of his mates asked me to do the same for them, and soon I had a small class to instruct. I found teaching them both pleasant and interesting, for they were such apt and diligent pupils. The gunner's mate, to show his gratitude for my instruction, undertook to clean my Mauser pistol, and show me how to take it to pieces, so as to be able to clean the mechanism myself when necessary. Another of my pupils presented me with two pictures, really well executed and painted entirely with the ship's paint. He apologised for the fact that the face wanted tinting, but, as he explained, the ship's paint did not include face colour.

Three big explosions, which, although twenty-five miles away, we plainly heard, and, indeed, felt, we learnt afterwards occurred at Double Dragon Hill. Three charges weighing two and a half tons were placed under three angles of North Fort. The first wrecked the moat, driving the defenders to another part of the fort; at the second, which quickly followed the first, the defenders were panic-stricken and rushed wildly hither and thither, while the third destroyed practically the whole side of the fort. Over two hundred Russian soldiers were blown up, and numbers were buried deep beneath thousands of tons of debris. An officer who witnessed the explosions told me that the Russian soldiers went up into the air erect, falling to the earth in all sorts of fantastic postures, like a troupe of acrobats.

We had two or three supernumerary lieutenants on board, and there were a great many naval officers, captains and admirals included, who were in want of jobs, which was remarkable after over a year's hard fighting.

The government report of the torpedo attacks on the *Sevastopol* was read out and listened to eagerly. The first attack was made on the morning of the 12th of December at 12.30, when the flotilla under Commander Kasama attacked, but failed. Two torpedo-boats, under the command of Lieutenant Masato, then ran into range, and discharged their torpedoes. They were met by a storm of shell from the quickfirers, but they felt the explosion of the torpedoes, and thought they had done for the *Sevastopol*; but when day dawned she showed no sign of injury. There were no casualties among the Japanese.

On the 13th, at 2.30 in the morning, another attack was made. The flotilla, under the command of Lieutenant-Commander Arakawa, dis-

LAST ATTACK ON THE *SEVASTOPOL. EARLY MORNING*

charged their torpedoes under a galling fire, but with what effect was not known. During this attack one of the torpedo-boats was struck in the funnel, and a shell entered the boiler room of another, putting her out of action, and she was towed back by her consort. On this occasion, also, no one was killed or wounded. At six o'clock on the same day a third attack was made by a flotilla under Lieutenant-Commander Saki, but the enemy's searchlight was worked so well, as were the quickfirers, that the flotilla returned without effecting anything, but two torpedo-boats under Lieutenant Adachi which ran in close to the Sevastopol at about the same time discharged their torpedoes, but with what result could not be ascertained. Both boats were struck by shells simultaneously, and three men on one of them were wounded.

An engineer officer who was in the fight told me that torpedo-boats Nos. 45, 47, 46 and 49 (a mixed flotilla, working in pairs in the manner I have already described) attacked boldly and approached within five hundred metres (easy tube range) of the *Sevastopol*. Five torpedoes were discharged from Nos. 45 and 47, which undoubtedly got home. The petty officer who fired said he felt in his hand that they had struck.

(This is a curious phenomenon, but every officer I spoke to on the subject assured me that it was a fact: when a torpedo strikes its mark the man who has fired it, if he keeps his hand on the button, experiences a curious feeling in the thumb, but when the torpedo misses he feels nothing.) On retiring the enemy's destroyers opened fire and Assistant-Engineer Koatanahe was slightly injured. Then No. 46 discharged three torpedoes, one of which exploded, but a Hotchkiss shell (47 mm.) struck her, and exploded in the engine-room, killing one of the hands and severely wounding another. No. 49 then made a dash, getting quite close to the Russian ships, which she found (owing to the darkness) with great difficulty. She discharged her torpedoes at the *Sevastopol* and the gunboat *Otvesi*, returning safely after hearing the explosions.

Lieutenant-Commander Esoe, in torpedo-boat No. 42, was in chief command of the flotillas, and his boat led another bold attack. As he was standing in the conning tower watching for the result of a torpedo which No. 42 had just discharged, a shell struck him, completely tearing away his chest and bespattering the conning tower with fragments of his flesh, and stopping the clock. On board No. 42, also, Lieutenant Nakehore and four petty officers were killed by another shell. The lieutenant-commander took command of the flotillas on the death of poor Esoe, and he made yet another attack and then drew off. On the following morning it was signalled that the *Sevastopol* was totally disabled, her bows being on the bottom.

Lieutenant-Commander Esoe was a genial, merry fellow, and when all that remained of him was laid out, his face wore the happy smile that had so often illumined it in his lifetime. His body was sent to Sasebo for cremation, and Japan's loss was a gain to one of the many unemployed officers who had been waiting long and patiently for a vacancy.

On Christmas Eve we went mine-searching as usual, finding two, which we succeeded in destroying, thus bringing up our total of mines to twenty-eight.

An English steamer, the *King Arthur*, succeeded in getting into Port Arthur with a cargo of supplies. She loaded at Shanghai, and coming on to Kinchow, made her way through the only open channel, the Russians having taken up the mines to facilitate their own escape. She lay between the *Sevastopol* and a sunken gunboat.

On Christmas Day Admiral Togo, in deference to the religious scruples of the Christians under his command, did little or no work, and the day was practically a holiday. My Christmas was a particularly happy one, for I received five letters from home and twenty-three presents of cards and flowers made by the Japanese sailors. One of the flowers was a wonderful work of art and also a curiosity; it was a chrysanthemum made of block tin and brass wire captured from the Russians at Dalny. Another of my presents was a beautiful little model of a Russian mechanical mine. The captain, before the officers and men, wished me the compliments of the season, and told me the gifts were from them all. To each gift was attached a card and a piece of coloured paper, folded in a peculiar way, which is called a *noshi*, and always accompanies a present.

The temperature was sixty to seventy degrees in the sun, and the country, glittering in its white mantle of snow, made an ideal Christmas scene. My health was drunk at dinner, which as nearly approached an English Christmas dinner as could be expected. There was roast beef, although no plum pudding, and I was annoyed with myself for not having thought of getting one sent out to me from England, as I should have liked to present it to the mess. Afterwards I was photographed with my presents, and some of the officers were also photographed, posed around the bow gun. Altogether I spent a pleasant and unique Christmas Day.

ROUND THE ARMSTRONG GUN OF A CRUISER.
OFF PORT ARTHUR.

ON THE DECK OF A CRUISER, WITH MY *BANZAI* PRESENTS.

We received news from Port Arthur on Christmas Day to the effect that the Russian second-in-command. General Falke, had died of his wounds, and that our army was preparing for what it was hoped would be the final assault. The enemy's forces were divided, and the Japanese threatened the communication between them.

Admiral Togo's fleet had become very much broken up, for the majority of the ships had returned to their various bases. It is a marvellous fact that, after over a year's active service one month was the longest period of time taken by the Japanese to repair the ships and render them fit for duty again.

I went into the ward-room on Boxing Day and found there the naval tailors from Sasebo. They were very busy showing the latest fashions and patterns, and were doing a big trade in warm clothing. There were a number of officers there, some fitting on warm gloves, others trying ear caps, and several were being measured for new suits. I wanted to buy some warm things, but they had nothing large enough for me, and my struggles in trying to get into the biggest they had caused a good deal of amusement.

I had a very pretty purse with a portrait of Togo on it given to me by my friend Kato, the chief engineer. He and Togo were shipmates twenty-five years ago, when the latter was commander of the emperor's yacht, a paddle-wheel vessel called the *Jingey*, which means "fast whale." Togo apparently has not altered greatly since those days, for Kato said he was always quiet and never talked very much.

A captain with a staff of officers came from Japan soon after Christmas to wait for a ship—probably one or other of the Russians. When I said, laughingly, to the captain, "Which battleship in Port Arthur is yours?" he smiled, but said nothing, and I guessed I had hit the nail on the head.

Six destroyers were now the sole representatives of the Russian Navy. They came outside nearly every day, returning at night. It was rumoured that the garrison was expecting the Baltic Fleet to arrive in about a week's time.

On New Year's Eve I had a new dish for supper—whaleskin. It does not sound inviting, but was not at all bad, well flavoured with vinegar and pepper, and it tasted very much like cowheel. We all sat up to see the New Year in and waiting to ring the bell. It is said that the man who rings it longest and loudest will have luck with his wife. The old custom was duly observed, and a young sailor dreamt that night of the unknown, beautiful, dutiful wife in store for him.

The chief engineer looked into my cabin in the morning to tell me that we should have a ceremonial breakfast. There was, I noticed, a greater variety of food than usual, and there were rice dumplings in the soup which were very tasty. A cup of sweet *saké*, drunk with great solemnity, was really the only ceremonial part of the meal. After breakfast I went to the captain's cabin. It was very prettily decorated in honour of the day, and the rice cake (which is made only on this occasion) was placed on the table with the little pine trees in front of it. Fruit, oranges and persimmons, with leaves of the pine, the bay, the fir, and the fern, were also on the table, which was festooned with strings of white paper and dry seaweed.

A little plum-tree of mine stood opposite the captain's dwarf fern. The rice signified plenty, the bay eternity, the fir evergreen, and so on. The captain and myself were photographed by the chief engineer, taking a five minutes' exposure on account of the darkness of the cabin. The captain paid an official visit to the flagship *Fuso*, bringing back a glowing account of the doings of the army. On hearing the news, the men started "*Banzai-ing*" and all on board were wildly excited.

The second day of the New Year I spent off Port Arthur. The harbour was vomiting forth dark clouds of smoke. There was no mistaking the cause of the smoke. The Russians were burning their ships. The *Sevastopol* we could still see, the water flush with her upper deck and the six torpedo destroyers hovering around her. General Stoessel, I heard, had moved his headquarters to Liao-tan-shan, where the last desperate stand would be made, unless, indeed, the fortress were surrendered, which, in view of what we saw and heard, did not seem improbable.

The next day we heard that the Russians had surrendered, although four destroyers had escaped to Cheefoo, where they were blown up by their own officers. The end had come at last. The determined defence the Russians had made had proved unavailing. Port Arthur was won. Loud "*Banzais*" floated over the sea as the good news reached the ships.

We steamed away to look for a steamer with contraband, which was known to have left Shanghai for Port Arthur and was, of course, unaware of the fall of the town. We could see nothing of her, however, and we heard afterwards that her skipper had thought better of it and returned.

At 4.35 in the afternoon of January 22nd the terms of the surrender of Port Arthur were arranged, being, with a few trifling ex-

THE BURNING OF THE RUSSIAN BATTLESHIPS, AS SEEN FROM RENDEZVOUS B ON THE TORPEDO
FLOTILLA. THE RETSIVAN OUTSIDE IN THE OUTER ANCHORAGE.

ceptions, quite in accord with the Japanese demands. Every detail in preparation for this result had been carefully thought out and provided for, and the chief engineer went in at once to take charge of docks, machinery, ships, etc., a staff of officers and men accompanying him. Each ship contributed to the chief engineer's staff, according to her size, our contribution being one officer and forty men. The necessary gear for raising the ships was already on the way from Japan. All the positions around Port Arthur were being permanently occupied, and the Japanese flag flew bravely from the lofty crown of Liao-tau-shan.

CHAPTER 11

Arrival at Port Arthur

As a big "*Banzai*" in celebration of the fall of Port Arthur was to take place in Dalny, I decided to go ashore and take part in it. When I came to the gangway the captain positively refused to let me go unless I changed my fur cap, because, he said, I looked so much like a Russian that, in the excitement, things might be made uncomfortable for me. So I had to wear my yachting cap, and this and the presence of two officers on duty was sufficient to protect me from any demonstration or insult from anyone who might not know that I was an Englishman. As to being subjected to anything of the kind by the Japanese I did not for a moment think it possible, but there were in the town a number of Chinese of a very low type who would probably think it a meritorious act to hustle or annoy a Russian, and it was the possibility of this that the captain wished to guard against.

The small dockyard tender came alongside, into which I stepped, and we glided off into the darkness. I could not fail to be struck by the brilliancy of the harbour as we neared the shipping, for, during the last few months no lights of any kind had been allowed, and on this evening the outlines of all the ships were illuminated with different coloured lights. The night was still, and although our movement through the air caused a slight chilliness, it was one of the most beautiful evenings of the many I had spent in Manchuria. The coloured lights gave a witchery to the scene, which held us in silent admiration of its fairy beauty.

The smoke from the vessels rolled slowly away in heavy plumes, with scarcely a break until lost in the gloom that surrounded the illuminated area. Dalny was transfigured. Innumerable paper lanterns decorated all the main streets. We made for the principal thoroughfare, through which the processions were to pass, and found ourselves in

IN THE ICE OFF TALIENWAN BAY.

Seppings Wright.   Kubo.   Aihara.

THE ARMSTRONG GUN ON THE CRUISER

the midst of a vast crowd composed of thousands of soldiers from the victorious army and the Chinese and townspeople, who had turned out *en masse*. All the soldiers wore their side arms, and their doing so was no danger to anyone, for there was never a quarrel amongst them, nor did I see a single drunken man. But the Japanese soldiers and sailors are tea drinkers, by choice and from long habit.

The members of the processions were principally Japanese workmen and dockyard hands, but there were many Chinese carrying big lanterns, ringing bells and beating gongs, and generally partaking in the excitement and joy of the occasion. The lanterns were of various designs. Those worn on the head like hats might have been modelled from the ordinary London street lamp. There were at least 2,000 of these "hat" lanterns. Others, of large size, and inscribed with patriotic words, were carried banner fashion and were of a wonderful variety of shape. Some were like the pennons of the knights of olden days, others resembled the ancient Roman eagles, pyramids and Chinese temples.

At intervals, emblematic cars and *tableaux* were carried shoulder high, instead of being drawn on wheels. The procession was, in fact, very like an illuminated Lord Mayor's Show. One of the most interesting things in the procession was a very good model of the *Tacachido*, one of the cruisers that helped to sink the *Rurik*, and the details were wonderfully modelled, even to the searchlight on the bridge, which sent forth its beams and swept and re-swept the faces of the crowd. Fireworks and a bonfire in front of the town hall were the concluding items of the "*Banzai*."

The prisoners at Port Arthur were removed from the town, and I have no doubt they were not sorry to leave the dreadful city where they had so long fought and suffered. I heard, too, that General Stoessel had received a very kind letter from the Emperor of Japan.

For some time, our ship had been short-handed, as a number of the crew had been to Japan for their periodical gun-drill. Throughout the war these drills seem to have gone on as usual.

The *Uji* gunboat captured six Russians in an open boat who were leaving Port Arthur and, no doubt, trying to escape to Chefoo. When the gunboat approached they were seen to drop their arms overboard. They were brought in to Dalny and handed over to the care of the harbour master. They said they were sailors, but from the appearance of their clothing, and the fact that they possessed field-glasses and valuable jewellery, it was suspected that they were Russian officers. Whether they were officers who had refused to give parole, making a

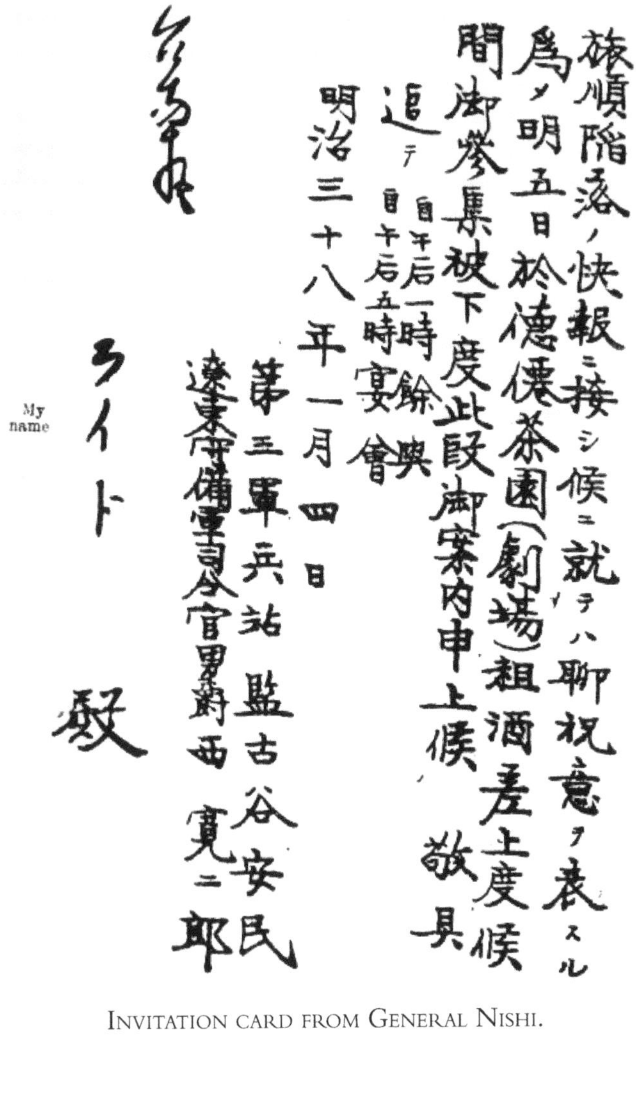

旅順陥落ノ快報ニ接シ候ニ就テハ聊祝意ヲ表スル

為メ明五日於徳儷茶園（劇場）粗酒差上度候

間御参集被下度此段御案内申上候　敬具

追テ　自午后一時餘興　自午后五時宴會

明治三十八年一月四日

第三軍兵站監古谷安民

遼東守備軍司令官男爵西寛二郎

My name

ライト　殿

INVITATION CARD FROM GENERAL NISHI.

dash for liberty, or had dishonourably broken parole, I was unable to discover.

I received an invitation from General Nishi, Governor-General of Liao-Yang, to the *"Banzai"* that was to be held there the same evening, and I went, accompanied by the Chief Engineer, who also had been invited. The Chinese theatre, being the largest available building, was chosen for the function, and we threaded our way to it through the narrow Chinese streets, which were crowded with people. The building was gaily decorated and the national flag floated from every prominent part of it. Presenting our invitation cards, we were shown upstairs to the admiral's box, which corresponded to the stage box in an English theatre. The interior of the theatre was very simple, having only one large balcony.

A number of tables in the arena were set out with fruit plates, *saké* cups and chopsticks, and at every place was a *noshi* with a box of sweetmeats. The entertainment was something in the nature of a music-hall performance, consisting of a long comic song, a little play in which the dresses were very gorgeous and there was a great deal of noise (the principal actor being a tyrannical parent who constantly interposed a fool's bauble of a little drum and three gongs between a loving pair whenever they seemed about to display signs of affection), and finally a lively play by some Japanese actors, which was very funny and clever. One of the actors burlesqued a foreigner sitting à *la Jap*, and the way he imitated the stumble that most Europeans make on rising from the unfamiliar position was very amusing.

While the entertainment was proceeding preparations for the feast were being made, and soon the tables groaned beneath the weight of eatables and an imposing array of bottles. Where everything came from was a mystery to me, for few London caterers could have done more. It was *"cold but capital,"* as Mr. Jingle remarked at the cricket dinner. The only other foreigner besides myself was Colonel Hume, one of the English *attachés* just come from Liao-Yang. He was passing through *en route* for Tokyo. The military bands entered and took possession of the stage, and this seemed to be the signal for the guests to take their places. There were, of course, no chairs. The band played the National Hymn, and we *"Banzaied"* long and loudly when the emperor's health was proposed. I was introduced to a number of officers, amongst them Commander Nishi, one of the staff officers, who said, genially:

"We have all heard about you, Wright, and you shall go to Port

Arthur tomorrow, before anyone else."

This was a most gratifying favour, but unfortunately I was prevented from taking the promised trip, for my ship was ordered on a three days' mining cruise in Kinchow Bay, and the next day the navy was to give a return *"Banzai"* to the army. Admiral Togo invited me to this Naval Banzai, which was held on the *Kimana Maru*, one of the biggest auxiliary cruisers. At 11.45 I left with the captain in the vedette boat, and we boarded the *Kimana Maru*, which presented a very gay appearance, being housed in with flags. Wonderful imitation trees were growing on mossy banks, paper flowers bloomed everywhere, and the whole shelter-deck was transformed into a garden, gay with the beautiful flowers of Japan, all made of paper. Cherry-trees were blooming and the scent of the blossoms filled the air (for even to this detail the wonderful imitation was carried). I was introduced to Admiral Kataoka, commander-in-chief, a small, spare, alert-looking man, and I was presented by him to Admiral Yamada and Admiral Togo— a relation of the great Togo. They all welcomed me warmly, and, as usual, tea and cigarettes were handed round.

The guest of honour, General Ujichi, commanding the division at Dalny, was received at the gangway with military honours, the band playing the usual number of bars of music accorded to an officer of his high rank. After I had been introduced to him we all entered the saloon, or banqueting hall. The smoke room, at the further end, had been turned temporarily into a sort of hall of audience, where the generals and admirals received several Chinese gentlemen, who presented their vermilion visiting-cards, as large as a sheet of ordinary note-paper. This ceremony was soon over, and we were shown to our places at the table. Admiral Kataoka took the head of the table. The variety of uniforms reminded me of the Lord Mayor's banquet, and when I saw the turtle soup and mighty barons of roast beef, the resemblance struck me still more forcibly. My health was drunk and I was called upon for two speeches.

The general gave me his cup, and we drank each other's health. The admiral pledged me, too, and both of them presented me with the bottles and cups from which we drank. Many of the other officers pledged me, and in each case the cup was handed to me as a memento. The captain of the ship made me a present of a lovely dwarf plum-tree, in full bloom. When I left the table, Arai staggered after me with his arms full of the gifts I had received. These included forty *saké* cups and two *saké* bottles, which, I need scarcely say, I value highly.

Aai. Kei. a complement . which couldn't be translated into any known language

a cold collation will be given on board the steamers menu

of them on the steamer instead to congratulate the fall of Port Arthur

will you please come . we ask you to join in Crying Banzai . humbly pay

January 6 & 38 Year 2 Meiji

Vice Admiral Kataoka Commander of the Third Squadron

Saippuge huy ti-Euge Sir Warham Swainson Wentworth & Co. Limited

here . near the Harbourmaster at . 11.30 A.M.

After dinner the band played on deck, and we sat smoking cigarettes and drinking tea. The Japanese do not need alcoholic liquors to make them merry, and there was as much hilarity and fun over the tea as at a "smoker" stimulated by whiskey and soda.

I returned to my ship about 5 o'clock, and Lieutenant Yamanashi accompanied me to talk about my trip to Port Arthur, for he hoped to go with me.

It was ordered that the Japanese sailors who had been captured in the blocking operations of last year and had obtained release at the fall of Port Arthur, were to join our ship. This caused us to postpone our three days' mine-searching in Kinchow Bay, so I went on shore to see the Russian prisoners arrive, having obtained the necessary permit.

We went to the railway station to await the train. Everything for the reception of the Russians was complete. The train drew up at the long platform, and the prisoners, sailors and soldiers, were all squatting down in trucks. The natural ferocity of the *Cossacks* had toned down considerably since their capture, and they obeyed the orders of the Japanese with promptness. The sides of the trucks were lowered to the edge of the platform to make a gangway, and the train was quickly emptied. The prisoners fell in in squads, many of them carrying a miscellaneous assortment of bags, boxes and tins, and nearly all had a kettle slung around their shoulders, and they moved to the clattering accompaniment of these articles.

The doctor inspected them, and those that were passed marched off towards the barracks at the other side of the dockyard, but any suspicious cases of sickness were sent to the quarantine hut for further examination and afterwards distributed in the various hospitals. On my way home I visited one of these hospitals, a long, low shed, the door of which opened on to the road. There were three Russians in the first room, one of whom had half of his face torn away by a shell, but in spite of his terrible plight he was able to ask for a cigarette, which we at once gave him. The others were sick, and seemed very weak. I tried to converse with them, but it was a difficult task.

"Where do you come from?" I asked in English, but none of them could speak the language. So I pronounced the words "Mukden," "Liao-Yang" and "Port Arthur." They understood the first two words because the pronunciation is the same as in Russian, and they shook their heads. Although they did not understand what I meant by "Port Arthur," I did not doubt that it was there they were taken prisoners. I endeavoured to get them to say the Russian name for Port Arthur,

KOJO-TAU.

to learn how they pronounced it. I repeated the words slowly and distinctly several times, and at last their eyes lighted up and they said, "*Port Artoie, Port Artoie.*" I smiled and nodded, and they smiled, too, and I left and entered the next room, where were five Russians. Four were wounded and in bed, and the fifth, who was sick, was sitting on a campstool.

One of these prisoners was a corporal in a *Cossack* regiment, and he seemed a very intelligent man and used the language of signs with wonderful skill. They all could speak a little Chinese. I adopted a different method for discovering where these men were taken. I mentioned General Stoessel, and the corporal promptly pointed to himself and two of the others. Pointing at the two remaining men, he shook his head to indicate that they belonged to some other general. I tried them with Kuropatkin, and the corporal, pointing to himself, shook his head, but waving his hand towards the two he nodded and said, "Kuropatkin, Kuropatkin." I wanted to photograph them, and they quite understood what was required, posing in various attitudes for the purpose. The corporal seemed to be a little vain, for he combed his long hair, put on his coat, which was very smart, and seemed determined to look his best. He apparently understood something of photography, too, and, because the room was rather dark, he made signs that it would be better to have his cap on his knee, so as to show his face.

We left after taking the photographs, with the blessings of these poor fellows and their valedictory "*Sayonora*" sounding in our ears.

The following morning, we steamed off for South Kojo-tau. About 1.30 we sighted what we took to be a large lump of ice, but as we neared it we discovered that it was a mine coated with ice. The hot sun had melted a part of it so that we were able to detect the mine, but it occurred to me that a new terror will be added to the seas if small icebergs with a heart of gun cotton drift over them. This mine was exploded by the first shot, the concussion of the coat of ice presumably breaking the contact tube.

We anchored about 4 o'clock in the big harbour of Kojo-tau. The Chinese brought some baskets of soles and showed complete confidence in the honesty of the Japanese by sending the baskets on board for us to select from before receiving any money. This was most unusual, as John Chinaman generally likes to feel his money before he parts with his goods. Our old friend the *Akagi* and a torpedo boat were at anchor under the lee of the smaller island. On coming to an-

THE CAUSEWAY AT KOJO ISLAND.
THE INHABITANTS HIDING THEMSELVES AT OUR APPROACH.

CURIOUS BOAT RAFTS OR LOGS, KOJO-TAU, GULF OF PECHELI.

chor our cutters were manned and lowered and pulled round the ship to verify all the soundings, the captain telling me that, however good the charts might be, he always satisfied himself that there was plenty of water for his ship to swing in. The group of islands is situated between Chefoo and Port Arthur, and had been the headquarters of a very lucrative blockade-running business. Liao-tan-shan, with its numerous small sheltered coves, is only twenty miles from Port Arthur, and on dark and foggy nights the *junks* could slip over to the beleaguered port and get big prices for vegetables and supplies.

The islands are of rather peculiar formation, and the perpendicular layers of slate with jagged tops were unlike anything I had ever seen. The inhabitants are mostly fishermen (when not engaged in privateering). There are a few farms, and altogether about 300 families. There are no means of communication with the mainland, save by the *sampans* and *junks* which make periodical runs to Chefoo to sell the fish. In spite of the apparent poverty and ragged appearance of the inhabitants I noticed a sleek, contented look about them suggestive of prosperity, and, no doubt, the siege of Port Arthur had been enormously profitable to them. Throughout China all the natives dress alike, but these islanders wore baggy breeches of untanned dog skin, which they never take off during the whole winter.

The next day we ran another course in Kinchow Bay, and one of the most dangerous for mines. Our cruise, however, terminated more quickly than we had anticipated, for the wind blew strongly from the north, making it impossible to detect the mines, and the danger of the weather suddenly getting thick determined the captain to make for the largest island in the group, Kin-shan-tao. It is an important fishing centre, doing a great trade in soles with Chefoo and other large towns on the coast of China. These islands will become necessary to Japan in the near future, and doubtless they will eventually become part of the Empire of the Rising Sun. Kin-shan-tao is two barren, desolate mountains of slate with a small belt of fertile land.

At 4 o'clock the captain and as many wardroom officers as could be spared went on shore with me. We filled two cutters and landed, to the astonishment and fear of the islanders, who promptly closed their doors. The beach was kept in very good order, the *sampans* being drawn up on one side, and the big junks on the other. A high causeway, rugged and irregular, fronted the beach, and on this the gates of the compounds opened.

Among the boats I noticed some that were very antiquated—mere logs with rough side-rails. Nets and other fishing implements were littered about the boats. As in Manchuria, there were no roads, only rough tracks leading from one part of the island to the other. Each small hamlet had its own temple or shrine, and the city of the dead lay close to the chief village in a small copse planted with trees at regular intervals. On a sort of terrace by the shore was stowed the working-gear of the big *junks*, which were themselves drawn up in regular file, their high, square prows throwing their shadows upon the strand.

We followed the western track, which led us over a rough shoulder of sharp, jagged slate, from the top of which we obtained a fine view of the cultivated area of the island and the cycle-shaped beach, ashy-grey where the tide ebbed and flowed. Beneath the shadow of the further mountain there nestled a small village, the land around which, consisting of from 20 to 30 acres, seemed to be common property, as there were no boundary lines. The captain had gone on ahead, and when we arrived at the village we found that he had gone on to the third and last village. We followed, and found him inspecting a *silo* with the old Chinese farmer, who was explaining its use.

This village, like the others, was crowded. As in most Chinese towns, the people seemed too many for the houses. We wandered round the place to see everything that was to be seen, the only member of the party who did not accompany us being the gunner's mate, who had borrowed my Mauser pistol and was busy stalking the village magpie, apparently the only bird on the island. There was some business going on in the village, and in particular we noticed a hawker sitting on a very small stool between two boxes, smoking his pipe and displaying his wares, but there was nothing very tempting, the goods being principally shoddy jewellery and imitation jade. It soon became evident that the inhabitants thought I was a Russian, for an evil-smelling crowd had collected around me to stare. I bore the ordeal pretty well until a man with dog-skin overalls joined the sightseers, when the stench of his half-cured, wet nether garments became too much for us and we all scrambled back to the beach, after having spent an hour and a half in one of the unknown parts of China.

We sighted no mines on that day's cruise, but kept a steady course, and 12 knots an hour brought us to the usual anchorage at 5.30, when Arai and myself were soon busy preparing for my trip to Port Arthur. Lieutenant Yamanashi came from the *Fuso* to tell me that the admiral had given him orders to accompany me, and he had called to ask what arrangements I had made. He apologised for the early hour that

KOJO-TAU ISLANDS.

BLOCKADE RUNNERS, KOJO-TAU ISLANDS, GULF OF PECHELI

it would be necessary to start, but for that, he said, I must blame the military authorities who controlled the train service.

"The train starts," he said, "at 6.30, and the picquet boat will leave in time to catch it."

He then presented me with a map of Port Arthur, as he said it would be interesting to mark out our course.

"And," he added, "I will write the names of the forts and places we visit in English for you."

It was dark when Arai called me, and I went aboard the picquet boat, which steamed alongside the flagship to pick up Yamanashi and an orderly. Dawn was just tinting the horizon as we reached the military pier, from which we walked to the railway station. At the further end of the town we met a number of naval and military officers, all bound for Port Arthur, and amongst them I met my old friend the captain of the *Kimana Maru*, bluff and hearty as ever. There was a long delay, as some trains of Russian prisoners were expected. These arrived at 9 o'clock, and at 9.15 when they had discharged their unhappy freight we steamed out. Soldiers were in charge of the stations all along the line. At the junction we met the train from Liao-Yang, which was made up of trucks and horse-boxes.

A number of wounded Japanese were packed in the horse-boxes, in the sides of which square holes had been roughly cut for ventilation and light. Our journey resembled a triumphal progress, for nearly all the Chinese in the country through which we passed turned out to see the train, and, of course, to "*Banzai*." I noticed that whenever I showed myself at the window the enthusiasm increased, and I was beginning to feel that my own estimation of my importance perhaps erred on the side of modesty, when Yamanashi said:

"They have all turned out to see General Stoessel, who is coming back in this carriage."

The people, clad in blue and red, made a fine splash of colour in the monotonous landscape. We passed a frozen lake, its glassy surface gleaming in the sun like a polished mirror, and all along the dusty roads were strings of horses and the celebrated Chinese transport-carts—clumsy vehicles drawn by miscellaneous teams of donkeys, horses and cows. In one instance I noticed a dog straining along as leader. Very few trees were to be seen, and those only grew in the villages and graveyards. Bird life was represented solely by chattering magpies, each village housing a pair, whose ragged nest was generally to be seen in the tallest tree.

證明書

英國「アームストロング」會社ノ員
英國人 「ライト」

右ハ從来觀戰ヲ許可シ聯合艦隊
ノ艦ニ乗艦セシメ居ルモノニテ確實ナル
人物ナリ今般旅順陥落ニ付其現況
視察致度者願出候ニ付右証明候也

明治三十八年一月五日

第三艦隊司令長官片岡

We stopped at a station to allow two trains full of prisoners to pass. I noticed that they contained mostly sailors, and I concluded that there must be very few prisoners left in Port Arthur, as the sailors were to be the last to leave. They were, on the whole, very quiet, but some were cheerful and jested with their sprightly guards. Children from the village trooped out to "*Banzai*" us, and the men of the regiment that was travelling in our train amused themselves by throwing pieces of biscuit and pickles to them. I saw one soldier lean down to give a paper of sugar to a little girl, who tasted it, threw the paper down and went off disgusted, making wry grimaces.

These poor little girls hobble along on their heels, their feet are so tightly bandaged, and the pain caused by walking must be excruciating, and they twist the poor, deformed stump at all angles to ease the pressure. On leaving this station the train skirted Pigeon Bay, with its picturesque islands, and the journey ended at a station about seventeen miles from Port Arthur, the remainder of the line being damaged. Here I met several of the correspondents who had come to see General Stoessel. As the crow flies, the distance from the town was only three Japanese miles, but the Japanese, liberal in this as in everything, give many furlongs to their mile, and measured by the English standard it was about fifteen miles.

There was a great deal of bustle and preparation at the station, which was decorated with evergreens, and it seemed strange to see a number of *droskies* driven by Russian drivers, clad in greatcoats, Russian boots and fur caps of the *Cossack* type. The train drew up between two lines of Russian prisoners, numbering about two thousand. They were standing easy, in some cases sitting down making tea.

Among them servants were pushing their way with portmanteaux, dressing-bags and other European baggage, which seemed strangely out of place on this dusty Manchurian station. A group of Japanese officers, drawn up at the door of the station-master's office, waited to receive the Russian commander-in-chief. Some temporary sheds had been erected to accommodate the earlier Russian arrivals, and it was a painful sight to see the ladies and children there, the former dressed in mourning and the children, in happy, careless innocence, playing merrily near, failing to realise the awful tragedy that had afflicted their mothers.

Presently the station was cleared, and everyone stood at attention as a tall, fine-looking man, upright, and with somewhat cynical features, marched through with firm, deliberate tread, acknowledging the salutes of the Japanese officers as he passed. It was General Stoessel, the hero of Port Arthur. The Japanese, with chivalrous consideration, avoided as far as possible anything that might emphasize the brave general's unfortunate position, and with the exception of the guard of honour and a few soldiers, whose duties necessitated their presence, the Japanese troops were drawn up among the foothills, a mile away. A special room had been prepared for the Russian general, to which he was at once conducted, and there he received his staff, giving them his last orders.

When the baggage had all been stowed on the train the officer in charge politely informed General Stoessel that they were ready to start, and the general and his wife and children at once took their places, followed by the staff. The remainder of the prisoners filed in and the train steamed out of the station amidst the hearty *"Banzais"* of the Japanese. All the Russian officers wore their swords, in accordance with the terms of the surrender, and were in new greatcoats, looking very smart and holding themselves proudly.

From the station Yamanashi and I, accompanied by a couple of Chinamen with donkeys bearing our baggage, set forth on foot towards General Nogi's headquarters, procuring on our way permits authorising us to pass the picquets. We reached the village close to headquarters, and made our way to the office of the naval *attaché*.

The road in front had been converted into stables, some rough sheds which had been erected sheltering the horses belonging to the staff. Two of these animals were pointed out to me as General Stoessel's chargers; one a serviceable bay, rough-coated, the other a grey Arab of about fifteen hands. Entering the house, we saw, in the front room, a fat woman engaged in cooking. The room seemed to be kitchen, dwelling and sleeping-room combined. Turning to the right, through a doorway, we found two small rooms leading into one another. In the first were some sailor orderlies, and in the second the commander, who was sitting on a high bench close to the window, studying a plan. A small brazier stood by his side, at which he lighted his cigarette, and warmed his fingers from time to time.

The room had quite a cosy appearance, hangings of matting concealing the dirty walls. On the floor, in a shallow depression about eighteen inches square, a charcoal fire smouldered, warming the atmosphere. The window was papered, instead of being glazed, in order to moderate the glare of the sun, and also to ensure privacy. By telephone and telegraph the commander was in constant touch with

THE NAVAL BRIGADE RETURNING FROM PORT ARTHUR

WOUNDED OFFICER GOING TO THE REAR.

the authorities, and could communicate with Tokyo in ten minutes. We drank tea, smoked and chatted pleasantly for about an hour, while a messenger was taking my card to General Nogi. He returned with the message that the general was away "on business" (in the Japanese services this expression is used instead of "on duty"). We discussed the situation and the respective advantages of pushing on to Port Arthur at once or stopping at the village for the night and resuming our journey in the morning. We decided to go on at once.

Preceded by the donkeys we left the village, my appearance creating much interest among the natives and Japanese soldiers, for my fur coat and cap gave me an appearance not unlike that of a *Cossack*. The Japanese soldiers, to use an American expression, could not "size me up" at all. We passed the artillery park, with its silent monsters whose mouths had so lately breathed forth shot and shell into the forts and trenches of Port Arthur, and I was anxious to take a snapshot of the great weapons, but the sentry forbade.

My friend pointed out the advantages of the place from a strategical point of view, but my sense of the artistic compelled me to appreciate more the marvellous beauty of the grand mountains than their adaptability to the requirements of modern armies. As the sun declined we entered a sort of *khor*, or defile, walking in the dry bed of a torrent. The valley was littered with scrap iron, the fragments of Russian shells harmlessly spent among the rocks and boulders. The Japanese big guns, using smokeless powder, were well sheltered behind the dip of the hills which ran into this gorge, and they were the guns whose slight fumes I could detect from my mountain top, but the guns themselves I had always failed to locate. It soon became evident that we should not reach Port Arthur that night, but Yamanashi comforted me by saying that we should be heartily welcomed in any of the camps. While inspecting a big gun and its carriage, which blocked our pathway, a naval officer rode towards us on horseback, and I at once recognised Commander Nishi.

"Why," he said, "if s old Wright! Don't you bother about walking, old chap, I can get you all the horses you want and you can ride the rest of the way into Port Arthur."

But I declined his offer, explaining that I could see more on foot than on horseback.

"But you can't possibly get to the town tonight," he said. "You had better go and call on my cousin, General Ichinohe, who will be very pleased to see you. He has already heard a lot about you. His camp is on the side of the next mountain, about 2,000 metres off."

He left us, saying that we should be sure to meet again ere long, and we continued our journey. The sun had just gone down behind the hill, and faint, gauze-like streaks of smoke hung over the defile, linking the hills as with fairy bridges.

As we turned into the valley a busy scene met our gaze. Soldiers were at work everywhere. Some were cooking, others washing, and there were all the cheerful sounds of a busy camp. Squads were falling in for picquet and night duty, and the sharp notes of the bugle rang loud and clear at the head of the valley, where a regiment was mustering for a march north. Batteries of artillery were also rumbling off, and in the distance a cloud of dust showed the position of the advance guard. These troops were destined to take part in the great Battle of the Shaho.

This camp, unlike the others, had been in the danger zone, and well within the range of the enemy's gun and rifle fire; consequently, the soldiers were all living in caves and bomb-proof shelters. Even the lavatories were in deep pits with bomb-proof roofs and sides. A few tents, however, had been pitched since the surrender. We witnessed a sad scene on the other side of the valley, where soldiers were performing the last sad offices for their fallen comrades, the bodies being disinterred and carried to the ovens for cremation.

We directed our steps to the headquarters of the 6th Brigade. I had heard often of General Ichinohe, the gallant officer who, sword in hand, was wont to spring to the head of his troops and personally lead them to the attack. He was remarkable for his habit of wearing a white *obji*, or band, which made him conspicuous to his men—and also to the Russians. He possessed to the full the spirit of the old *Samurai*. We ascended to his quarters by a number of steps, roughly cut over the flat roofs of the bomb-proofs, threading our way to a second steep pathway, at the end of which, on a little platform quarried out of the hillside, was the general's house. The New Year customs had evidently been strictly observed by the general, for half-a-dozen young fir-trees were planted in the cases of shells which had failed to burst and made excellent flower-pots.

The house was half cave and half hut, leaving a tiny space for a garden—surely the most unique garden in the world. In the small enclosure, besides the trees, Russian shells of various sizes and shapes were arranged like a small shrubbery, and against the low fence trailed a solitary spray of hardy creeper. The door opened at the side into the little garden. The interior was a model of a Japanese house, the floor being raised a few inches, leaving a square depression by the doorway for the removing of boots. The general was writing, seated on the floor in front of the usual low table. He had, apparently, just finished his supper, for the remains were on another table beside him. He protested at my taking my boots off, but I insisted and crept forward, saluting him in Japanese style, that is, bowing in a kneeling position.

Tea was served, and through Yamanashi I entered into conversation with him. He said he had heard of me, and was very pleased to meet me. Would I sleep there? If so, he would at once give orders for my accommodation, although he was afraid his means of making me comfortable were very limited. He asked me a number of questions about my family, and told me of his. I then asked him to tell me something about his fighting exploits, but on this subject he was extremely reticent.

"If you wish to see the forts," he said, changing the subject, "I will send my orderly with you tomorrow. He has been through all the fighting with me and can explain everything."

I thanked him for his kind offer, and he handed me cigarettes and cigars, himself smoking the small silver pipe. Hot *saké* was brought in, and we pledged each other, and then, remembering that he was busy when I entered, I took leave of him. He sent his *aide-de-camp* to take charge of me, a charming young fellow, who had been wounded in the head by a piece of shell during the final attack, and was still wearing a bandage. He found us quarters in a bomb-proof on the second tier. It seemed rather insecure, wobbling whenever we moved, but it was very comfortable. It was draped with mats, and a pile of red blankets and a glowing brazier made it a cosy place in which to pass the chilly night.

Cigarettes, oranges, sweetmeats, and a bottle of *saké* were sent to us by the general, to which Yamanashi, the *aide-de-camp*, and myself did full justice. But these were merely a preliminary, for the dinner that followed was as good as if we had been in Tokyo. There was ham, eggs, rice, fish, omelettes, and last, but not least, a sort of haricot of beef and Chinese cabbage. This final dish was sent not merely to satisfy our hunger, for the Japanese attach to it a special significance. It is intended to express the sender's feeling of great friendship for the recipient, and I much appreciated the general's kindly sentiment. The *aide-de-camp* apologised for the unavoidable absence of his chief, saying:

"I am deputed to represent him, and we are going to eat together

351

a dish of stew which we shall also cook."

A brazier of charcoal was brought in, and on this was placed a pan. Slices of raw beef, cut very thin, vegetables, sauces and condiments were placed on a table by the side, and with our chopsticks we placed the meat and vegetables in the pan and added water, sugar, salt and *soyu*—an excellent sauce peculiar to Japan. The meat was turned over from time to time, and when it was cooked, each of us selected the piece he fancied, and of course could suit his own taste as to whether it was well cooked or underdone. It is a dish that is only eaten by intimate friends. Having heard of the custom I understood its significance, and felt much honoured at such a mark of esteem.

The orderly brought in more blankets and another brazier, together with candles and matches, and I lay down and fell into one of those pleasant, dreamless sleeps that generally follow a fatiguing day.

The sharp sound of the bugle awoke us in the morning and we arose at once. Everything necessary for my comfort had been thought of, even to an extra large basin of hot water. I only managed to get a "lick and a promise," however, for the water froze on my towel. Icicles, too, quickly decorated my tooth-brush, and I was glad when my toilet was finished. Outside, groups of men were trying to perform their ablutions at the ice hole in the stream. Every man was most particular about cleaning his teeth, taking a long time over it and walking about with the toothbrush sticking out of his mouth and giving a vigorous scrub from time to time.

After breakfast I went to wish General Ichinohe "*Syanora*." I found him outside his quaint garden. We chatted together for some time and he again expressed his pleasure at meeting me. He also made me a present of some warm red flannel underclothing and a pair of mits, knitted by one of his daughters. In such weather a more acceptable present could not have been made. His orderly turned up in heavy marching order, and with final adieux I left him and started on my tour of inspection.

Masses of troops were mustering in companies and regiments preparatory to marching north, and also a number of men were practising the various bugle calls. I asked the orderly why there were so many buglers, and he said that such a large number of buglers got killed that they were constantly compelled to train new ones. We made our way up the dry bed of a *spruit*, at every angle of which were holes and shelters and also shell splinters, caps and bloody rags—striking evidence of the heavy gun fire which had been brought to bear on the place.

THE DOCKYARD, DALNY.
THE FIGURE IS MYSELF, IN FURS.

ENTRAINING GUNS FOR HARBIN

MOAT ROUND THE DOUBLE
DRAGON FORT. THE WALL IS
SIXTY FEET HIGH AND DEFENDED
AT THE BOTTOM BY QUICKFIRERS.

RUSSIAN GUN ON DOUBLE
DRAGON FORT. NOTE THE
BREECH BLOCK IS OUT, AND SHOT
IN TRAY, SHOWING THE HURRIED
FLIGHT OF THE RUSSIAN
ARTILLERYMEN.

But the Japanese soldiers were fast clearing everything away, for the importance of hygiene is fully realised in the army, and nothing is ever left to become a danger or even a nuisance. To this is largely due the wonderful health of the army, which has astonished everyone.

Where this *spruit* narrowed and became too small, the Japanese sappers' wonderful work began, and we entered miles of rifle trenches and parallels which were a marvel of human industry. The work involved by this extensive sapping must have been enormous. In some parts the ground was tunnelled, in others huge beams of wood and sand had afforded the soldiers shelter from the storm of projectiles. We followed the trenches of these marvellous approaches until we came to a fort which was named after General Ichinohe. It was not a permanent work, but it had been a position of great strength, being covered by machine guns and rifles from a dozen other forts, and, further, it had a bolt hole (a deep, well-protected trench as broad as a Devonshire lane) through an opening in the old Chinese wall. This Chinese wall was, with the addition of sandbags, a perfect defence for riflemen and for machine guns.

A deep ditch outside added to its strength, and shellproof dens were excavated on the inside which afforded shelter for the defenders. In almost a straight line, about three hundred yards higher, was Signal Hill, with the Japanese colours blowing bravely out in the south wind and a *kharki* sentinel standing motionless between two guns of large calibre. One of these guns had about three feet knocked off the muzzle, the elevating gear of each was destroyed and they were seared and scored, and in some places actually fused by the Shimosi powder. Port Arthur harbour, with the dockyard and sunken battleships, lay beneath us.

Following the ridge built up of sandbags with loop holes, and further protected by barbed wire, we turned downwards to the military road, which was beautifully made and strongly fortified. There we halted to survey a scene of devastation unparalleled in the annals of the world. For miles the whole of the mountain tops had been converted into piles of debris, their original character and shape being completely destroyed. In places the earth was so riddled that it actually quaked like a dry quicksand as we walked over it. It seemed as if some Titanic stonebreaker had been at work. Here and there lay fragments of guns and their carriages, and shells, bloodstained clothing, and all the litter of a battlefield mingled with the mass of debris. By the side of the road a trench ran, and caves had been excavated in the mountain side and supported by huge beams. Several heaps of brick and portions of masonry showed the positions of the kitchens, for it was in these dens that the heroic Russian defenders lived.

We followed the road to Double Dragon Fort, the scene of the disastrous explosion. The broad moat would have disheartened any other soldiers in the world, but the Japanese Army attacked it again and again, yet it was only when the mines had done their work that they were able to enter. The original shape of this fort was difficult to discover, for it was as if a volcanic eruption had occurred altering the contour of the land. We entered the fort through a small door hewn in the rock, and a steep incline with steps at long intervals took us to the top.

On entering the doorway, we noticed a long gallery, loop-holed for machine guns, and a similar gallery ran around the summit. The battlements were of solid concrete, but they and the guns were quite destroyed and looked as though a tidal wave had passed over them. I entered one of the bomb-proofs, beneath the bed of the guns. It was lined with big baulks of timber and was designed for the gunners to creep into when the fire became too hot. It reminded me of Cardinal Balne's cage, for it was impossible to sit, stand, or lie down in it.

We made our way to where the northern corner of the fort had been, but nothing was visible but debris, shreds of flesh, bones and scraps of uniform—grim testimony to the awful nature of the explosion. At the other corner a deep hole had been blown out of the side of the mountain. We climbed down the hundred yards or so of slope to see the subterranean passage, but found it choked with rubbish.

We returned to the military road, for we had seen enough at Double Dragon Fort. The whole road and the trenches were a continuous line of wreckage, and we noticed bloodstained stretchers, half-eaten pieces of black bread, and boots scattered everywhere. As we reached the gates of the city we saw that the last formidable obstruction was a number of trees, laid boughs outwards, *zareba* fashion, and barbed wire. It was there that the Japanese made a rush to capture the city with their swords, but they had to retire, leaving the plain strewn with their dead and the wire entanglement broken down by the weight of its ghastly burden. We passed through the gates, which were merely rough pointed stakes with a palisade of the same material on either side. A number of quickfirers studded the hillside from the emplacements that commanded the entrance.

Outside, a ditch and glacis completed the defence works. A short

MY DROSKI IN PORT ARTHUR.

RUINED BY A SHELL. THE
WRECKED MUSIC HALL IN WHICH
THE RUSSIAN OFFICERS WERE
ENJOYING THEMSELVES ON FEB. 8,
1904.

FRIENDS AND FOES. JAPANESE
SOLDIERS ASSIST THE WOUNDED
RUSSIANS, PORT ARTHUR.

JAPANESE PICKET IN PORT
ARTHUR.

distance inside the gate on the left was the site of one of the arsenals, a heap of cartridge cases, quickfiring and rifle, showing the completeness of its destruction. The heap had a mildewy appearance from the effect of the guncotton, and there were lumps of brass which had melted and cooled into curious shapes. A few hundred yards below there were more bomb-proofs and cave dwellings, and nearby was the Russian hospital. Since the surrender, however, the town had become full of hospitals, the Red Cross and the Japanese flag, flying side by side, denoting their positions. The road wound round the foot of a hill, on which some very handsome houses stood, not much damaged, but the old town, which was built by the Chinese, had suffered severely.

In the square a solitary *drosky* stood, and Russians, Chinese and Japanese crossed and recrossed the *plaza*, and ladies and children walked and drove about in perfect confidence and security. No houses had been looted, for the Japanese sealed them up immediately on taking possession. Anyone found in one was at once arrested and taken before the authorities. We passed through the square and found ourselves in the main street. There many of the houses showed signs of the terrific bombardment. The music hall was smashed in and completely wrecked, being, like most of the places where the chief damage was done, in a direct line with the dockyard and ships, and, in consequence, struck by the shells that fell short of the harbour. In the roadway huge holes had been torn by these shells.

A sharp turn brought us to the esplanade and harbour. The Russian ships were lying aground, the masts and funnels being upright, which made me think that they were not seriously damaged. Along the waterside were warehouses, offices and the railway station, with a number of engines and rolling stock. These had been damaged principally by the Russians themselves, but there were some characteristic markings of Japanese shells. The anchor of the *Retsivan*, which had been planted in the roadway, had dragged and ploughed through the hard macadam with the weight of the ship as she sank. The *Bayan* cruiser faced the harbour entrance, which was still draped with a torpedo net.

We crossed another bridge and, entering the dockyard gate, reported ourselves to the officer in charge. The dockyard staff were occupying the official residences of the late harbour-master, and Yamanashi and I were told off to the quarters of the chief engineer. We entered a long puzzling passage, rather like a cloister, at the end of which was a small hall, which had been turned into a kitchen. We were then ushered into a dining-room of fine proportions, divided in the centre by a handsome carved open-work screen, supported on two massive pillars. One side of the room was bulging in from the effect of an explosion outside. In the left-hand corner, standing against the wall, a Russian stove reached as high as the ceiling and gave a generous warmth.

Two beds, with a press between, stood by the side wall, the further end was furnished with a very handsome sideboard, and by the side of it was a third bed. Two windows lighted the apartment, and at one was a writing table, and under the second were two box mattresses. There was also a very handsome cockatoo in a cage, which one of the officers was teaching to say "*Banzai*," but, being a Russian, he found it difficult. In the centre of the room stood the dining-table, seven chairs, a settee and two saddle-bags. Two occasional tables in black lacquer ornamented with designs of mother-of-pearl completed the furniture of the room. The engineer and some officers were seated around the table smoking cigarettes and doing their business. The chief engineer greeted me very warmly, and introduced me to the other members of the mess.

In the evening I walked along the water's edge to the new town, where all the houses seemed to be turned into hospitals. The harbour is very beautiful, and Liao-tau-shan, with its 1,500 feet, dominates the whole bay. Tiger Island lies right in front of the town, forming the two entrances to the harbour, and Golden Hill, on the opposite side of the harbour's mouth, protects the dockyard from the sea. The sunken *Palada* was lying just beneath, and four iron smoke stacks rising from a blackened heap of scrap iron was all that remained of the great floating oil tank. The sunken battleships—helpless monsters—seemed to fill the small anchorage. Three hospital ships, one half sunk, were anchored just under Tiger Island, and funnels and masts projecting from the water marked the graves of several small craft.

The new town is beautifully laid out with fine streets and boulevards, and there is also the beginnings of a public garden. It was very pathetic to see the number of masterless dogs, and I noticed a beautiful Gordon setter wandering restlessly round the cemetery, every few moments sitting down on his haunches hopelessly and howling dismally. But these poor animals had kind protectors in the Japanese.

It was difficult to realise that the town had changed hands so recently, for perfect order was maintained and many of the tradespeople were doing a brisk business. There was no looting or rioting, and children went to school and ladies walked about in perfect security. There was a fair number of *droskies* on the stands, but of course the military had the first claim on these, and they had ordained that no one might hire one for more than three hours. This was a necessary precaution, so that if any emergency arose and the government required the horses, they could be collected in a very short time.

We got into a *drosky* driven by a good-looking young Russian, who was a bit of a humourist. He rattled us along at ten miles an hour, shouting at everybody and everything in the way. A regiment of soldiers was coming along in front of us, and I naturally expected our noisy *droskyman* would give way, but not a bit of it! He continued his noisy ejaculations and the whole regiment made a half turn out of our way! I mention this incident to point out the absence of anything approaching arrogance on the part of the conquerors. A military occupation usually results in a certain amount of official tyranny, but these model soldiers seemed to efface themselves, leaving most of the policing of the city to the Chinamen.

DECK OF THE *POLTAU*, SHOWING BAGS OF COAL AND SLACK FOR
SHELL PROTECTION, WHICH PROVED INEFFECTUAL.

INSIDE THE BARBETTE OF A RUSSIAN BATTLESHIP AT PORT
ARTHUR HARBOUR. THE TOP WAS BLOWN OFF BY A MINE,
PLACED THERE BY THE RUSSIANS.

CHAPTER 12

I Visit Admiral Togo

At 7.0 the next morning our household awoke. There were no baths, but in the hall—or kitchen—outside our sailor-men provided us with a big basin of hot water. After breakfast Yamanashi and I discussed our plans, and the Chief Engineer very kindly placed one of the captured steam launches at our disposal, so that we might inspect the battleships.

We first visited the *Palada*, which lay exactly opposite the harbour-master's house on the other side of the inner harbour.

We got on board, and found that she had been set on fire. Coals, coal-bags and old hawsers, all covered with sheets of iron, had failed to protect the decks, one shell going through the lot as easily as if it were sheets of paper. Everything had been soaked in oil, and the wood of the deck burnt, buckling the iron deck beneath and leaving the lines of rivets sticking out, making our walk over her very unpleasant, being constantly tripped up by them. The upper works were much damaged, but the bottom seemed to be sound.

The *Peresviet* was the next, and we boarded her with some difficulty, as the accommodation-ladder swung loosely and all the gratings were gone. The deck was a scene of confusion. As in the case of the *Palada*, it had been saturated with oil and burnt out. The fore-turret, or barbette, was partially destroyed and the guns and gear smashed, although the guns seemed as if they might be rendered serviceable. The upper part of the barbette was partially blown off, and one of the heavy top plates had been deposited on the deck. The remaining part of the barbette was loosened and looked like a bursting pomegranate. The bridge was destroyed and the conning-tower completely wrecked.

The fire had scorched and blackened everything and apparently a shell which had burst in the conning-tower had also perforated the deck in many places. All the ironwork in the vicinity was cut to ribbons, like the rags of a topsail blown from its bolt ropes. What the Japanese shells left, fire had made havoc with. In one place on the bridge the fire still smouldered, as one of our sailors accidentally discovered by standing on the spot. The funnels, too, had suffered, one of them being but a distorted mass of scrap iron. The after-bridge was much in the same condition as the fore-bridge, but most of the shell damage had been obliterated by the fire. The bottom of the ship was sound, but what had happened in the engine-room was a mystery which could only be revealed when the water had been pumped out.

On the *Retsivan* the damage was very similar. The tops of the barbettes were completely blown off, and the working gear of the guns smashed. We got up on the top of the ruined turret and walked round, at the risk of our necks, to have a thorough look into this well of destruction. The bridges were not so much damaged as in the *Peresviet*, but they were in a very dilapidated and charred condition.

The fate of these ships proves beyond doubt that to use wood in battleship construction is a mistake, for, had there been no wood, the damage would have been comparatively small. The tide being high at this time, I could not go below, but merely glanced down the open hatchway. About the deck there was a miscellaneous collection of various articles which had escaped the fire, including instructive and valuable documents and charts, novels, magazines and newspapers, clothes, linen, hair brushes and combs, soap, towels, and all sorts of cabin furniture. This seemed to point to the fact that the decision to abandon the ships was arrived at suddenly, and that the arrangements for burning them were hurried and, in consequence, faulty. I arrived at the conclusion that these battleships would all be floated within a few months.

The *Poltava* had a big hole in the bottom, which was all the damage the diver could discover. Her bridge was in pretty much the same condition as that of the others. The sides of all the ships looked very smart, as the boiling oil had run down, making an even polish to the water's edge.

We went to the mouth of the harbour, to see the blocking ships. On the port side, going out, two ships of the first attempt were aground beneath Golden Hill fort, the nearer of the two, rusted and slimed with a year's growth of seaweed, was the one that was commanded by the gallant Hirose. The Russians, towards the end, had sunk half a dozen more vessels right across the entrance, and the masts and fun-

DECK OF THE *PERESVIET* SHOWING COAL BAGS TO PROTECT THE DECK.

DECKS HEAPED WITH COAL AND GRAVEL; PORT ARTHUR TOWN AT THE BACK.

THE BARBETTE OF THE *POLTAU*.

AMONGST THE RUINS OF THE *POLTAU*,

nels had the appearance of the stunted remains of a primeval forest, making the navigation very difficult for anything larger than the vedette boat, which, since the Japanese occupation, had brought supplies from Dalny every day.

We returned to the landing-place where the Red Cross hospital corps was assisting the wounded and sick Russian soldiers who were being brought from the hospitals on the island of Manjusan. The gentle care with which the Japs helped their stricken foes up the steps of the landing to the stretchers was a touching sight and one that I shall not easily forget.

Making a tour of the dockyard we found that the buildings had suffered considerably, one big shell having caused nearly as much destruction as a mine. The machinery was damaged, but a great deal of it could, no doubt, be repaired. The fine pair of shears was not damaged, with the exception of two 6-in. shot holes, about nine feet from the top. In the dry dock the *Amur* mine-ship lay on her side like a helpless whale, riddled with shot, the funnels and mast resting on the edge of the basin. But the greatest damage had been done at the entrance, where dynamite or mines had blown the gates out of existence and completely wrecked the hydraulic gear. Already, however, there was a new dock-gate ready to be launched. In the basin two or three steamers and other vessels were sunk, but about twenty small steamboats, from pinnaces to tugs, and one good steamer of 400 tons (probably the one that plied to Chefoo), were in excellent condition and most of them in use.

The bands were playing, for General Ichiji was taking over the town as Governor-General of Liao-tang, and I procured a *drosky* and drove to the square to see the ceremony.

It was foggy the next morning, but towards noon it cleared a little and I hired a *junk*, as the steam launch was not available, and went to the *Pobieta*. The first-named battleship looked a pitiable object and was much knocked about. All her 6-in. guns were destroyed, evidently by the Russians themselves. The muzzles were blown off, the turrets were roofless, and an attempt to destroy the barbette had evidently been made, although unsuccessfully. Gun cotton had been used, making a slight mark on the muzzles, but much of the explosive had come out and was scattered about the deck. They must have been good guns to stand such a test.

Fire had done the chief damage in this instance as in the others. The mainmast had bent and was lying right over the water, and the great umbrella top had evidently been wrecked by shells. The tide being out I went below. The oily planks, at an angle of 25 degrees, were not easy to walk upon. The course of the shells was easily traceable by shafts of brilliant sunlight that streamed through the holes. One 11-in. shell had apparently pierced but not burst, although fragments of other shells were scattered everywhere. Generally, the shells had ripped through both decks and, probably, down through the bottom. Over the engine room torpedo nets were spread, but as no shell had come that way the efficacy of such a protection could not be gauged.

The ironwork about the hatchways was cut and gashed, and a huge copper kettle, capable of holding about a hundred gallons of tea, was cut right through. Papers, sailors' bags full of clothes, loose clothes, hammocks, blankets, all preserved in oil, lay in confused masses about the deck. The armour, so far as I could see, was untouched, and as the fire had been what is known as a plunging fire, it was not likely the sides would be put to the test. Around the funnel casings a large pile of spars and beams were placed, five deep, but the shells had gone right through them. The bulwarks had suffered and a heavy crane derrick had been snapped off by a shot.

What I saw on the *Pobieta* convinced me that no battleship can venture with safety near any harbour with high land, for these plunging shells, I believe, would go through even an armoured deck if there were such a thing. An experiment with armoured plates firmly fastened to a deck and tested by means of a plunging fire would be interesting and instructive.

We went from the *Pobieta* to the *Palada* again. She lay with her bow to the harbour entrance, almost in a direct line with the two white beacons on the hill. The daring of the Japanese torpedo officers had been thoroughly appreciated by the Russians, for a torpedo net was spread in front of her. I do not think the Japanese commander-in-chief would have allowed any of his torpedo boats to run the gauntlet of the mines, booms and quick-firers to torpedo a vessel in the harbour, but I am certain that any of those torpedo commanders would not have hesitated a moment if ordered to do so, and the Russians seemed to have been of the same opinion. Two big spars spread the net, keeping it clear of the ship, the ends being looped up like curtains.

There was the same wreckage that I had observed in the other vessels, the rigging was hanging in bights, and the quick-firers had all been removed. On the after-bridge, on the port side, the last quick-firer had apparently been removed in a desperate hurry, for a box of

DESTROYED GUN ON THE
POBIETA

DIRECTION OF A JAPANESE SHELL,
THROUGH UPPER AND MAIN DECK.
★Sheets of iron proved no
protection.

ON THE AFTER-BRIDGE. THE
BLACK ARCH AT THE TOP IS THE
ANGLE OF THE MAST WHICH FELL
OVER THE SIDE.

THE *AMUR*, RUSSIAN MINE SHIP,
WRECKED IN THE DOCK AT PORT
ARTHUR. ALEXIEFF'S HOUSE ON
THE TOP OF THE HILL.

engineers' tools lay open, and some of the instruments were lying beside the circular mark on the wood where the gun had stood. There was a big upheaval on the after-deck just by the captain's cabin, which was caused by a torpedo that had been run at the stern to damage the shaft and steering gear, but had struck high, blowing a hole large enough for a rickshaw to drive through and doing much damage to the captain's cabin. All the handsome uniforms, linen, etc., were hanging about in shreds. As I left the ships I noticed that the anchor hanging at the bows of the *Pobieta* was broken off at the neck by a shot.

The weather having quite cleared we decided to visit 203 Metre Hill. We secured the services of a bright, intelligent-looking young Chinaman to carry our coats, our orderly being loaded with rations and water, and started out across the new city until we came to the main road, which took us to the top of one of the fortified hills. From there we struck straight across in the direction of the hill of tragic memory, but we made rather slow progress as our path was obstructed by wire and rifle trenches. At 1 o'clock we sat down beneath the hill to lunch, our meal consisting of army biscuits. Armour ration and a pot of pickles, washed down by cold tea. Groups of soldiers and strings of *coolies* were wandering about the top of the hill, and what their object was we could easily guess. That hill had cost Japan 20,000 men and the Russian loss was nearly as heavy. From a lower ridge, dark, sullen clouds of smoke arose at intervals.

"They are burning the dead," said Yamanashi.

The top of the hill is slightly saddle-backed, on the higher hunch the monument stands out clear and shining. We ascended by a military track, which was, in places, rendered easier for traffic by means of sandbags. A small convoy of pack-horses passed us, guarded by some soldiers, and we halted and saluted as it passed. A long open box, like a wash-tray, stood near, in which lay a soldier sleeping the long sleep with his face to the sky.

The side of the hill was pitted and dented by shell marks as though preparations were being made for a plantation of young trees. On the crest of the range and to the left 203 Metre Hill rose still higher. Every inch of the ground around us had been ploughed by the projectiles. The remains of gun-pits and emplacements covered the side of the hill. The knowledge of the tragic drama which had been performed there filled us with awe. The rocks were ground to powder and the hill was little more than a great mound of soft, yielding dust. A slight breeze stirred, lifting this dust, which was so fine that it floated upward

FRAGMENT OF THE MIGHTY DERRICK ON ONE OF THE RUSSIAN
BATTLESHIPS AT PORT ARTHUR.

* These bolts are all that remained of the deck except the iron
floor, which was buckled up, the woodwork being entirely destroyed.

and remained suspended in the air. The discs of Japanese shells were thick upon the ground, and rags and splinters of rock and wood lay everywhere.

The trenches on this side could scarcely be traced, for they were filled to the level of the ground with Russian corpses, burnt beyond recognition. Such a terrible sight I had never looked upon. I have seen death on many battlefields, but never such wholesale slaughter as I saw that day on 203 Metre Hill. Death must have come terribly suddenly to many of the poor human beings whose corpses filled the ghastly trenches. In one place I saw the naked legs and part of the stomach of a man still in the crouching position in which death found him, while, far down the slope, the other half of the body lay strung together by the entrails. Fragments of human flesh strewed the hill, and everywhere scorched faces with hideous death-grin looked up at us with unseeing eyes from the awful debris.

The monument was merely a square wooden post, painted white, on which was written a list of the heroes who had fallen in the great battle. It stood upon a base of sand bags. Nearly three weeks had passed since the battle was fought, but the searchers were still busy and the funeral fires constantly burning. The Russian dead remained where they fell, for there had been no time to bury them. In two respects the battlefield was less horrible than is generally the case when the dead have been left unburied, for there was no stench of putrefaction nor flies rising in clouds as we approached. The rarefied, cold air of the north was the cause of the absence of these additional horrors.

Port Arthur and its bay lay beneath us, a beautiful panorama, and I shall never forget the scene with its ghastly, haunting foreground. As we turned to leave, one of the Japanese soldiers, who spoke a little English and evidently thought I was a Russian, pointed to a dead Muscovite and said sympathetically:

"Is that your dear friend?"

We descended, passing Russians and Japanese walking together in perfect amity. Along the shore-front parties were busy making bonfires of infectious rubbish, and the dead-carts were busy with their burden of wash-tray-shaped, shrouded bodies. There was no mistaking the palsied motion of the rigid shapes beneath the white sheets, as the carts bumped over the rough ground. At the foot of the hill we were fortunate in securing a *drosky*, which carried us the remainder of the way home.

I paid a visit to Alexieff's house—an elegant mansion overlooking

A BATTLEFIELD HORROR. 203 METRE HILL.

FIELD CREMATORY, 203 METRE HILL. SOLDIERS IN THE DISTANCE AT WORK, CREMATING THE BODIES OF THEIR DEAD COMRADES.

ALL THAT REMAINS OF THE RUSSIAN SOLDIERS KILLED BY A JAPANESE SHELL, 203 METRE HILL. THE MONUMENT IN THE DISTANCE, BEYOND THE SEATED SOLDIER.

A RUSSIAN TRENCH, ACTUALLY FILLED WITH DEAD.

the dockyard. Two or three large gaps in the high walls enabled the public to view from the road the beautiful garden. A well-paved road from the dockyard leads to the main gates of the house, which stands well back, and is a fine two-storied building with verandahs. The windows are double-sashed, and *jalousies* shield the room from the summer sun. The garden is well laid out and planted with beautiful shrubs and trees, and reminded me of the quadrangle of a first-class German hotel. Most of the furniture had been stacked underneath the portico. We entered from the side through the kitchen, a fine big room, and through this we passed to a passage that led to the front hall.

A spiral staircase with a very handsome balustrade was the means of ascending to the second storey. The first room we entered was the dining-room, and on the very handsome sideboard still stood the liqueur stand and tray, and some half a dozen glasses. Two handsome screens took up one side of the room, one being ornamented with heavy gold dragons on black, and the second with golden birds and flowers. This room opened into another handsomely-furnished apartment. The screens here were of brilliantly-coloured silk, decorated with chrysanthemums and birds and obviously executed by skilled workmen of the East. Another piece of furniture that was worth a day's journey to see was a remarkably handsome table of polished green jade, evidently for writing.

Darkness was coming on, and we left Alexieff's house and returned to our quarters. We went to bed at once, worn out with our long day.

"Tomorrow—" began Yamanashi, drowsily.

"Let tomorrow come," I said, and fell asleep.

The nearest station was seventeen miles away and there were only two trains a day, one at 1.30, the other at 8. At 9 our man told us that he could not get a *drosky* for love or money, so we hired a couple of coolies and a *jinrickshaw* to carry our baggage; and, with a last look at the sunken Russian ships, we bade farewell to our hosts and started forth on our journey.

The brisk morning air was delightful, and a tramp of twenty-five miles or so seemed no hardship. We had decided to visit some more forts on our way to the station, so we stepped out briskly. On passing the market square, however, I saw two *droskies* evidently waiting for a fare, so I approached the driver of one of them and pointed over the distant fortresses to the Dalny road. The driver nodded, and we got into the *drosky* and left Port Arthur behind two magnificent animals, fresh and fast, passing everything on the road.

A SHRINE ON 203 METRE HILL.
LIEUT. YAMANASHI DOING
HOMAGE TO THE DEAD.

TEMPORARY MONUMENT ON THE
SUMMIT OF 203 METRE HILL.

GUARDS IN CHARGE OF BURIAL
PARTY, 203 METRE HILL.

WIRE ENTANGLEMENT, *CHEVAUX
DE FRISE,* AT THE GATES OF PORT
ARTHUR.

One *drosky*, which we overtook, contained a wounded Russian officer and his wife, and a little black terrier which barked his delight at leaving the place, thankful, no doubt, for not having been made into soup. We met regiments of soldiers, Chinese beggars, and trains of the little Japanese transport carts on the road.

After a couple of hours' driving we saw a cloud of white steam on the distant ridge as the incoming train entered the station, and soon after we arrived. There was a great deal of bustle and excitement there, for artillery and stores were being entrained for the north and there were, besides, a number of passengers for Dalny. We all squeezed into a baggage truck, in which we made the journey, and on reaching Dalny I at once went on board the old *Tainan Maru*, walking across the ice to the ship. There had been several changes made in my absence, and the paymaster and two or three of my friends had been promoted and appointed to other ships.

On February 2nd we received sailing orders, our destination being Kure, and we were not sorry at the prospect of soon reaching the warmer climate of the Inland Sea. My pleasant sojourn with the Japanese Fleet was coming to an end.

The ice melted from the sides of the ship as we steamed through the Strait of Gun, Togo's first rendezvous, and we felt comparatively warm when; on February 7th, we glided into Kure.

I remained with the ship, and two days later saw the Japanese Nelson go aboard his flagship preparatory to sailing south to meet the Baltic Fleet.

On February 12th (which was a public holiday, being the anniversary of the birth of Nippon's first emperor, who saw the light 2,500 years ago) I went to the *Mikassa* to call on Admiral Togo. He received me in his cabin and we had a long talk, and he sent me over the ship to see the places that had been damaged. A big shot had passed through the sick room, but without doing much harm, and one of the casemates was injured by a shell which had exploded on the deck above and damaged the mainmast. Two-thirds of the girth of the mast had been shot away, leaving very little to support its great weight.

Soon afterwards I was ordered to Tokyo. Captain Takahasi, with his wife and their boy and as many officers as could be spared, came with me in the dockyard launch to see that I was properly settled on the little steamer that was to bear me away, perhaps for ever, from my dear Nippon friends. I remained on the deck of the steamer until the launch, with its waving crowd of the best and truest friends I have

Togo in Straits of Tsushima

ever made, passed out of sight, and a few days later I was on my way home to England.

★★★★★★

While preparing for press this account of my experiences with the Japanese Navy, news reached England of the overwhelming success of that navy in its last encounter with the Russian ships—a success which completed and crowned the arduous and gallant work which I had witnessed the brave Japanese sailors performing off Port Arthur. By this great victory the Japan Sea becomes the moat of Tokyo, and under the protection of the flag of the Rising Sun, merchant ships of all nations will sail in security through those Eastern waters. New ports, too, will be thrown open to the world, and territory whose inhabitants have been crushed beneath the weight of a Russian occupation will come under the beneficent sway of Japan, and the light of civilization, peace and prosperity will shine over the land. *Banzai!*

LESSONS OF THE WAR.

Sea Battles of today, as in the past, and possibly in the near future will be decided by guns. We have no such reports about the Japanese Artillery, which is entirely Armstrong's, as makes such painful reading in the daily-papers of *defects* in our guns. The *system* only is to blame; and this ought not to be, when we have British firms of such high repute as Elswick, Newcastle-on-Tyne. Surely the British Navy and Army ought to be provided with the very best ordnance; from what I have seen "and heard from various Japanese naval officers," Elswick guns are the first in the world, and that they have fully sustained their world-wide reputation under the most severe test, *viz., that of actual war service.* After hearing these opinions, and, seeing what I have seen I have no hesitation in stating that the whole of our armament ought to be renewed.

I claim to know something of this subject, as I watched carefully for seven months the working of these guns, having been on nearly every type of ship during that time.

To me the doom of the big battleship has already sounded; her future place will be on the ocean; fur with up-to-date methods of coast defence—which must be the "burning question" of the immediate future—properly defended narrow seas are unsafe for large craft. Mines, torpedo and submarine will keep them at a distance. So, even in ocean fighting, history is repeating itself, and the day of mosquito craft has again dawned.

LEONAUR

ALSO FROM LEONAUR

AVAILABLE IN SOFTCOVER OR HARDCOVER WITH DUST JACKET

THE FALL OF THE MOGHUL EMPIRE OF HINDUSTAN *by H. G. Keene*—By the beginning of the nineteenth century, as British and Indian armies under Lake and Wellesley dominated the scene, a little over half a century of conflict brought the Moghul Empire to its knees.

LADY SALE'S AFGHANISTAN *by Florentia Sale*—An Indomitable Victorian Lady's Account of the Retreat from Kabul During the First Afghan War.

THE CAMPAIGN OF MAGENTA AND SOLFERINO 1859 *by Harold Carmichael Wylly*—The Decisive Conflict for the Unification of Italy.

FRENCH'S CAVALRY CAMPAIGN *by J. G. Maydon*—A Special Correspondent's View of British Army Mounted Troops During the Boer War.

CAVALRY AT WATERLOO *by Sir Evelyn Wood*—British Mounted Troops During the Campaign of 1815.

THE SUBALTERN *by George Robert Gleig*—The Experiences of an Officer of the 85th Light Infantry During the Peninsular War.

NAPOLEON AT BAY, 1814 *by F. Loraine Petre*—The Campaigns to the Fall of the First Empire.

NAPOLEON AND THE CAMPAIGN OF 1806 *by Colonel Vachée*—The Napoleonic Method of Organisation and Command to the Battles of Jena & Auerstädt.

THE COMPLETE ADVENTURES IN THE CONNAUGHT RANGERS *by William Grattan*—The 88th Regiment during the Napoleonic Wars by a Serving Officer.

BUGLER AND OFFICER OF THE RIFLES *by William Green & Harry Smith*—With the 95th (Rifles) during the Peninsular & Waterloo Campaigns of the Napoleonic Wars.

NAPOLEONIC WAR STORIES *by Sir Arthur Quiller-Couch*—Tales of soldiers, spies, battles & sieges from the Peninsular & Waterloo campaingns.

CAPTAIN OF THE 95TH (RIFLES) *by Jonathan Leach*—An officer of Wellington's sharpshooters during the Peninsular, South of France and Waterloo campaigns of the Napoleonic wars.

RIFLEMAN COSTELLO *by Edward Costello*—The adventures of a soldier of the 95th (Rifles) in the Peninsular & Waterloo Campaigns of the Napoleonic wars.

LEONAUR

ALSO FROM LEONAUR

AVAILABLE IN SOFTCOVER OR HARDCOVER WITH DUST JACKET

THE 9TH—THE KING'S (LIVERPOOL REGIMENT) IN THE GREAT WAR 1914 - 1918 *by Enos H. G. Roberts*—Mersey to mud—war and Liverpool men.

THE GAMBARDIER *by Mark Severn*—The experiences of a battery of Heavy artillery on the Western Front during the First World War.

FROM MESSINES TO THIRD YPRES *by Thomas Floyd*—A personal account of the First World War on the Western front by a 2/5th Lancashire Fusilier.

THE IRISH GUARDS IN THE GREAT WAR - VOLUME 1 *by Rudyard Kipling*—Edited and Compiled from Their Diaries and Papers—The First Battalion.

THE IRISH GUARDS IN THE GREAT WAR - VOLUME 1 *by Rudyard Kipling*—Edited and Compiled from Their Diaries and Papers—The Second Battalion.

ARMOURED CARS IN EDEN *by K. Roosevelt*—An American President's son serving in Rolls Royce armoured cars with the British in Mesopatamia & with the American Artillery in France during the First World War.

CHASSEUR OF 1914 *by Marcel Dupont*—Experiences of the twilight of the French Light Cavalry by a young officer during the early battles of the great war in Europe.

TROOP HORSE & TRENCH *by R.A. Lloyd*—The experiences of a British Lifeguardsman of the household cavalry fighting on the western front during the First World War 1914-18.

THE EAST AFRICAN MOUNTED RIFLES *by C.J. Wilson*—Experiences of the campaign in the East African bush during the First World War.

THE LONG PATROL *by George Berrie*—A Novel of Light Horsemen from Gallipoli to the Palestine campaign of the First World War.

THE FIGHTING CAMELIERS *by Frank Reid*—The exploits of the Imperial Camel Corps in the desert and Palestine campaigns of the First World War.

STEEL CHARIOTS IN THE DESERT *by S. C. Rolls*—The first world war experiences of a Rolls Royce armoured car driver with the Duke of Westminster in Libya and in Arabia with T.E. Lawrence.

WITH THE IMPERIAL CAMEL CORPS IN THE GREAT WAR *by Geoffrey Inchbald*—The story of a serving officer with the British 2nd battalion against the Senussi and during the Palestine campaign.

LEONAUR

ALSO FROM LEONAUR
AVAILABLE IN SOFTCOVER OR HARDCOVER WITH DUST JACKET

ESCAPE FROM THE FRENCH *by Edward Boys*—A Young Royal Navy Midshipman's Adventures During the Napoleonic War.

THE VOYAGE OF H.M.S. PANDORA *by Edward Edwards R. N. & George Hamilton, edited by Basil Thomson*—In Pursuit of the Mutineers of the Bounty in the South Seas—1790-1791.

MEDUSA *by J. B. Henry Savigny and Alexander Correard and Charlotte-Adélaïde Dard* —Narrative of a Voyage to Senegal in 1816 & The Sufferings of the Picard Family After the Shipwreck of the Medusa.

THE SEA WAR OF 1812 VOLUME 1 *by A. T. Mahan*—A History of the Maritime Conflict.

THE SEA WAR OF 1812 VOLUME 2 *by A. T. Mahan*—A History of the Maritime Conflict.

WETHERELL OF H. M. S. HUSSAR *by John Wetherell*—The Recollections of an Ordinary Seaman of the Royal Navy During the Napoleonic Wars.

THE NAVAL BRIGADE IN NATAL *by C. R. N. Burne*—With the Guns of H. M. S. Terrible & H. M. S. Tartar during the Boer War 1899-1900.

THE VOYAGE OF H. M. S. BOUNTY *by William Bligh*—The True Story of an 18th Century Voyage of Exploration and Mutiny.

SHIPWRECK! *by William Gilly*—The Royal Navy's Disasters at Sea 1793-1849.

KING'S CUTTERS AND SMUGGLERS: 1700-1855 *by E. Keble Chatterton*—A unique period of maritime history-from the beginning of the eighteenth to the middle of the nineteenth century when British seamen risked all to smuggle valuable goods from wool to tea and spirits from and to the Continent.

CONFEDERATE BLOCKADE RUNNER *by John Wilkinson*—The Personal Recollections of an Officer of the Confederate Navy.

NAVAL BATTLES OF THE NAPOLEONIC WARS *by W. H. Fitchett*—Cape St. Vincent, the Nile, Cadiz, Copenhagen, Trafalgar & Others.

PRISONERS OF THE RED DESERT *by R. S. Gwatkin-Williams*—The Adventures of the Crew of the Tara During the First World War.

U-BOAT WAR 1914-1918 *by James B. Connolly/Karl von Schenk*—Two Contrasting Accounts from Both Sides of the Conflict at Sea D uring the Great War.

Lightning Source UK Ltd.
Milton Keynes UK
UKHW040720151122
412232UK00001B/141